ADMIRAL VAT SMITH

The extraordinary life of the father of Australia's Fleet Air Arm

Graeme Lunn

Admiral VAT Smith

The extraordinary life of the father of Australia's Fleet Air Arm

Graeme Lunn

ISBN: 9780645700480

First published 2024 by Avonmore Books
Avonmore Books
PO Box 217
Kent Town
South Australia 5071
Australia

Phone: (61 8) 8431 9780
www.avonmorebooks.com.au

A catalogue record for this book is available from the National Library of Australia

Cover design & layout by Diane Bricknell

Official ship and unit badges are reproduced with the kind permission of the Australian Department of Defence and the UK Ministry of Defence.

Aircraft profile artwork by Juanita Franzi Aero Illustrations.

The front cover image is reproduced from a painting titled *A Gallant Failure* by artist Drew Harrison. The painting depicts Fairey Swordfish of Nos 821 and 823 Squadrons, Royal Navy, undertaking a daylight torpedo attack against the German battlecruiser *Scharnhorst* on 21 June 1940. Flying as an observer, VAT Smith led the attack with pilot Lieutenant John Stenning. The full image can be seen on page 91.

Limited edition prints of *A Gallant Failure* can be purchased from Drew Harrison's website: www.drewharrison-art.com

CONTENTS

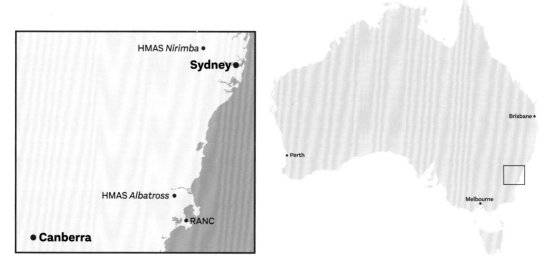

While VAT Smith's naval career spanned almost five decades and a vast number of geographic locations, a handful of locations close to Sydney played a key role. Sydney Harbour is the headquarters and main fleet base of the Royal Australian Navy. Approximately 170 kilometres to the south is the town of Nowra in the Shoalhaven region which is home to the Australian Fleet Air Arm and its base of HMAS Albatross. A short distance south of Nowra is the picturesque Jervis Bay, home to the Royal Australian Naval College. Inland from these locations is the Australian capital city of Canberra where VAT Smith spent the latter part of his career and lived in retirement. VAT Smith also spent time at the Navy Office in Melbourne, before it was relocated to Canberra in 1959.

Author's Note

In 1991 the Chief of Navy, Vice-Admiral Ian MacDougall AO (1954 RANC class), approached a long-retired Sir Victor Smith (universally known as VAT after his initials) about writing his memoirs but, ever self-effacing, the response was a firm no.[1] Commodore Thomas "Toz" Dadswell AM (1946 RANC class) was recruited, suggesting that VAT should write about his "interesting" life, getting a fatherly talk in return on why he didn't want to do it. VAT had always shunned self-promotion and had no interest in advancing any "legacy" by writing an autobiography, commenting that:

> I could see no good purpose in this as my experiences in the service were, to a degree, similar to others.

Dadswell then recruited Lady Nanette Smith, and an outflanked VAT had interviews recorded, from which Lieutenant-Commander Peter Jones (1974 RANC class) compiled the booklet *A Few Memories of Sir Victor Smith*, published by the Australian Naval Institute in 1992.[2, 3] It is hoped that this biography will help fill the many omissions VAT made in that too modest recounting of his life.

Graeme Lunn

January 2024, Auckland, New Zealand

---

1 Initially a supply officer Vice-Admiral Ian MacDougall (1938-2020) transferred to the Submarine Branch and was commissioning executive officer of *Oxley* and commanded *Onslow*. Later he commanded *Hobart* and *Supply*, and then the Australian Submarine Squadron, before becoming Maritime Commander. In retirement he was Commissioner of the NSW Fire Brigade.

2 Later Vice Admiral Peter Jones AO DSC (b 1957), who commanded *Melbourne* and then the Maritime Interception Force during the 2003 Gulf War. An eminent naval historian and Adjunct Professor of Naval Studies at the University of NSW, it was at his urging that this biography was initiated.

3 After names, future references in this book in the form "(1974 class)" refer to the RANC entry class of the individual.

GLOSSARY & ABBREVIATIONS

A	Air
AC	Companion of the Order of Australia
AFC	Air Force Cross
AG	Air Gunner
AJASS	Australian Joint Anti-Submarine School
AM	Member of the Order of Australia
ASV	Radar, Air-to-Surface Vessel
ASW	Anti-submarine warfare
BA	Bachelor of Arts
BSc	Bachelor of Science
BWC	Bridge Watchkeeping Certificate
CAG	Carrier Air Group
CAM	Catapult Aircraft Merchantman
CAP	Combat Air Patrol
CB	Companion of the Order of the Bath
CBE	Commander of the Order of the British Empire
CH	Order of the Companions of Honour
CMG	Companion of the Order of St Michael and St George
CNS	Chief of Naval Staff
CPO	Chief Petty Officer
CVO	Commander of the Royal Victorian Order
DAWOT	Director of Air Warfare Organisation and Training
DCNS	Deputy Chief of Naval Staff
DFC	Distinguished Flying Cross
Divisions	To organise a ship's company for work and discipline they are divided into divisions under a divisional officer. Individual divisions will be further organised into watches and assigned their action stations
DMZ	Demilitarised Zone (Korea and Vietnam)
DSc	Doctorate of Science
DSC	Distinguished Service Cross
DSO	Distinguished Service Order
Dumbo	USN code name for an air-sea rescue mission
FAA	Fleet Air Arm
FCS	Fighter Catapult Ship
FDO	Flight Deck Officer
FOBAA	Flag Officer, British Assault Area
FOCAF	Flag Officer Commanding Australian Fleet
FRS	Fellow of the Royal Society
G	Gunnery
GBE	Knight Grand Cross of the Order of the British Empire
GCB	Knight Grand Cross of the Order of the Bath
GCMG	Knight Grand Cross of the Order of St Michael and St George
GCVO	Knight Grand Cross of the Royal Victorian Order
H	Surveying
HF/DF	High-frequency direction finding
HFV	Helicopter Flight Vietnam
HMAS	His/Her Majesty's Australian Ship
HMS	His/Her Majesty's Ship
IJN	Imperial Japanese Navy
KBE	Knight Commander of the Order of the British Empire
KCB	Knight Commander of the Order of the Bath
KCMG	Knight Commander of the Order of St Michael and St George
KM	King's Medal
MA	Master of Arts
MC	Military Cross
MiD	Mentioned in Despatches
MONAB	Mobile Naval Air Base
MP	Member of Parliament
MVO	Member of the Royal Victorian Order
N	Navigator
O	Observer
OBE	Officer of the Order of the British Empire
OM	Order of Merit
OOW	Officer of the Watch
P	Pilot
PC	His Majesty's Most Honourable Privy Council
RAAF	Royal Australian Air Force
RADM	Rear-Admiral
RAF	Royal Air Force
RAN	Royal Australian Navy
RANC	Royal Australian Naval College
RANVR	Royal Australian Navy Volunteer Reserve
RFC	Royal Flying Corps
RMC	Royal Military College
RN	Royal Navy
RNAS	Royal Naval Air Service
RNZN	Royal New Zealand Navy
S	Signalling/Wireless Telegraphy
SAR	Search and Rescue
SEATO	South East Asia Treaty Organisation
SGM	Sea Gallantry Medal
SOBS	Senior Observer
SM	Submarines
T	Torpedo
TAG	Telegraphist Air Gunner
TAS	Torpedo and Anti-Submarine
US	United States
USN	United States Navy
VADM	Vice-Admiral
VC	Victoria Cross
W/T	Wireless/Telegraphy
WWI	World War One
WWII	World War Two

FOREWORD

T**HE NAVY AND THE NATION ARE INEXTRICABLY LINKED.** Since Federation, as an island nation Australia has had a dependency on the sea for its trade and subsequent prosperity. It has sought to raise and maintain a navy to assure that outcome. But the task has not been a simple one and whilst acknowledging the competing national defence priorities, the development of the navy has relied on the strength of character and the persuasive arguments of a few seasoned men.

This book has a part to play in describing the navy's development, from its inception to the recent past through the story of one of those seasoned men – Admiral Sir Victor Alfred Trumper Smith AC KBE CB DSC MiD RAN. His entry into the service was just over a decade after the creation of the Royal Australian Navy. His period of service traversed some of the most dramatic changes within the service until his retirement in November 1975. He did not merely witness these changes but was fundamental in the planning of some and the leading of many as he assumed more senior roles. His story reflects so much of the navy's story.

As such, this book can be read on three levels; as part of the history of the nation's emergence from its colonial roots, struggling to find its future role in an uncertain century of geo-political turmoil; as a description of the navy's response to these challenges and the consequences for our national security; but mainly, as a record of achievement by one of the navy's best – a thirteen-year-old cadet midshipman from the "Class of 1927" who rose to lead the navy and then the Australian Defence Force as the Chairman of the Chiefs of Staff Committee; the first RAN College graduate four star admiral to do so. His story cannot be fully appreciated without an understanding of the other two levels and all three are carefully interwoven here to paint a true picture of the man.

Sir Victor was a fiercely proud Australian; he portrayed all the characteristics that most people would ascribe to great Australians. Strong, dependable, courageous but with a hint of good humour (when required). In his early years he was not the leader of the pack, but with deepening experience in his profession, under wartime conditions, he took on all challenges with a determination that sharpened his skills at every opportunity. He became adept at collaborating across the other services, and those services of other nations. His network of colleagues and friendships was extensive, and he used them to great effect. He was well regarded as a disciplined thinker, firm but fair, understanding of tradition but progressive in nature. These characteristics equipped him well to leadership roles at the highest levels.

Finally, Sir Victor can truly be described as the father of the Fleet Air Arm. He developed a passion for naval aviation and pursued it throughout his career, with skill, courage and with a genuine collaboration in a deft approach to ensure naval aviation was prized within defence. It was not always smooth sailing and debate over the navy's role and that of naval aviation continues to be had. And so, to the aviators who continue to walk past his portrait, proudly hanging in the wardroom at the Naval Air Station at Nowra, and who one day may be called upon to lead that debate – you would do well to remember these characteristics.

Vice Admiral Tim Barrett AO CSC RAN (Rtd)
December 2023

INTRODUCTION

A portrait of Admiral Sir Victor Alfred Trumper Smith AC KBE CB DSC MiD RAN.

Looking at the plain weathered face, left, you see an ordinary Aussie bloke of the best kind. Not handsome by any means but dependably solid, a mate who would stand by you. A neighbour that would rush to your aid and remain calm, perhaps almost laconic, in the face of stress or danger. But if you look a bit closer there is an encompassing assessing glance in his eyes, a determined line to the mouth, a long-faded scar on the cheek, and you begin to wonder if he is quite so ordinary after all. As your eye moves across the uniform he wears comfortably, the sleeves with stripes of gold braid seemingly reach towards his elbows and the badge on the shoulder proudly proclaims Australia as his country of service. Perhaps he was indeed a man of consequence?

When your eye then drops to the five rows of medal ribbons under the wings of a naval aviator on his left chest you recognise that he cannot be, in any sense, ordinary after all. You find yourself anticipating the varied stories from his life of service to the nation that each of those medals represents.

VAT Smith's medals.

Retirement Day: 23 November 1975

On this day Admiral Sir Victor Alfred Trumper Smith AC KBE CB DSC MiD RAN retired from his appointment as Chairman, Chiefs of Staff Committee. In this position - nowadays titled Chief of the Defence Force - Sir Victor had, for half a decade, guided the Navy, Army and Air Force of Australia through both war and peace. Widely known as the "Father of the Fleet Air Arm", he was the first graduate of the Royal Australian Naval College to achieve four-star Admiral's rank.

Fittingly his Defence Force Service Medal, awarded for long service in the Australian Defence Force, had on the obverse the Naval anchor, Army crossed swords and Air Force eagle superimposed above a boomerang to represent all three armed services. The medal ribbon, in the traditional national colours of blue and gold, sported the rarely seen two silver Federation Stars to signify the six clasps awarded for more than 45 years of service. Admiral VAT Smith had served continuously in the permanent armed forces of Australia for almost 49 years, a unique span that will never be equalled because no longer does the nation call on children of thirteen to don naval uniform as the young Victor had 17,826 days previously.

Day 1: 2 February 1927

A group of boys from five Australian states warily assembled on a platform of the Central Railway Station in Sydney. Farewelled by local parents, they were directed to a train heading south, down the picturesque New South Wales coast via Kiama, to the small station of Bomaderry where they were met by a naval Chief Petty Officer. From Bomaderry there was a Cadillac charabanc coach into the night some 40 kilometres across the Shoalhaven River to Nowra, and then along the rough bush road to the remote Royal Australian Naval College, situated on Captain's Point at Jervis

Left: VAT Smith's Defence Force Service Medal. Right: The logo signifying all three Australian defence services, as featured on the obverse of the Defence Force Service Medal.

Bay. It is not recorded if that CPO made the traditional stop at the Nowra pub while telling the boys he needed "to collect some mail"!

The thirteen new cadets were met on arrival by the College's two Year Officers. After biscuits and cocoa, they were then taken to their dormitory, where beds and sea chests were allocated in alphabetical order. Cadet-Midshipman Victor Smith, thirteen years and eight months old, would have turned in at the end of his first day in the Navy simultaneously excited and exhausted. In his tired boyish dreams that night could he have possibly fantasised the improbable – that almost eighteen thousand days of service later he would be an admiral, knighted by his sovereign and decorated for repeated acts of bravery in the air against his nation's enemies.

The Royal Australian Naval College at Jervis Bay in the pre-war era.

CHAPTER 1

FAMILY & CHILDHOOD

IN THE GOLDEN AGE of cricket none shone brighter than the Australian batsman Victor Trumper. Visiting the Australian dressing room at Lord's in 1899, after Victor's maiden test century against England, WG Grace presented his own bat to the young Aussie with the words "From the past champion to the future champion". Australia won eight out of ten tours with Victor considered the country's "best and most brilliant" batsman. His career statistics of 42 centuries and 82 half-centuries ensured Victor was a popular hero to the young nation in that antipodean *belle époque* before those grimmer heroes of the First World War emerged.

With Trumper slowly succumbing to kidney disease, a benefit match was played on his behalf in 1913 which raised almost £3,000. Several days later, on 9 May 1913, his sister Una Smith gave birth to a boy who was

Australian batsman Victor Trumper.

immediately named in his honour - Victor Alfred Trumper Smith. Baptised at St Pauls Anglican Church in Chatswood, New South Wales, the young Victor never knew his famous uncle who died, much mourned by both family and a sporting nation, in 1915 at the young age of 37.

In a nation that had not yet reached the level of urbanisation that was its future, Victor Smith was largely the progeny of a country family with an ethos of hard-work and regular worship. His paternal grandfather, plainly named John Smith but later known as Charles John Smith, was born in Norfolk, England, in 1835, the middle of ten children. His mother Emila Rose, worn-out from childbirth, died aged 43 when John was eight years old. John's father was Richard Smith, who as a widower farrier/veterinary surgeon in 1851, was farming 250 acres. At home Richard had a female servant to help look after the younger children. The farm employed twelve men and three boys in that census year, including a seventeen-year-old John. His was a farming family at a time when farmers, graziers and agricultural labourers made up the largest sector of the British workforce.

Free settler opposition to transportation saw the final convict ship to Sydney offload its wretched cargo in 1850. In 1851 gold was discovered in the colony and the subsequent gold rush saw one in four of the English population clamouring for passage to the Australian colonies. This rush of emigration caused the European population to double, from 450,000 in 1851 to over a million a decade later. Among those who emigrated to the colony of New South Wales was Charles John, but not for him the allure of the gold fields. He remained true to his rural roots and became a grazier.

Charles John Smith

In 1859 Charles John married Sarah Cock at Wallabadah in the Liverpool Plains area (south of Tamworth, New South Wales). The same year the young couple settled on a property further west, near the small settlement of Tambar Springs. This run of just under four square kilometres they named *Bomera Creek* after their vital water source. Four hundred kilometres north-west of Sydney the area had only recently been opened for sheep grazing, with the nearest railhead in the town of Gunnedah 67 kilometres away.

At *Bomera Creek* Charles John ran sheep and grew wheat. He was a straightforward God-fearing man, well respected in a rural community where respect was hard earned. Work was unrelenting as the carrying capacity of the run was increased with dams, tanks, fencing and clearing in addition to cultivation. The land was occasionally dangerous with snakes, bushfires and floods. Their postman, John Harrison, drowned crossing a high-running Bomera Creek in the winter of 1874. His horse survived and the mail bag was recovered.

Sarah Smith

Himself one of ten siblings, Charles John, with Sarah, in turn raised ten children, three of whom died young. Wool was a booming commodity into the 1880s and the market at the Sydney Wool Exchange was bullish. Life at *Bomera Creek*, though hard, proved relatively prosperous. The 1890s brought drought with economic depression and by the second half of the decade sheep numbers in the colony had halved. These were hard times which caused a rise in industrial action by shearers for better wages and conditions, leading to the formation of the Australian Workers Union in 1894 which later helped found the Australian Labor Party.

By this time half of Australians lived in cities and towns. This last decade of the nineteenth century, while economically harsh, was politically buoyant with the constitutional conventions and referendums moving the colonies towards federation as the Commonwealth of Australia on 1 January 1901. The market for good wool recovered, and in 1903 the district around *Bomera Creek* sent 4,000 bales to the Sydney Wool Exchange. When the auction results were telegraphed through to Tambar Springs Charles John learned that his wool clip had achieved the top sale price of 11¼ pence.

The youngest of the ten Smith children at *Bomera Creek* was George, born in 1886. As a boy he went to the government school at Tambar Springs which involved riding on horseback twelve miles each way. After four years of secondary education, with older brothers already working on the property, George decided to head for Sydney where he obtained employment in a pastoral firm and completed his final years of secondary education part-time. He eventually became a pastoral agent and auctioneer, settling into a job so compatible with the rural interests instilled in his childhood at *Bomera Creek* that he remained with the same firm until he retired.

George Smith

On first moving to Sydney George boarded in Paddington where, in his spare time, he was an avid cricket supporter. Also living in Paddington was Charles Thomas Trumper who had emigrated from England via New Zealand and set up a factory manufacturing shoes and boots. Charles Thomas was a quiet, kindly man who was devoted to his family and whose passion was cricket - a passion he passed on to his three sons, of whom Victor Trumper was the first born.

Family lore is that George became mates with one of the Trumper boys. The Trumper parents kept an open house welcoming their children's friends. It was in that home that George met one of the daughters of the household, Una Margaret. Her father's health had declined in the early 1900s leading Charles Trumper to sell the family business. Obeying doctors' orders the Trumper family moved to Chatswood on Sydney's north shore, where the increased height above sea level was hoped to be beneficial for Charles's health. George, still living in Paddington, made sure he did not lose touch with Una.

George and Una were married on 9 November 1909, at St Paul's Anglican Church, Chatswood. After their marriage, as was common custom of the day, they rented a house close to where Una's parents had built their home. Chatswood, traditional land of the Cammeraygal people, was a northern suburb in a city that would remain divided by an unbridged harbour for another 23 years. One-third of Sydney's population lived to the harbour's north, so for his work commute George would walk six minutes to Chatswood Station, catch the steam train to Milsons Point and then board a ferry across the harbour to Circular Quay. The street lighting in the suburb was still gas and tradesmen called at the back door to take orders and deliver the household's meat, vegetables, milk and bread. Life was decidedly more leisurely, even genteel, on the North Shore.

Una Smith (nee Trumper)

The couple had three children, Charles "Bill" born in 1911, Victor in 1913 and Una "Bess" in 1919. Victor, called "Mick" by his siblings, was the middle child of a solidly middle-class family. There were frequent outings for the children and no deprivations. The open house policy of the Trumpers was continued in the Smith household, making welcome any friends the children brought home. Their annual Christmas beach holiday stretched over five idyllic summer weeks and was always keenly anticipated. Victor's memories, as those of his siblings, were of a very happy childhood.

While life was remote at patriotic Tambar Springs, the upheaval of the Great War was still momentous. In 1915 the Belgian Consul in Sydney reported that Mr CJ Smith of *Bomera Creek* had donated one bale of sheepskins to Belgium's Relief Fund. Ninety-one men of the area stepped forward for service, the highest number per capita from any rural community, with eighteen of them killed in action. The local War Memorial, erected in December 1918 and said to be the first in Australia, included three Smiths among the inscribed names. Victor always remembered the joy and relief of the 1918 Armistice celebrations. Held in both the city and on Chatswood Oval they marked the end of a war whose tragedy, from Gallipoli onwards, had seared the Australian ethos deeply and moved all political parties towards disarmament and pacifism.

Weary from 58 years of rural toil Charles John felt he was now too old to run the property, so Alfred as the oldest son took over. Victor accompanied his mother and older brother when they went up to *Bomera Creek* in 1918 to bring the old couple back to Chatswood. While waiting at Gunnedah to board the train for Sydney a large crowd of well-wishers gathered. As Charles John and Sarah boarded the train the crowd spontaneously burst into the hymn *Abide With Me*, giving the five-year-old Victor an indelible memory of a rural community where faith, toil and service were paramount. Retirement was short as Charles John died the next year.

The adult Victor would look back on his childhood from 1922 to 1926 as "so very busy"! In addition to years of piano lessons Victor's boy treble singing voice was put to use in the church choir. Tuesday after school was Wolf Cub band practice, which with his parents' commendable forbearance was held in their home, while Thursday night was choir practice. Wolf Cubs met on Friday evening with their Cub outings on Saturday afternoon. Sunday, with its choir commitments, meant three services for Victor. And, of course, there was sport throughout the week. Initially playing rugby and cricket he soon realised that, despite maternal Trumper genes, his talent for cricket was minimal and he switched from bat to tennis racquet. Rugby, however, was to remain a passion throughout his life.

After family, the major influence of Victor's young life was the scouting movement. As soon as he turned nine in May 1922, Victor joined the local Wolf Cub pack overseen by the 1st Chatswood Scout Troop. When Colonel Baden-Powell's *Scouting For Boys* was published in 1908, scout patrols spontaneously formed in Australia, starting with Sydney's 1st Mosman. The governor-general's son promptly joined and, with imperial patronage, the movement's growth in the Commonwealth was assured. A Wolf Cub movement for the Scouts younger brothers commenced in 1916. Participation was popular with 6,074 Cubs and Scouts in 1922 almost doubling to 11,651 by 1926.

The Wolf Cub promise was to "Do My Best. To do my duty to God, and to the King" and Victor took it to heart. He was a stalwart of the Wolf Cub pack for almost five years, eventually becoming the pack leader. When it was decided that the pack needed a drum and fife marching band Victor's proven musicality saw him appointed teacher of the band and he was proud of its accomplishments. Being one of the larger boys, not for him the flute, triangle, snare drum or cymbals; the big bass drum was to be his particular instrument. While marching he would have a smaller cub in front of him sharing the weight while he vigorously plied the calfskin with his mallet. Victor would later muse on how that boy had got on in life, foretelling that "he is probably stone deaf by now"!

The 1st Chatswood was known as "Lord Forster's Own", with Lord Forster being the governor-general since 1920 and Australia's Chief Scout. The 1923 annual northern suburbs Corroboree was held at Beauchamp Park in Chatswood where the Wolf Cubs gave a gymnastics display for their patron. During 1925's Scout Week the Chatswood Cubs again performed, this time in Sydney's Theatre Royal as part of a Boy Scout Matinee in front of Admiral Sir Dudley de Chair KCB KCMG MVO RN, the governor of New South Wales.[1] Eight weeks before Sir Dudley had presided at the laying of the 2½ ton granite foundation stone for the ambitious Sydney Harbour Bridge. Scout Week that year culminated in a 4,000 strong march through the city by Cubs and Scouts with the Chatswood Troop leading the throng past the saluting base where the governor-general, in scout uniform and accompanied by the District Naval Officer, Commander Harold Quick RAN, took the salute.

A Universal Military Training Scheme had been introduced in 1911 for all boys from the age of fourteen. The Scout movement by contrast was consciously less military and strove for a "moral" tone while harnessing a boy's natural energy into fun outdoor activities. Emphasising as it did the qualities of honour, duty and respect along with self-discipline and self-reliance, the movement provided a firm foundation for Victor's developing character.

April 1924 saw the seven warships of the Royal Navy's Special Service Squadron, led by the world's largest warship, "The Mighty *Hood*" (48,000 tons) visit Sydney. Some half a million people watched the squadron's arrival from clifftop and foreshore, while 156,000 stepped aboard the battlecruisers *Hood* and *Repulse* on their open days. Few in Sydney would not have been aware and excited at the squadron's visit and its example of Royal Navy might.

In 1925 the family gained the major status symbol of the day, a motor car. Their Model T Ford was hand cranked and cantankerous, particularly in cold weather. This would cause George great irritation and the children, discreetly amused, learned to retreat well away from their father when he was trying to get that Model T started. Perhaps this was where a lack of patience with poor performance was initially ingrained into the son?

---

1   Dudley de Chair commanded the 10th Cruiser Squadron maintaining the Northern Patrol out of Scapa Flow in WWI.

It was a direct result of his Wolf Cub activities that first steered Victor towards a naval career. Like many with European heritage, his family's only contact with the sea had been their ancestors voyage out in emigrant ships. But occasionally, at the Friday evening Wolf Cub meetings, engineer Lieutenant Percy Sims RAN appeared. Percy and his wife lived in the area, and he was responsible for the warships in reserve on Sydney Harbour. When not teaching knots and hitches to the youngsters he talked about his service life. As an artificer engineer Percy had been instrumental in keeping the obsolescent cruiser HMAS *Pioneer* operational during the enervating 1914-1916 East African campaign.[2] Reminiscing about exotic Zanzibar or helping hunt down the German cruiser SMS *Königsberg* in the Rufigi Delta, it is easy to imagine the enthralled Cubs gathered around. The more Victor heard of naval life the greater its attraction.

His interest in the navy aroused, Victor discovered that the son of one of his teachers at Chatswood Primary School, Mrs Bowden, had joined the Royal Australian Naval College in the 1925 class. Mrs Bowden's son Harold, also a keen rugby player, was able to meet with Victor and told him a lot about a cadet's life at the college.[3] With these influences Victor declared, when he finished his primary education at the end of 1925, that he wished to join the navy. His father sensibly decided in that case he would not follow his brother Bill to Sydney Grammar School. Rather he was sent to the local Chatswood Intermediate High School for the 1926 school year and received special coaching for the RANC academic entry exams.

For the family of a prospective cadet, the naval college had a lot to commend. Consciously more egalitarian than the British Royal Naval College *Britannia*, there was no call for funds from the boy's father. The entire cost of a cadet's outfitting and training was borne by a paternal commonwealth, even down to the payment of pocket-money (1/- shilling per week in the first year), a clothing allowance and traveling expenses. The only cost would be a bond repayment if the cadet was withdrawn as unsuitable or for academic failure. A cadet could not voluntarily withdraw himself without the consent of the Naval Board.

Meanwhile *Bomera Creek* was put up for auction but failed to sell and in 1926 George and Una, after years of renting, built a house opposite the Trumper grandparents which they named *Bomera*. George formally applied to Navy Office in Melbourne for his son's appointment to the Royal Australian Naval College by the 30 June deadline. The application was supported by a certificate of moral behaviour from their Anglican minister, and a certificate of conduct from Victor's school principal. One father's application was rejected as the mother was not a natural-born British subject, although the boy was the Australian-born son of an Australian-born father who had served in the war with the Australian Imperial Force. All applicants had to be of "substantially" European descent.

---

2   Engineer Commander Percy Sims (1874-1957) transferred to the RAN Emergency List on retirement in 1930. He was mobilised in August 1940, aged 66, as the Assistant Inspector of Ordnance in Sydney.

3   Midshipman Harold Bowden (1911-1992) served in Australian cruisers and the Royal Navy battleship *Royal Oak* (nicknamed "Woody"). His appointment was terminated in 1931 as the Navy contracted during the Great Depression. Harold joined the Public Service as a clerk. Commissioned a pilot officer in WWII Harold saw operational service as a navigator on Ansons with No. 73 Squadron RAAF.

22595
HMS PIONEER

The light cruiser HMS Pioneer which was transferred to the RAN in 1913 as HMAS Pioneer and subsequently saw service in East Africa in WWI.

Every year towards the end of October the captain and headmaster of the college would conduct a three-week selection tour around Australia's capital cities. In each city they would be supplemented by a third naval officer of at least commander's rank. For Victor the academic entrance exams were invigilated at Sydney University. At 31 centres around the country 110 boys sat the exams, 63 successfully.

A few weeks later Victor reported to rooms in the Commonwealth Bank Building on Martin Place in Sydney. There he underwent a medical so comprehensive that 20 boys out of the 63 were rejected. Victor, along with the other healthy state candidates, was directed upstairs to where the interview committee was sitting.

When Victor sat in front of Captain Richard Lane-Poole OBE RN, and college's Director of Studies Dr Frederick Wheatley for the formal interview, they were probably joined by Captain John Robbins RAN, Captain Superintendent of Sydney. Victor was amazed but not fazed at the amount of gold braid opposite him and found all of the questions straightforward. No doubt he had been well coached by Sims and Bowden on demeanour and what questions to expect. With leadership in the Wolf Cubs likely giving him a pleasing directness without being forward, coupled to sporting prowess and perhaps even some interest around his Trumper name, Victor would have scored solidly with the committee. There were only 13 places available, so the 43 boys needed ranking in order of merit and whittling down.

The coming year of 1927 was to be a year of change for the Smith family. That cantankerous Ford gave way to a new Essex Super 6, *Bomera Creek* was finally sold and uncle Alfred bought the adjoining property of *Brooklyn*. George Smith received a letter from Paymaster Commander Charles Spurgeon OBE RAN, Acting-Secretary to the Australian Commonwealth Naval Board in Melbourne:

> Dear Sir,
>
> In connection with your son's candidature for entry to the Royal Australian Naval College, I am directed to inform you that he has been selected for appointment as Cadet Midshipman and will be required to take up appointment at the Royal Australian Naval College Jervis Bay early in February 1927.

CHAPTER 2

CADET MIDSHIPMAN 1927 – 1930

Disarmament was a committed government principle under the National Party of Stanley Bruce, the prime minister of Australia since 1923. Bruce had been both seriously wounded and decorated at Gallipoli in 1915. The "Five Powers Treaty" between the British Empire, France, Italy, Japan and the United States, resulting from the 1922 Washington naval conference, formalised the general dictum of "disarm some of what you have and limit what can be built" to prevent a new arms race. At London's Imperial Conference of 1923 these disarmament obligations were given dominion accord when Bruce agreed to the scuttling of the 17,000-ton battlecruiser HMAS *Australia*, off Sydney Heads in April 1924. The tonnage counted towards the British tally for scrapping.[1]

The Sea Lords had lobbied Bruce for Australia to build a modern naval force able to secure vital trade routes, while awaiting the concentration of a British battle fleet against the "enemy" in the Far East. Bruce, who campaigned under the slogan "Men, Money and Markets", was partial to these defence-of-trade priorities and accepted his country's Empire defence responsibilities. Committed to this Royal Navy policy for the dominion's navy, on his return Bruce announced in parliament a five-year defence plan from 1924-1929 that was heavily naval-centric and consequently costly. Two new cruisers at 10,000 tons each were to be the heaviest vessels with the largest armament allowed under the Washington Naval Treaty. It was expected that those cruisers would carry spotting aircraft and the proposed submarines were to be the latest ocean-going design. The concurrent upgrading of the specialist schools, dockyards and supply infrastructure necessary to sustain a modern force made this, at £4.25 million, the most ambitious peacetime defence program per capita in Australia's history.

The battlecruiser Australia is scuttled off Sydney Heads.

---

1   In a public relations reassurance, the scuttling occurred surrounded by the powerful warships of the Royal Navy's Special Service Squadron, on an official visit to Sydney as part of their "World Cruise" - sometimes described, not unfairly, as the "Booze Cruise"!

For Australia 1926 was a year of economic well-being: the country was prosperous and with no real intimations of the coming difficulties. Melbourne, where commercial radio broadcasts had only been heard for three years, was the seat of the Australian parliament as it had been since federation in 1901. The district of Yass-Canberra, selected as the site for the new nation's capital in 1908, still appeared as a small country town overlaid on a sheep station straddling the Molonglo River, with every second building seemingly under construction.

As 1926 closed, back "home" in Great Britain the General Strike had caused months of social unrest. Europe had seen the governments of Poland, Portugal and Lithuania overthrown. In Germany the Nazi Party, two years after Hitler had been released from prison, held no seats in the Reichstag and Nuremberg had yet to see a rally. Republican China was chaotic with brutal warlords holding sway over most of the country. The decade long tragedy of the civil war in Russia finally ended, giving way to the unfolding greater tragedy of monolithic rule under the General Secretary of the Communist Party, Josef Stalin. Japan, the harsh occupying power in Korea, had commenced the year shelling China's Taku forts yet again, and Toyota Industries was founded. In December Emperor Taisho died and his son, Hirohito, acceded to the throne as the Emperor Showa.

The Navy in 1927

The Royal Australian Navy of 1927 was perched on the south-eastern perimeter of the continent. Navy Office, at Victoria Barracks along Melbourne's St Kilda Road, was presided over by Rear-Admiral William Rawdon Napier CMG DSO RN, on loan service from Britain as the First Naval Member of the Commonwealth Naval Board.[2] Napier, responsible for the final three years of the ambitious five-year plan, was struggling with the complexities of an ambitious building programme overlaying a small manpower base. Facing significant construction costs his spending for 1927-28 was £5.05 million, compared with £2.42 million in 1924-25 at the start of the five-year plan. Subject to regular Treasury demands to reduce previously agreed estimates, the outlook for Australia's Navy still remained upbeat. Navy Office was located within easy walking distance of the federal public service departments, which had not yet fully relocated to the new capital of Canberra.

There were small naval depots around Port Phillip Bay at Port Melbourne, Williamstown, Geelong and Swan Island while some 48 kilometres away by train lay Flinders Naval Depot with its newly constructed barracks to support the Engineering, Signals, Gunnery and Torpedo Schools. Sydney's Port Jackson hosted the Dockyard, Naval Depot and Stores Depot at Garden Island, the Naval Armaments Depot at Spectacle Island and the Royal Edward Victualing Yard in Pyrmont. Alongside were the depot and receiving ships *Penguin* (5,880 tons) and *Platypus* (3,476 tons).

---

2   Later Vice-Admiral William "Bill" Napier CMG DSO (1877-1951), an 1891 *Britannia* cadet and decorated veteran of minesweeping off Gallipoli and in the North Sea. It was a mine that had sunk the returning hospital ship *Anglia* in 1915, drowning his wounded older army officer brother. Napier's numerous commands included torpedo boats, monitors, sloops, cruisers and the battleship *Royal Sovereign* (nicknamed the "Tiddly Quid" by her crew) as well as specialist training schools.

The final class of fourteen- to sixteen-year-old boys had joined the training ship *Tingira*, moored in Sydney's Rose Bay. Bound to serve until the age of 25 these young sailors were the solid backbone of the squadron. Recognising local democratic sentiments, the Naval Board would annually reserve places at the Naval College for one or two *Tingira* boys who, if found suitable, would join the second-year class at Jervis Bay.

Around the continent could be found small District Naval Officer establishments and Naval Drill Halls in each state. "Girt by sea" Australia was encircled by 34,000 kilometres of coastline, much of it inadequately charted. Off remote sections of the continent could be found *Geranium* (1,250 tons) and *Moresby* (1,320 tons) steadfastly surveying.

The unreconstructed second verse of *Advance Australia Fair* in 1927 still proclaimed "Britannia rules the waves" and the RAN considered itself intimately included in this Empire sentiment.[3] Coupled with a sense of manifest destiny since federation, with its surging nationalism where defence of empire was self-evident, this had helped the strategic vision of an Australian Navy able to assume a mature role in that empire's defence.

The warships of the squadron were concentrated in Sydney Harbour when not away on their seasonal training cruises. Commodore First Class George Hyde CBE RAN flew his broad pennant as Commodore Commanding the Australian Squadron from his flagship, the famous cruiser *Sydney*.[4,5] Hyde was the first RAN officer to command the squadron. Among the many RANC trained junior officers in the wardrooms of the squadron were the first two to be promoted lieutenant-commanders that October. When their ships were in Jervis Bay these officers would inspect with interest the latest batch of cadets boarding for a sea-training day.

The Royal Australian Naval College

With Sydney and Melbourne's contending claims to become the new nation's capital a compromise was necessary. In 1913 the capital city was formally named Canberra, located within the newly proclaimed Australian Capital Territory which lay 160 kilometres southwest of Sydney. Meanwhile on New South Wales's southern coast the Jervis Bay Territory had been ceded by the state in 1915 to the Australian Capital Territory. It was intended to give the landlocked capital a deep-water port that could be reached via an inland railway. Well isolated from city enticements and distractions Jervis Bay was the natural choice for the site of the Royal Australian Naval College. With the sea an integral part of the environment, and protected waters in which the warships of the RAN would often anchor, its location could not be bettered, although the railway was never built.

---

3   When *Advance Australia Fair* became the national anthem in 1984 the original four verses became two. Expunged were such lines as "True British courage bore him on" and "Then here he raised Old England's flag, the standard of the brave".

4   Later Admiral George Hyde KCB CVO CBE (1877-1937). English born; Hyde had transferred to the RAN in 1912 as a commander. He had been captain of HMAS *Brisbane* and later the Second Naval Member before promotion to commodore of the squadron. In 1932 he was appointed Rear-Admiral and First Naval Member of the Commonwealth Naval Board.

5   HMAS *Sydney* had been victorious at the Battle of Cocos against the cruiser SMS *Emden* on 9 November 1914.

A modern view of the Royal Australian Naval College at Jervis Bay. The site was selected in 1911 and construction of the main buildings was completed four years later.

Jervis Bay had been sighted by Captain Cook in 1770. When the convict ship *Atlantic* of the Third Fleet entered in 1791 Lieutenant Richard Bowen named it after his patron, Rear-Admiral John Jervis.[6] Captains Point on the western side of the bay occupied a postcard-worthy position overlooking two kilometres of pure silica sand, the whitest in the world. The college was purpose-built with enviable facilities for academics, naval instruction and sport.

Twenty-three midshipmen of the 1913 Pioneer class had graduated on its grass quarterdeck at the end of four years training in December 1916. Sailing for WWI in January 1917 they joined the battleships and battlecruisers of the Grand Fleet at Rosyth in Scotland and Scapa Flow in the Orkney Islands. Most had yet to celebrate their eighteenth birthday and the college had become a symbol of the young nation's willingness to shoulder the burdens of naval self-defence.

When Victor was woken at 0630 on his second day, he discovered that even time was different in the navy. He had heard from his dormitory the imposing clock tower overlooking the quarter-deck/sports-field striking the bell strokes of the naval day.[7] It was five bells in the morning watch. Like all naval shore establishments, the routine and nomenclature paralleled shipboard life so Victor would have hastened along the passageway to the heads before falling-in for scran.[8] The newly designated Flinders Year were rapidly made aware that their navy life had commenced.

There was a single day of orientation before the senior classes returned to the college. After breakfast the boys were issued uniforms and all clothing down to service pyjamas. There were

---

6   Admiral Jervis, known to his crew as "Old Jarvie", was ennobled as Earl St Vincent after the Battle of Cape St Vincent in 1797. Captain Richard Bowen died assaulting the town of Santa Cruz de Tenerife that same year. During this assault Rear-Admiral Nelson lost his right arm and believed his career was finished.
7   Naval Time or Ship's Time - one stroke of the ship's bell for each half-hour of a four-hour watch. Hence eight bells, rung in double cadence, marked the end of that watch.
8   i.e., down the corridor to the toilets before mustering in ordered ranks for breakfast.

lectures about life at the college and its do's and don'ts. Naturally, as the most junior cadets, it was mainly don'ts. After changing into their new uniforms, instruction commenced in the basics of saluting, marching and doubling. They soon learnt that junior cadets would always default to doubling when not marching - they rarely walked.

Victor had joined a service institution that believed early novitiate-style moulding of a boy cadet would produce a dutiful, efficient and self-disciplined naval officer. The Naval Defence Act of 1910 authorised the formation of an Australian Navy from the old Commonwealth Naval Forces and on 10 July 1911, shortly after his coronation, King George V approved "with pleasure" the title Royal Australian Navy.[9] At the inception it was the intention that RAN and RN officers should be so alike in their training that, apart from their accents, they would be totally indistinguishable and interchangeable. The British cadet joined *Britannia* Royal Naval College, Dartmouth, at thirteen, therefore the Australian followed suit. Not all considered their service would be a life's vocation but each cadet on graduation was expected to serve twelve years until the age of 30.

On day three the college really came alive with the arrival of the second-, third- and fourth-year cadets, respectively the Cook, Phillip and Jervis years, making 50 cadets under training at an establishment whose capacity was triple that. Although the Pioneer 1913 class had numbered 28 cadets, yearly entries had peaked at 36 in 1918, before post-war reductions had drastically cut each year to an average of thirteen.[10] Smith was the 332nd naval cadet to enter the college. While each of the Flinders Year, in the careful manner of young boys, eyed the twelve other strangers gathered from five states it would not take long before the shared stresses of that junior year would see them form lifelong bonds of mateship.

At the college four years of study under the professorial staff saw the cadet achieve matriculation standard. Tertiary study was decades away from being considered necessary, or even desirable, for a seaman officer. With over ten years of professional training and technical courses until achieving his chosen specialisation, the sooner started the better.[11] Compared with public service clerks where promotion was based almost solely on seniority at their departmental desks, the naval years of technical and staff courses were notably more formalised and rigorous.

Heading a devoted academic staff was the Director of Studies Dr Frederick Wheatley BSc BA DSc. A Doctor of Science degree was then rare in Australia and Smith found Dr Wheatley's academic regalia at Sunday Divisions most impressive. Smith would always remember his

---

9   As a boy of twelve in 1877 King George V had, himself, joined *Britannia* as a cadet. He visited the Australia Station in 1881 aboard the corvette *Bacchante*. In his fifteen-year naval career Prince George commanded torpedo boat *TB.79*, the gunboat *Thrush* and the cruiser *Melampus*.
10   Thirty Cadet-Midshipmen were retired by the Naval Board at the end of 1921 and 32 graduates resigned by invitation.
11   Against a seaman officers name on the Navy List the letters (G) Gunnery, (H) Surveying, (N) Navigator, (O) Observer, (P) Pilot, (S) Signalling/Wireless Telegraphy, (SM) Submarines and (T) Torpedo took a minimum of ten years to achieve and were all hard earned. For example, the RAN's original observer, Henry Chesterman (1915 class), was not awarded an (O) designation until 1928 after consolidation flying training off HMS *Eagle* in the Mediterranean.

The thirteen boys of the 1927 Flinders class with their Year Officer, Lieutenant Maurice Lancaster, (centre). VAT Smith is on the far right, standing.

masters who, given the reduced numbers at the college, easily ensured a high standard of tuition. They included the history master, Mr Frank Eldridge BA and the physics master Mr Hugh Simpson BA BSc, while he recalled the English master Mr Hector Macleod BSc mainly as a very good cricketer.

French was patiently taught to Smith by Mr Geoff Adeney MA, and Mr Leonard Morrison MA. To keep the foreign language relevant, it had a preponderance of naval ranks, warship types and seamanship terms just as history had included numerous naval actions. Smith's academic results would remain solidly average for four years. At the end of 1927 he was ranked fifth out of thirteen but, most remarkably, was the only one of his year to have avoided any official punishments.

Among the college buildings and around the marine section were workshops and other facilities for the naval staff to progress, in tandem with their academics, the cadets' nautical training. Overlaying all was sport of every variety. As well as fitness, each day was begun with a run and sea swim at the end of the breakwater. The sporting ethos of teamwork and leadership were considered essential foundations for a young officer.

The commanding officer was Captain Richard Lane-Poole OBE RN, and the executive officer Frederick "Jack" Durnford RN. Although Royal Navy officers would continue in senior positions for some years yet, the first RANC trained officers were starting to return in naval staff positions, with Smith's Year Officer being Lieutenant Maurice Lancaster RAN, of the 1916 class.[12] The captain, by definition, was a high and remote person ashore as much as afloat. Smith did not see much of Lane-Poole before he returned to the UK that April but his replacement, Captain Herbert Forster MVO RN, took great interest in all the sports played and was more in evidence. Whether hockey, football or cricket, and always if the college was playing another team, Forster would be there as an onlooker and active supporter.

Life for junior cadets was not easy. In addition to the normal punishments of unyielding naval discipline there was sanctioned beating, usually with a sandshoe. A second year could beat a first year, and so forth to the top where a fourth year could beat a third, second and first year. This veered too easily into bullying instead of a justified punishment, and an older Smith would express firm support when it was finally proscribed. The young Smith soon discovered that some of his seniors had very strong arms. While unacceptable today, only the excessive striking, not the actual, was then frowned on. It would appear to have never degenerated into the viciousness and occasional serious injury experienced by the first-year staff cadets at the Royal Military College, Duntroon, who emulated the West Point hazing tradition.

The British system of fagging was also operating at this time. Common in public schools and the gunrooms of the RN it was a form of minor servitude to senior cadets. Running the gamut from shining a senior's shoes to doing errands, Smith, with such tasks intruding on the already overfull life of a junior cadet, believed it was taken to an unnecessary degree. When given a mundane task from a senior, such as fetching a football from the sports store, he would rebelliously think "Why cannot the silly fool do the thing himself!" First year were fags for third year, second year fags for fourth year, and were at their seniors' beck and call.

A highlight of 1927 for the college was participation in one of the seminal moments in Australian political history, the opening of Parliament House in Canberra on 9 May. Smith did not appreciate the full significance at the time although finding it memorable. He was, however, quite interested in what Duntroon cadets did for social activities. On enquiry Smith was told that several of them had bicycles, but as all the reasonable girls seemed to live so far away it required serious consideration whether it was worth a bicycle ride to go calling.

Remote Canberra was a long drive for the college vehicles through the Kangaroo Valley and past Goulburn. On arrival it was still a very rural capital with the only suburbs being Civic, Ainslie and Kingston. They were accommodated at the Military College for six days before the opening. The long hours of drilling and rehearsing were enlivened by the roar of the aeroplanes from the nearby air force camp. These aircraft fascinated the cadets and there were at least four forced landings and several crashes. The day before the ceremony leave was granted to join the throngs of visitors and do the small amount of sightseeing possible.

---

12   The Year Officers were responsible for the leadership, naval training and administration of the cadets. A casualty of the depression, Lancaster was placed on half-pay in 1932 and then transferred to the Emergency List. He returned to the college staff on the outbreak of WWII. Lieutenant-Commander Maurice Lancaster (1902-1983) served in *Bungaree*, surveying the Torres Strait, before commanding the corvette *Maryborough* in 1945.

It was a cold clear day when the Naval Guard of Honour, commanded by Lieutenant John Armstrong RAN (1914 class), joined the army and air force guards opposite the main entrance to the new Parliament Building.[13] Facing these guards-of-honour the staff cadets flanked the main entrance on one side and the cadet midshipmen the other. As they braced in position an RAAF formation flew overhead.

The Duke and Duchess of York, the future King George VI and Queen Elizabeth, had voyaged out to Australia in the battlecruiser *Renown* whose royal marine band and sailors contributed to the day's pageantry.[14] As the royal party alighted from their coach a fanfare was blown by the marine buglers. His Royal Highness's speech was made audible to the crowd with the recently introduced system of amplifiers, which the world-famous opera singer, Dame Nellie Melba, eschewed when she sang the National Anthem *a capella*. Prime Minister Bruce presented the duke with a golden key to open the door of Parliament House and further ceremonies continued inside.

The cadets ate lunch at the army camp and then joined the naval brigade and the other services for the royal review of three thousand servicemen in the newly named York Park.[15] As they marched past the saluting base *Renown*'s band played the stirring official march of both the RN and the RAN, *Hearts of Oak*.[16] Tragically an SE5A inexplicably rolled away from the formation overhead and crashed 600 metres from Parliament House.[17] Flying Officer Francis Ewen, RAAF, (27) died from his injuries.

Life back at the college continued its rigid routine enlivened by the occasional visits of squadron warships. There was the annual regatta in October and the cadets returned to Parliament House for Armistice Day ceremonies in November. When *Sydney*, *Melbourne* and *Success* were in the bay, Commodore Hyde took the opportunity to inspect the cadets at Divisions.

At the 1927 passing out graduation parade his excellency the governor-general gave a speech whose essential elements Smith was to hear from the monocle-wearing Baron Stonehaven GCMG DSO PC, over three consecutive years. He was congratulated on joining the King's Navy, and for having found in Australia the opportunity to qualify for such a profession:

> (1927): I say King's Navy because the Royal Australian Navy is part of the Royal Navy, and

---

13   Later Commodore John Armstrong DSO MiD US Navy Cross (1900-1988). Executive Officer of the college in 1938, he commanded the armed merchant cruisers *Manoora* and *Westralia* in 1942. Armstrong was captain of the cruiser HMAS *Australia* during the invasion of Luzon when his ship was hit by kamikazes on each of four successive days in January 1945.

14   The Duke of York, Prince Albert, came bottom of his Osborne Naval College class in 1911. A turret officer aboard the dreadnought battleship *Collingwood* at the Battle of Jutland, chronic seasickness and health issues saw him transferred to the Royal Naval Air Service and then the Royal Air Force. He qualified as an RAF pilot in 1919. By 1927 Prince Albert had been consulting the Australian speech therapist Lionel Logue for two years, and subsequently his speech was delivered without stammer or undue hesitation.

15   The area of Kings Avenue and State Circle in modern Canberra.

16   Come cheer up, my lads, 'tis to glory we steer,
       To add something more to this wonderful year;
       To honour we call you, as free men not slaves,
       For who are so free as the sons of the waves?

17   This was not the first RAAF crash the duke had witnessed. Two weeks beforehand, while inspecting an air force guard-of-honour in Melbourne, two DH9s in the 30 strong formation overhead collided and crashed. Glimpsing the collision over the guard commander's shoulder, the duke involuntarily exclaimed, without stutter, "Two of your buggers gone!".

Parliament House, Canberra, in a very rural setting during the opening ceremony on 9 May 1927.

you are all members of one family... the Navy is one of the few tangible and visible links between the different parts of the Empire ... Whether at peace or war, the guarding of the seas, protection of the great trade routes of the Empire, the maintenance of order, has been, is, and always will be, the duty of the Navy.

(1928): You share the history and tradition, the rights and responsibilities of British citizenship in its widest sense ... defend first Australia, and second the British Empire; and in practice it will be found impossible to separate the two.

(1929): The College was the nursery of the Australian Navy.[18]

Smith found his second year was a welcome relief from the pressures of being the most junior. There was now some little authority and hard-won privileges, such as the eagerly anticipated camping expeditions at half-term. To make life a little less harsh a second weekend leave per term was introduced. With his first-year experience behind him, Smith, ever practical, now knew what corners might safely be cut to improve his still lowly lot, only receiving a single minor punishment over the whole year of 1928 while doing so.

In January 1928 Commander Edward Fogarty Fegen SGM RN replaced Durnford as executive officer. The third generation of an Anglo/Irish naval family Fegen had served in destroyers during the war and, before his loan to the RAN, had trained Dartmouth cadets in seamanship. An arresting character, decorated for the daring rescue of a crew from a blazing oil tanker, he was also a capped international rugby player. Unsurprisingly all the cadets hero-worshipped him.

Smith, yet to experience his growth spurt, was playing in the Junior Rugby XV (under 48 kilograms) in a three-quarters position and gratefully received personalised coaching from

---

18   While such sentiments strike the modern Australian as lacking in patriotism, not so for the contemporary listener. When six colonies became the Commonwealth of Australia the population retained British nationality. This meant that when Harold Bowden joined the RAAF in 1942, he attested for service not as an Australian but as a British subject. Australian nationality was not legislated until the Nationality and Citizenship Act of 1948 and Australian passports bore the word "British" on the cover until the 1960s.

The Duke of York inspects the cadets ranked behind their Year Officers at the opening of Parliament House ceremony. He is accompanied by the college's executive officer Lieutenant-Commander Durnford and Rear-Admiral Napier.

Fegen. The improvement in his play was shown when Smith scored three tries against Blue Mountains Grammar.

Whether they were competitive or not all cadets were expected to participate in as many sports as possible. The annual boxing championship was compulsory but Smith, perhaps sensibly, never progressed past the first heats. In the 1928 athletics he managed a second in the long jump and seconds in the 50-yard breaststroke and freestyle at the swimming regatta. Smith also sailed skiffs in the sailing regatta. Forty-eight cadets participated in the annual cross country and Smith, with the benefit of the junior year's handicap start, came a commendable fourth.

The Naval Board had approved £80 to purchase a replacement piano which Smith, with several years of piano tuition, was soon playing regularly. To help produce a well-rounded officer and gentleman there were weekly dances on Wednesday night for the cadets. The married officers' and the masters' wives, very long suffering, would come along to have their feet politely trodden on by the cadets. With not enough partners to go around the remaining cadets would have to dance together. This embarrassment Smith avoided as he was playing the piano, the other instruments being drums and a tin whistle. He would recall that the quality of the dancing reflected the quality of the music.

Smith's musical tasking did not end with the weekly dance. Every weekday morning Divisions were held at 0900 (two bells in the forenoon watch) and evening prayers in the chapel on Sundays. At both Smith would be the organist for the hymns. He would also have been co-opted for the end-of-year concert which coincided with graduation functions. Smith was learning early that naval service would lead to some extraordinary and unusual duties at times.

The lovely sight of the Argentinian three masted sail training ship ARA *Presidente Sarmiento* appeared in Jervis Bay in July 1928.[19] In a speech Lieutenant-Commander Müller, seeing the British navy as the teacher and the young Australian cadets as brilliant pupils, eloquently declaimed:

> We are officers of one ship which is also a part of a naval college of a young country, and through which have passed as pupils all the chiefs which today direct the fates of the Argentine Navy … the joy and pleasure it gives us in visiting the naval college of another young country, and through which have passed the officers which tomorrow will direct the destinies of the Australian navy.

While his remarks proved accurate for Smith and two other cadets listening who became admirals, there were also seven in that cadet body sadly fated to be killed in action.[20] In September 1928 Flinders Year saw the first of their number have his appointment terminated. Patrick George's parents were informed in September 1928 of his unsatisfactory progress, and he was withdrawn.[21]

In June 1928 Charles Kingsford-Smith MC AFC, along with his co-pilot/navigator Charles Ulm AFC, flew the first transpacific flight via Hawaii and Fiji.[22] It was recognised as a great aviation feat by the cadets, but the future ramifications were not really considered. While Smith's later memory was that people in naval service then looked upon anybody who had anything to do with aircraft as being rather unusual, the college archives give a different story.

While serving with the Grand Fleet in 1918, seven of the 1913 Pioneer class had volunteered for the Royal Naval Air Service but were not used. Meanwhile, back at the college the growing importance of "aeronautics" had seen a short course of lectures on the subject introduced in the fourth year. When a Fairey seaplane from Point Cook arrived in Jervis Bay for fleet co-operation exercises with *Sydney, Anzac, Success, Swordsman* and *Platypus* on 2 March 1928, the cadets were enthralled until it left 28 days later.

In the annual college magazine Lieutenant Vincent Kennedy (1915 class), a pilot seconded to the RAAF, wrote of flying for the 1926 Barrier Reef survey embarked rather precariously on *Geranium.* On 18 August 1928, a large and impressive Supermarine Southampton flying boat

19 Armada de la República Argentina (ARA) *Presidente Sarmiento* of 2,750 tons and four 120mm guns.
20 Rear-Admiral Morrison (1925 class), Admiral Smith (1927 class) and Vice-Admiral Peek (1928 class).
21 A West Australian entry Patrick George (1913-1985) returned west to a pastoral life, farming under the surname George-Kennedy. He married in 1939 and raised a large family.
22 To be followed by the first non-stop flight across Australia in August and the first trans-Tasman flight in September.

An RAAF Supermarine Southampton flying boat, one of which visited Jervis Bay in August 1928.

raised much interest when it brought Air Marshal Sir John Salmond KCB CMG CVO DSO* RAF, to visit the college.

The 1928 passing out graduation saw the standard round of sport and social activities attended by the governor-general and first naval member. Over several days there was a sailing regatta, captain's dance, passing out dance and a gymnastics display.

In 1929 Smith, now in his third year, was approaching the upper hierarchy among the cadets. He was feeling well experienced in the routine, hewed without effort to the discipline standards expected, accepted uncomplainingly the one major and four minor punishments awarded, and was seemingly comfortable with all aspects of his cadet existence.[23] The new cruiser *Australia* had arrived in her namesake country on 23 October 1928. The submarines *Oxley* and *Otway* followed shortly afterwards and then the cruiser *Canberra*. When *Canberra* entered Sydney Harbour on 16 February 1929, she was carrying the oak figurehead from Cook's *Resolution*.

The arrival of the *Australia* and *Canberra* in Jervis Bay Smith found terribly impressive. To see these newly constructed County Class treaty cruisers with their elegant lines steaming in and anchoring only a few cables off the college proved unforgettable.[24] On 8 March 1929 the cadets visited *Australia* and *Albatross*. It was almost as memorable when, on 13 March, during a sea day onboard *Albatross* the majority of the Cook and Flinders Years experienced *mal-de-mer*. Their sea training day aboard the submarine *Oxley* in June, after a lecture by her commanding officer Lieutenant-Commander Frank Getting, left no major impression on Smith.[25]

On Anzac Day, 25 April 1929, all the cadets attended a ceremony in Canberra where the

---

23   It was not many years since a cadet could be tied over a vaulting horse and publicly beaten.
24   Ten cables equals one nautical mile, making one cable length 185 metres.
25   Getting was the first of the 1913 Pioneer class to gain a command. In June 1942 he would be appointed captain of *Canberra* with Smith as his embarked observer.

governor-general laid a commemoration stone for a memorial Smith would always consider unsurpassed by any other country - the Australian War Memorial.

In the pre-season rugby training of the college First XV Fegen made time to continue his personal coaching of Smith. Moving him from the left wing he told Smith he would be playing full-back in the coming matches. Initially lacking confidence in this new position Fegen's coaching was suitably patient and apropos. Smith valued that coaching enormously.

Navy versus Army Rugby Match

The annual rugby match against the Royal Military College (founded in 1911, two years before the naval college), was the highlight of the sporting calendar. Both institutions were proudly seen as vigorous examples of the new nation's desire for defence self-reliance. Unlike the pristine surrounds at Jervis Bay the military college huts in the cleared bush outside Canberra were said to resemble a prison farm. The staff cadets joined RMC at the age of seventeen so there was, inevitably, a physical mismatch where the oldest of the naval team would be outweighed by the youngest of the army.

This higher age of the RMC staff cadets meant that on the declaration of war in 1914 their two senior years were immediately posted to active units. When the First XV from the remaining two junior years lost the inaugural Navy versus Army match at Jervis Bay under the gaze of their commandant, Major General John Parnell, on 1 September 1916, he blamed the 20-9 loss on the war. Every annual match was gritty, and the navy did not win again until the 1920s when, in recognition of the size disparity, RMC only selected from their two junior years. If the match was being played at Jervis Bay, all ex-cadets in any nearby ships would come ashore to see it.

With navy wins in 1922, 1924 and 1925 the statistics stood at nine victories for the army and four for the navy when the RANC First XV motored to Duntroon on 27 July 1929. It takes physical bravery to stand up to a taller and heavier opponent on a rugby field, more so with the inevitable hard tackling and rough rucks and mauls of a navy versus army match. In the First XV were five Flinders Year cadets: Anderson, Hancox, Innocent, Ridley and Wilson. With numbers down due to injury Smith stepped into the breach at full-back as the whole team prepared to demonstrate their physical courage in abundance.

With a slight breeze across the ground Navy kicked off and immediately applied pressure. A penalty was awarded against Army; however, Hancox missed the penalty attempt. Army pushed back from their 25 with a clearing kick. From a scrum the Navy backs commenced a long passing movement, which Logan punted ahead and beat the Army full-back to a try under the posts. Hancox converted to make the score 5-0. For long minutes Army was dangerously on the offensive in the Navy 25 until Wilson intercepted and ran over half the length of the pitch to score in the corner. Logan converted to make the score 10-0.

After half-time a smarting Army made a heavy onslaught but a tackle by Smith, and a swift dive by Ridley, prevented what had seemed a certain try. Wilson, with a dummy pass, sent

Logan on to score near the posts but the conversion attempt was unsuccessful (13-0). Army then scored from a five-yard scrum but also could not convert (13-3). Maintaining a forward battle Army used their weight but were unable to get over the line, until a fine passing rush by their three-quarters ended in a try. Again, they failed to convert (13-6). Grinding play in the Navy 25 required the solid tackling of Menary, Smith and Langford to keep the score down. The final ten minutes saw Army in striking distance through a defensive wall of stubborn white until eventually forcing themselves over through sheer weight. The converting kick was disallowed, however, and Navy had won 13-9.

Surprising the soldiers, as well as themselves, this was the only naval victory ever on Army's home ground at Duntroon. Four of Smith's Flinders Year classmates were awarded rugby colours while Smith and Anderson received honorary colours. Just rewards for a tenacious team with the guts to endure through the gruelling they received from the heavier Army XV. A delighted Smith, nursing a battered nose, helped record the win with poetry:

The Conquerors of Duntroon
Tho' we were small, alas! and light,
We hoped (in hours before the game)
That we'd enhance the College name,
By vanquishing the soldier's might.
The ground was hard, the day was cold,
But as we waited our desire,
Excitement warmed our blood like fire,
And made us confident and bold.
Three times we scored ere half-time came,
And then our enemy awoke,
But to their onslaught seldom broke
Our one of white. To end the game
The whistle seemed triumphantly
To scream a hymn of victory.

Life at the college continued in an insular manner. Outside national and international events were, understandably, not of great interest to the cadets who were kept so very occupied. The National Party had submitted its first deficit budget in 1927. Subsequent Treasury economies meant that the 4,777 officers and men of the navy allowed for in the 1927-1928 estimates could not be supported. Napier stopped general navy recruiting in October 1927 and some "weeding out" took place. Hopes for a second five-year plan to confirm a further two cruisers and four submarines foundered at the Council of Defence meeting in April 1928 when it was decided to preserve what was existing until better financial conditions prevailed.

The international market for wool was declining with the price of the vital wool clip down 30%. More alarming was that the London underwriters in June 1929 could only cover 84% of

The winning 1929 Navy team - Smith is standing in the third row with his nose bandaged. Circled are those cadets who did not survive WWII.

a proposed Australian Government loan of £8 million. The London Stock Exchange plunged in September which increased doubt about the economy across the Atlantic. On 24 October 1929 Black Thursday marked the start of the Wall Street crash with the greatest sell-off of shares in US history. The decade-long world-wide Great Depression had commenced.

Napier's replacement as First Naval Member, Rear-Admiral William Munro Kerr CBE CB RN, arrived in Melbourne at the end of October 1929. Briefed on the seriousness of the financial situation, Kerr spent his first month paying off the survey ship *Moresby* and closing the naval establishments in Geelong, Newcastle and Launceston as the RAN contracted to its main bases in the capital cities.

Theodore Landon's parents were required by the Naval Board to "withdraw him forthwith" for unsatisfactory progress on 4 October 1929, and Flinders Year now numbered eleven.[26] When Kerr attended Jervis Bay for the passing out parade of 11 December 1929, he was astonished at the size of the establishment that was graduating only ten cadets. With 48 cadets on parade Kerr thought it was an extravagance with the financial position so bad, writing that:

> The cadets were very smart but it is rather absurd to see this handful of boys and contrast it with the large establishment which is maintained for them.

The writing was on the wall for the college at Jervis Bay.

---

26   Theodore Landon (1913-1980) led a peripatetic life. In 1937 he was a salesman in Perth and during WWII signed on as a crewman with various merchant ships, later settling in Wales.

Recognising his above-average leadership potential, Smith was made a cadet captain responsible, under the Year Officers, for much of the day-to-day routine at the college. His classmates Dowson and Wilson were also made cadet captains and Hancox, to no-one's surprise, was made chief cadet captain.

The October 1929 election changed the government by a landslide from National to the Labor Party. Prime Minister James Scullin, who visited Jervis Bay in February 1930, quickly grasped the position as Kerr proposed moving the college to Flinders Naval Depot. At Jervis Bay it had cost £65,000 a year to run whereas costs were estimated at only £15,000 per year at Flinders. Since the college closure was politically sensitive, and deeply unpopular within the navy itself, Kerr, to hasten government agreement, indicated he was willing to shoulder the responsibility. The announcement on 30 June 1930, stressed that it was at the First Naval Member's recommendation "due to the present financial condition of the Commonwealth". The Royal Military College, also in the throes of economic stringency, moved from Canberra to the old convict-built Victoria Barracks in Sydney's Paddington.

By mid-1930 Kerr's sea-going charge had been reduced to four ships: the heavy cruisers *Australia* and *Canberra*, the destroyer *Anzac* and the seaplane carrier *Albatross*.[27] A reduction scheme was introduced to cut manpower down to 3,200 and the two submarines were to be offered back to the Royal Navy at the 1930 Imperial Conference. This was the much-reduced squadron that Smith would be graduating to in six months time, albeit containing two of the most modern large cruisers in the world and a built for purpose seaplane carrier. The cadets went on leave from Jervis Bay on 26 June 1930, and reported to Flinders Naval Depot on 7 August. Kerr arrived a week later to inspect the new surroundings and *Albatross* delivered the remaining stores from Jervis Bay in October.

For Smith the upheaval of moving to unfamiliar surroundings was profound. Instead of being part of an institution whose sole objective was the training of future RAN officers, the naval college was now one unit in a much larger training establishment. He was especially disdainful of the restricted Hanns Inlet after the magnificent open waters of Jervis Bay. Overall, however, once settled into the new environment Smith considered things worked out reasonably well.

During these six months at Flinders, Smith, on an unfamiliar cross-country course and no longer benefitting from a junior's handicap start, came in twentieth place. Now in an Australian rules football playing state, rugby matches were against the depot officers, and once against a combined metropolitan team, with Smith continuing in his full-back position. Still steering clear of cricket, Smith's name appeared for hockey as a forward against a United Services team and he played in the spring tennis tournament. He still wisely continued to lose the first round of the annual boxing tournament and was unplaced in the annual swimming sports. He did participate in life-saving training which he would put to good use in the Mediterranean a decade later.

---

27   In reserve were: *Adelaide, Brisbane, Geranium, Mallow, Marguerite, Moresby, Stalwart, Success, Swordsman, Tasmania* and *Tattoo*.

The Flinders Year passing out parade was on 17 December 1930. Missing from the graduation were William Anderson and David Innocent, who had that same day had their appointments terminated as part of the reduction scheme, leaving only ten to graduate.[28,29] There were nine survivors from the 1927 Flinders Year, plus Bill Langford of the 1926 Cook Year, who had failed mathematics and joined Flinders for a remedial year.[30]

Awaiting the appointment of the first Australian governor-general, Sir Isaac Isaacs, the interim administrator of Australia and governor of Victoria, Lord Somers KCMG DSO MC took the salute.[31] In his speech he acknowledged sadness at seeing the reduced numbers but declared that "the fewer the number the greater the responsibility for the defence of Australia". These numbers were to be fewer yet as the coming lean years meant there was no 1931 entry to the naval college.

At the prize giving ceremony Peter Hancox was the outstanding cadet. The Chief Cadet Captain, an all-round sportsman who had gained six blues, he was later awarded the King's Medal.[32] Smith respected his classmate's sporting prowess and found him a chap of great charm. Fellow Cadet Captain Norman Wilson was awarded the Governor-General's Cup. Smith himself, still solidly average, was not in the running for any academic prizes although he placed third for the Otto Albert Prize for Seamanship. To recognise their leadership over the previous twelve months Smith and the other cadet captains were presented with silver cigarette cases, reflecting a time when smoking equalled maturity rather than cancer. Smith admired his greatly.

It was now "cruiser" time aboard *Australia* or *Canberra* for the graduating cadets to start putting into practice the nautical knowledge and skills the college's naval staff had striven to instil. In 1992 VAT Smith looked back six decades to his naval college years and wrote:

> I think the training was very soundly based. With the small total of cadets … it was almost approaching personal tuition, so there was every opportunity for cadets to become very well versed in any particular subject. The balance between the purely academic and the naval profession subjects was about right. It is probably unavoidable, but today it seems that some of the good points in a junior officers' training have disappeared, compared to the 1930s. Perhaps this is just an old sea dog growling!

---

28   William Anderson (1913-1980) worked his passage as a seaman aboard the *Discovery* to England where he joined the RAF on a short service commission. He was decorated with a Distinguished Flying Cross during tribal skirmishes on India's North West Frontier. William's DH.84 Dragon II passenger aircraft was shot down by a He-111 off the Scilly Isles on 3 June 1941, killing all six aboard.

29   David Innocent (1913-2004) became a farmer like his classmate Patrick George.

30   The graduating class was: Dowson, Drew, Hancox, Harvie, Knox, Langford, Ridley, Robertson, Smith and Wilson.

31   Chief Scout of Victoria (and Grand Master of the State's Freemasons), Lord Somers became Chief Scout of the British Empire in 1941.

32   Awarded annually to the cadet exhibiting the best character, officer-like qualities and good influence among his peers.

CHAPTER 3

JUNIOR OFFICER UNDER TRAINING 1931 – 1934

HMAS *Canberra* 20 January 1931 to 24 June 1932

The decade prior to 1931 had been bracketed by two disarmament treaties, their naval tonnage obligations underlying the defence polices agreed at the three Imperial Conferences of 1923, 1926 and 1930. Following on from the Five Powers Treaty of 1922 the further efforts made at the London Naval Conference of 1930 were ratified in that October's "Treaty for the Limitation and Reduction of Naval Armament". Looming economic recession had consigned the second Five Year Plan for the next two cruisers and four additional submarines to fading memory. For 1931-32 Rear-Admiral Munro Kerr had a budget of only £1.7 million but he, and his squadron commanders, were determined to maintain peak efficiency and squeeze maximum training value from that sum. There might only be a rump of four warships in commission, but three were new and they would work and train hard, recognising that they would be the nucleus of future expansion.

It is a truism of any navy that new ships are of little use without trained manpower, with that training taking considerably longer than any ship's construction. It had been three years to build and commission a new cruiser, but her efficient manning had required nine years to train a sufficient number of skilled ratings, longer for the senior sailors and officers. Cadet Midshipman Victor Smith was now commencing those long years of training. His initial junior officer training, in its fundamentals of task book and journal, would be recognisably familiar to the modern midshipman.

The County-class heavy cruiser HMAS Canberra circa 1931, the year in which Cadet Midshipman Victor Smith joined the ship.

After leave with his family in Chatswood, Victor joined *Canberra* - a cruiser he was to join three times over the years - on 21 January 1931. Two days later *Canberra*, *Albatross* and *Anzac* followed the flagship *Australia* to Hobart for the summer cruise and the Australian squadron's annual regatta. In his first journal entry Victor comments on how "interesting" it all is, although a few days later at "brightwork stations" polishing for captain's rounds he wrote that "although the brass assumed a magnificent lustre it at first did not satisfy the new sub-lieutenant Fogarty". Not long afterwards Victor saw *Oxley* and *Onslow* sail for the China Station and their permanent transfer to the RN.[1]

An early HMAS Canberra badge used from 1928, as the coat of arms of the city of Canberra had yet to receive royal approval. This badge features the letter "C" with a background of wattle. A subsequent badge design featuring the coat of arms is shown in chapter four.

Over the next seventeen months Victor experienced the annual round of seasonal cruises, interspersed with periods in home port, common to the inter-war years. Becoming flagship at the end of May, *Canberra*, after exercises in Hervey Bay north of Brisbane, had a three-month Pacific cruise to Fiji and New Caledonia which returned to Sydney via Newcastle. Her spring cruise encompassed Adelaide and November's Melbourne Cup with its accompanying Fleet Week. *Canberra* returned to her Farm Cove mooring on 26 November with harbour routine for the ship's company until January when she docked at Cockatoo Island for maintenance, where the stokers even polished the propellers with Brasso and soft cloths. Newly painted, *Canberra* was ready to commence the next summer cruise on Australia Day 26 January 1932, and the annual cycle recommenced.

Settling into the crowded life of a gunroom Victor would have been lectured by his Year Officer that this was one of the most valuable times in a young naval officer's career.[2] After four months training and further exams his college results, conduct and ability would be considered with this initial cruiser time and up to three months "time gained". This time would be applied on promotion to sub-lieutenant, backdating his seniority, and starting the ranking that figures so strongly in a naval officer's career.

Being junior, Victor discovered that the officers of the ship were very tolerant and made allowances for his mistakes. Just as valuable was the help that the young midshipman found he got from the sailors. Victor had no hesitation at all in asking sailors to explain something he could not understand. When, for example, he was midshipman of one of the ship's boats and taking liberty men ashore he found the crew would be quite happy to talk to him. He was learning far more about sailors and life on the lower deck during this period than during any later opportunity.

---

1   The RAN did not operate submarines again until 1967, although the RN's Fourth Submarine Squadron operated out of Sydney's Neutral Bay from 1949.
2   The gunroom was a single crowded compartment for the under-training junior officers in which they slept, messed, studied and occasionally relaxed.

These photos show an RAAF Supermarine Seagull III being craned aboard the seaplane tender HMAS Albatross.

In Hobart for the fleet festivities Victor and his classmate George Langford would see the sights ashore together when possible. All the members of the gunroom were required to escort debutantes at the Matron's Ball and put their college dancing lessons to good effect. Away from Hobart there were unending naval evolutions, often in Storm Bay, and keen training for the pulling regatta. Held in North West Bay the regatta always aroused strong competition between the ships with even the rear-admiral putting hands to oar in the veteran officers race.

With the rumour that 65 officers were to go in further manpower reductions Victor entered a rather forlorn caveat "providing we are still in the service" in his journal on 21 March. Throughout 1931 and 1932 he refers to the confused political and banking crises in Australia and the UK, just as he mentions contemporary aerial feats such as the delivery of the imperial mail by Kingsford-Smith or a Schneider Cup aircraft reaching 404 miles per hour. In April there was the excitement of both cruisers firing their broadsides of 170-kilogram projectiles at the obsolete destroyer *Huon*.

When Rear-Admiral Evans gave his lantern slide lecture "South with Scott" to interested groups in various ports, all the gunroom not on duty were obliged to attend. Victor got to know "South with Scott" very well. Captain Holbrook wrote after Victor's first four months onboard that he was a "keen officer of the stolid slow type". While having energy and zeal he continued to be found solidly average, although Holbrook noted that Smith's physique was good and that he played games well. All of Flinders Year were promoted to midshipman on 1 May with only John Dowson being awarded the maximum time gained of three months.

Canberra had arrived in Australia with an aircraft catapult mounting but no catapult. Most of Victor's early exposure to naval aviation was to be second hand, gazing across at the seaplane tender *Albatross* and watching her aircraft during squadron torpedo firings and gunnery shoots. Now two years into her first commission *Albatross*'s aviation capabilities were fully integrated within the squadron. The seaplane carrier was also *sans* catapult and used cranes to lower and raise the embarked flight of four Seagull IIIs of No. 101 Fleet Co-operation Flight, RAAF.

No. 101 Flight embarked eight pilots under Squadron Leader Joseph Hewitt RAAF (1917 class), who had transferred from the RAN rather than convert from pilot to observer. Attached to *Albatross* were five observers under the senior observer, Lieutenant-Commander Henry Chesterman RAN. Three of these observers were RN exchange officers while three other RAN observers were training and consolidating in the UK. The flight made good use of the amphibians in gunnery spotting, torpedo tracking and reconnaissance as well as the always welcome mail-run. While the Seagull III could scout out to 100 miles, this was well beyond W/T range for the early radio set carried in the aircraft and such distances were rarely ventured.

Victor experienced the first trial embarkation of a Seagull III in an Australian cruiser when A9-1 was transferred from *Albatross* in Hervey Bay on 3 September 1931. He had already noted in his journal the day before that *Canberra* had taken on aerial stores in preparation. Lacking a catapult, the aircraft was stowed on the catapult's mounting with wings spread. Over the next five weeks flights occurred over Gladstone, Noumea and Fiji. Seas had to be calm enough to hoist the seaplane outboard for take-off and inboard for recovery, with Victor seeing a wing damaged when it bumped the ship's side just before hoisting off Noumea on 16 September. No flights were possible in the rough seas around Norfolk and Lord Howe islands. Having a wood and fabric airframe made the amphibian vulnerable to prolonged exposure aboard a cruiser, and the Air Board was anxious to husband their few remaining airframes. This made them reluctant to embark a Seagull over the following depression years when there was no immediate prospect of funding for replacements.

The gunroom where the midshipmen lived was an entirely separate mess from the officers' wardroom. President of the gunroom mess was the senior sub-lieutenant, called the "sub of the gunroom". Because pay was scarcely adequate the gunroom sat down to a different menu to the wardroom to save money. Midshipmen were traditionally referred to as "snotties" so naturally the officer in charge of the midshipmen was known as the "snotty's nurse".[3] Being the flagship cruiser there was instructor Commander Francis Rednall MA to keep an overall eye on the midshipmen's continuing education within the squadron. Rednall had been on the staff at the college for most of Victor's time there.

The sub of the gunroom was Kevin Fogarty, keen to specialise as an observer, followed by Rupert Robinson.[4,5] The snotty's nurse was Lieutenant Thomas Godsell (T) who was the assistant torpedo officer. As snotty's nurse Godsell ensured that the training, behaviour and appearance of the midshipmen were up to expectations. He inspected their journals every month. In *Canberra* any real or perceived dereliction of duty was met with the arbitrary award of extra duty or stoppage of leave from which there was no appeal.

---

3   The traditional three buttons on the sleeve of a midshipman's uniform were supposedly to stop the young teenager wiping his dripping nose on his sleeve.

4   Kevin Fogarty (1923 class) completed the 23rd Naval Observer's Course in 1933 and was *Australia*'s (O) in the first year of the war.

5   Rupert Robinson (1923 class) was awarded a DSC at the Battle of Matapan serving in *Stuart*, and commanded *Voyager* when she was lost in September 1943 disembarking Australian commandos off Timor.

Alcohol was allowed in the gunroom but a strict eye was kept on consumption. The president of the mess would examine the wine book every week, and the snotty's nurse did it every month. In any event, Victor recognised that with the pay for midshipmen being only six shillings per week, there was not much chance of anyone going off the rails. Even that lowly pay was about to suffer a further cut. The Financial Emergencies Act of June 1931 reduced all government salaries and pensions by twenty percent and Rear-Admiral Munro Kerr's weekly £57.14 became £49 while Victors six shillings became five. When similar cuts to salary in the Royal Navy were applied unequally across all ranks it led to the September mutiny in the Atlantic Fleet at Invergorden. This panicked the London Stock Exchange and was a factor in the abandonment of the gold standard.

Any midshipman, especially in a large cruiser serving as flagship, is kept very active. A typical day would see hands turned to at 0600 which Victor would attend if not at physical training. There would be Morse or semaphore practice before breakfast. After seeing the watches turned to and the day's duties allocated for the ships company there could be Divisions at 0900 followed by organised instruction. When not attending lectures or practical demonstrations Victor would be undertaking his duties as Midshipman of the Watch on the ship's bridge or at the gangway. He would also be relegated some divisional work seeing to the welfare and training of a group of junior sailors.

Time in port was just as hectic for Victor as days at sea. Whether in a state capital or small city there would be official calls for the senior officers, mandatory social events, open ship days and Fleet Week activities in addition to team sports against the locals. While the captain would make his call on the mayor, or the governor would call on the commodore, Victor as Midshipman of the Harbour Watch or running one of the ship's boats to and from shore, would have been fully occupied. Whether firing a 21-gun salute for Queen Mary's 64th birthday and dressing ship overall or marching through a town, duties were varied and spare time unusual.

An obligatory daily task for Victor was the writing up of his midshipman's journal, adding a weekly or fortnightly sketch. The journal entries would be inspected regularly by the snotty's nurse and occasionally by the captain. Entries would range from seamanship and ship's sports results to ports visited. Given the state of the world in the early 1930s often current affairs would be commented on. In one single journal entry in June 1931 Victor commented on both Al Capone being sentenced to prison and that communists were causing troubles for the NSW police. Once all the midshipmen were required to produce an essay on the current conditions in Germany.

That world was looking increasingly dark. There was famine in Russia that would eventually cause the deaths of over five million people. In the United States 2,500 banks had failed while in Germany, where the Nazi party had increased their seats in the Reichstag from twelve to 107, there was a run on the mark. Benito Mussolini was celebrating ten years of rule by the National Fascist party in Italy. Japan invaded Manchuria in October 1931 and at year's end a

Korean patriot and eleven junior naval officers prepared to assassinate the Emperor Showa and Prime Minister Inukai Tsuyoshi respectively. Hirohito lived but the death of Inukai subjugated the civilian government to the military from then on.

While these events would seriously influence Victor's later life, it was still all very remote. Of immediate concern was his E190. Later called a Task Book this was a training book which the midshipmen commenced as soon as they arrived onboard. Detailing the training to be undertaken in all ship's departments, each task needed comment and signing off by the appropriate officer when the training was completed. With sections encompassing torpedoes, gunnery, navigation, astro-navigation, seamanship evolutions and engineering, completing the E190 ensured comprehensive knowledge of the cruiser. With each book periodically inspected by the captain, the instructing officer and snotty's nurse would make sure the progress of the midshipmen was steady.

The aspect of this junior naval life that Victor remembered most fondly was the opportunity for organised sports. Competition could be intense and rules sparse with Victor writing after his first round of deck hockey "In the dog watch we played deck hockey - a game where only the fittest survive". When in harbour many afternoons were a make-and-mend which meant that the ship's teams would be out playing. Whether interdepartmental, wardroom versus gunroom, against other ships in the squadron or civilian teams, participation was mandatory for the junior officer. This was welcomed by Victor, and winning results were keenly striven for. In his later years he would regret the passing of this sporting intensity that was so much a feature of shipboard life during the inter-war period.

In 1931 the Statute of Westminster established the legislative equality of the self-governing dominions. In the Dominion of Australia, a political crisis saw James Scullin's Labor Party ousted by the United Australia Party of Joseph Lyons. That March Ben Chifley was appointed Minister of Defence.[6] The depression meant Chifley concentrated on finding departmental savings which could be redirected to unemployment relief, while more officers and sailors were offered the generally unwelcome opportunity of discharge to shore. A bright spot was when Peter Hancox, serving in *Australia*'s gunroom, went ashore the short distance to Government House where the Governor of New South Wales, Air Vice-Marshal Sir Phillip Gain GBE KCB DSO RAF, presented him with the gold King's Medal on 29 July 1931.

With the new year of 1932 Victor, although the same seniority as George Langford, was made senior midshipman of the gunroom when six cadet-midshipmen of the 1928 year joined after their graduation at Flinders Naval Depot.

On Monday 14 March the cruiser *Diomede*, approaching Sydney from the New Zealand Station, was ordered to "attack a convoy" inbound from Hobart.[7] This "convoy" was escorted

---

6   Chifley was treasurer of Australia through four wartime years and prime minister from 1945 to 1949.
7   The captain of *Diomede* was Commander Victor Crutchley VC DSC RN and she was flying the flag of Rear-Admiral Geoffrey Blake CB DSO RN commanding the New Zealand Squadron. Crutchley would later command the wartime ANZAC Squadron.

FROM FARM COVE — H·M·A·S· CANBERRA — 19-3-1932.

Canberra moored in Farm Cove in March 1932, awaiting the opening of the Sydney Harbour Bridge.

by the Australian Squadron returning from its two-month summer cruise. Once sighted by the destroyer *Tattoo* the cruiser was badly damaged by salvoes from *Canberra* and *Australia* in the mock engagement which followed, before being finished off by bombs from *Albatross's* aircraft. All five warships then formed up to enter Sydney Harbour. This gathering of warships presaged the opening of that most iconic of Australian emblems, the Sydney Harbour Bridge.

Seven years after Admiral de Chair had seen the foundation stone laid at Dawes Point, and almost two years after the arch had been joined, the suspended roadway was finally complete. The final Bridge Lottery prize of £20,000 had been drawn. Train speed tests were conducted over the expansion sliding joints which could cope with 42 centimetres of movement as the 52,781 tons of steel and five million rivets expanded in the sun. The roadway included four train and tram tracks plus six car lanes and two pedestrian walkways. It remains the tallest arch bridge in the world.

At a time of economic depression and political tension in the state of New South Wales the opening of the long-awaited bridge took on heightened symbolism. The Honourable John Lang, State Premier, had aroused commonwealth ire by raiding his own State Bank rather than pay interest to bondholders in London when so many were on the breadline. With right-wing paramilitary formations of Old Guard and New Guard brawling against unionists and communists, times were fraught. When Lang announced that he would cut the ribbon at the bridge's opening instead of the King's representative, Governor Sir Phillip Gain, the conservatives were outraged. While the King was later reported to be annoyed, Sir Phillip himself remained quietly amused rather than offended.

In the more florid descriptions of the time the iconic span was seen as a *Colossus of the Southern Hemisphere*, the arch of a new era whose stately pillars represented national strength and stability. As 50,000 schoolchildren walked across the bridge three days before the opening their smiles were a timely, albeit brief, release from the prevailing economic depression and pessimism. Tolls had been announced, cars were to be charged six pence to cross, double the threepence for a horse and rider, while any sheep mustered across would be charged at one penny per head. It was hoped that the joining of the city would be symbolic of renewed unity in the state's social fabric.

The commodore and captain were run ashore from *Canberra* to join their wives for the North Sydney Mayoral Ball which began the official celebrations on 17 March. Thousands of visitors had poured into Sydney for the opening, which coincided with the annual Royal Show, horse racing at Randwick, inter-state cricket and a regatta on the harbour of the famous Sydney eighteen footers. It was a busy time for the ship and for Victor, although he did not make the height minimum of six feet for the guard of honour at the official ribbon cutting. The ship's company helped decorate a pontoon for the Venetian carnival under the bridge and prepared for their major role in the evening's light show.

Canberra was at the flagship buoy in Farm Cove, *Australia* and *Albatross* were alongside in East Circular Quay where they had been open for visitors, *Diomede* was in Neutral Bay and even the old cruiser *Adelaide*, in reserve at Garden Island, had a power cable laid to her and her searchlight platform was manned. At 1930 the warships illuminated and at 2000 they commenced a searchlight display around the harbour and its new bridge while fire floats were set off in the surrounding waters crowded with yachts. Fifteen searchlights, including three from Cockatoo Island dockyard to the west, formed a kaleidoscope pattern and Victor, as senior midshipman, was most likely on a searchlight platform. He wrote that the night was "a fantasy of colour".

After all the official obligations *Canberra* held a celebratory ship's company dance onboard at No. 1 Buoy the following Monday "to commemorate the opening of the Sydney Harbour Bridge". On Tuesday Victor went ashore with the landing party for a squadron march past the Governor-General Sir Isaac Isaacs, who took the salute in Hyde Park.

On 25 May 1932, the governor-general was to present the King's Medal to its latest recipient, Midshipman (E) Stuart St Vincent Welch of the 1928 class. Joined by the midshipmen from *Australia*, all were in *Canberra*'s crowded gunroom preparing for the parade on the

Canberra is illuminated during the Sydney Harbour searchlight display on 19 March 1932.

quarterdeck. Informed that Sir Isaac might visit the gunroom after the presentation, Victor, with only minutes available, oversaw the hurried rush to square away the compartment. Unfortunately, Welch's cap got stowed away in the confusion and could not be immediately located. A quick-thinking Victor designated Clive Hudson as a suitable substitute to receive the medal. Unluckily, also at the presentation was the governor-general's secretary, Captain Leighton Bracegirdle DSO RAN, who knew Hudson. When the plot was revealed under questioning, some were amused and some were very unamused. Welch got his medal eventually and the incident failed to appear in Victor's midshipman's journal but later formed the basis of a story in *The Strand Magazine*.

The third Flinders casualty of the manpower reductions occurred when Norman Wilson had his appointment terminated in April 1932.[8] Shortly before the others were due to depart for the Mediterranean an Imperial Japanese Navy training squadron visited Sydney in May 1932. Victor wrote that "war between Japan and China is regarded as almost certain" but, in common with most, had no conception of a wider conflict.

After Australian cruiser time the 1927 year were to join the Mediterranean Fleet for their final twelve months as midshipmen. In the event only five of the Flinders Year embarked for passage on 25 June 1932. Athol Robertson, who had beaten Victor to the Seamanship Prize, was due to take passage but was invalided out of the service for defective eyesight.[9] William Drew stayed on in Australia for a further six months before sailing to the Mediterranean and the cruiser *Sussex*. Keith Ridley, appointed a paymaster midshipman, also remained in *Australia* and continued his training in that branch. Bruce Harvie had elected to specialise as an engineer so had already been in the UK for six months, undertaking the four-year course at the Royal Naval Engineering College in Keyham.

---

8   Norman Wilson (1913-2004) studied medicine at Melbourne University for two years and then worked as a factory manager. On the outbreak of war, he tried to rejoin the RAN but was rejected for colour blindness. When his application for RAAF aircrew was rejected for the same reason, he joined as an aircraftsman. After service in the South West Pacific with an airfield construction squadron Norman was commissioned a Flying Officer. Post-war he became managing director of Preston Textiles.

9   Athol Robertson OAM (1913-2003) became a doctor. Appointed a surgeon lieutenant in 1940 he served with Australia's "Scrap Iron Flotilla" in the Mediterranean aboard *Stuart* and *Voyager*. At war's conclusion he was Senior Medical Officer New Guinea. Surgeon Commander Dr Athol Robertson RANVR transferred to the Retired List in 1973.

A trio of Fairey IIIFs over battleships and cruisers in Malta's Grand Harbour.

As Victor departed *Canberra* Captain Charles Farquhar-Smith RAN, setting aside the King's Medal fiasco, recorded that Victor, as the senior midshipman onboard, had been a good leader and a good influence. He was noted as tactful, loyal and of good sound common-sense. Farquhar-Smith still found Victor rather slow but, slightly more upbeat than his previous report, recognised that he was improving and forecast, accurately, that he would develop into a sound and useful naval officer.

Sailing with Victor aboard the Orient liner RMS *Otranto* were Dowson, Hancox, Knox and Langford. As officers their passage was first class but, as midshipmen, their pay needed careful budgeting to partake of even a few of the luxuries available. Not surprisingly, being young men of good appetite, the excellent standard of the meals was a highlight of each day. Victor enjoyed the comfort and revelled in the deck games and swimming pool.

Arriving at Malta's Grand Harbour the Australians spent three days in *Egmont*, the depot "ship" which was Fort St Angelo. Victor's first sight of the Mediterranean Fleet was overwhelming to eyes that had rarely seen more than four warships together. Among the battleships, aircraft carrier and cruisers was the heavy cruiser *London*, the flagship of the First Cruiser Squadron, which all five Australians were to join.

London was initially short of berths, so Victor and John Dowson went to the destroyer *Boadicea* for two weeks from 3 August. Joining at 1500 the ship sailed at 1700 and the next day passed the Italian fleet at summer manoeuvres. The Fourth Destroyer Flotilla then anchored in Tivat Bay, Montenegro, surrounded by battleships and destroyers. The only difference to the four ships of the Australian squadron conducting their annual regatta in Tasmanian waters was one of scale and exotic location. For six days the sporting battle was fought. *Boadicea* came last in her destroyer flotilla regatta so were supporters only in the next day's inter-flotilla regatta where the Third Destroyer Flotilla beat the Fourth and First. Then it was the turn of the cruisers followed by the battleships. Victor saw his first game of water polo during the dog watches, a sport he was to have a lot to do with over his years with the RN, in addition to his usual rugby and tennis.

Before returning to Malta, fleet exercises were held off Corfu and the Prince of Wales inspected the big ships while his younger brother Prince George inspected the depot ships, submarines and destroyer flotillas. The size of the task meant he only had ten minutes aboard *Boadicea* to meet the officers and inspect the assembled divisions. It was the second time Victor had paraded for his future king, the first being at the opening of Parliament House. On Monday 22 August the two midshipmen joined their three classmates in *London*.

HMS *London* 22 August 1932 to 27 September 1933

Flag Captain Henry Harwood RN and the executive officer Commander John Edelsten ran a very smart ship.[10,11] *London* had also been fitted the previous June with a Type EIIH catapult to launch a Fairey IIIF when embarked from No. 447 (Fleet Spotter Reconnaissance) Flight. By 1933 seven battleships and fourteen cruisers had been fitted with catapults.

Being on foreign service, the ship's company was stable, with very few draft changes during the commission. This cohesive gathering, from the start of a commission until the ship paid off back in her home port, was of great import to the ship's *esprit de corps* and morale. The officers and sailors got to know each other very well, which proved of enormous benefit during ship evolutions and ashore on the sports fields of Malta. Since few junior sailors or officers were married in those days, or had their families in Malta, the focus was ship centric. Victor would regret that posting policies in the later years of his service prevented this remembered stability.

With the intense rivalry that had existed between *Australia* and *Canberra*, the Australians felt right at home aboard *London* as she strove to be top ship afloat and ashore. Also a County class heavy cruiser, *London*'s layout and routines were entirely familiar and their duties

---

10   Later Admiral Sir Henry Harwood KCB OBE (1888-1950). As the commodore of Force G comprising *Ajax, Achilles* and *Exeter* with their 8-inch guns he fought the December 1939 Battle of the River Plate against the Deutschland-class *Admiral Graf Spee*'s 11-inch guns.

11   Later Vice-Admiral Sir John Edelston GCB GCVO CBE (1891-1966), Commander-in-Chief, Mediterranean Fleet after being Rear-Admiral (Destroyers) of the British Pacific Fleet against Japan in 1945

The heavy cruiser HMS London in the 1930s, with an embarked floatplane visible just abaft of the three funnels.

The HMS London badge.

onboard proved no different. Although flagship of the First Cruiser Squadron, Victor proudly felt that she was no smarter than *Canberra*, or any more efficient or professional in her drills and evolutions. *London* was just part of a much larger fleet although he did admit that the "talkie" equipment in the ship was excellent, allowing for very enjoyable film evenings.

In October *London* entered dock for several months and its floatplane disembarked. Another ship of the squadron, *Sussex* under Captain Hugh England, had an embarked flight and her flight commander probably wished he had followed suit. Captains could be famously eccentric, and Victor expressed no surprise when he wrote that Captain England, infuriated when *Sussex*'s Fairey IIIF was buzzing his ship prior to landing alongside, sent his steward to fetch his shotgun and took potshots at the aircraft. All were relieved when his aim proved as variable as his temper.[12]

HMS *Glorious* 9 October 1932 to 25 October 1932

Munro Kerr, returned from Australia to be vice-admiral of the reserve fleet, had enthusiastically embraced aviation. When captain of the early aircraft carrier *Eagle* in 1925, among his many recommendations Munro Kerr, a wide-thinking navigation specialist, had advocated aviation instruction be included within a junior executive officer's general education. This became formalised into a two-week air course for midshipmen aboard a carrier with lectures and exposure to embarked operations. His commander-in-chief wrote in appreciation that Kerr contributed to a steady progress in naval aviation whilst commanding *Eagle*.

When *London* anchored near the aircraft carrier *Glorious* off Mudros in the Aegean - where

---

12   Later Rear-Admiral Hugh England CB DSO* (1884-1978). His DSOs were awarded for the Sicily and Normandy invasions.

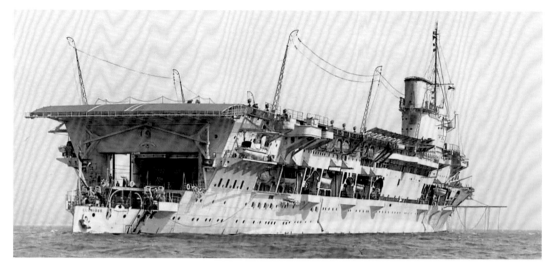

Victor's view approaching Glorious for the first time in a ship's boat. Palisades to catch veering aircraft are lowered, W/T masts are raised and the rear hangar door is open.

The HMS Glorious badge.

the Anzacs had practised their Gallipoli landings in early 1915 - the midshipmen were transferred by ship's boat for their air course. This fortnight was to be a momentous one for Victor who found life aboard *Glorious* as she exercised with the fleet exciting and "absolutely absorbing".

The Washington disarmament treaty limits for tonnage had a loophole that allowed some capital ship conversions into aircraft carriers rather than being scrapped. The WWI battlecruiser *Glorious*, whose main machinery was capable of propelling her 22,500 tons at 30 knots, was initially placed in the postwar reserve. Then in the 1920s she was rebuilt as an aircraft carrier. Recommissioned in February 1930, *Glorious* featured a double hangar design above the original main deck with a starboard side island overlooking her new flight deck.

The flight deck stopped well short of the stem of the ship. Underneath the edge were two large upper hangar doors which, when opened gave sufficient run for a small fighter such as the Fairey Flycatcher to take off between others launching overhead. Although fitted with two accelerators aircraft predominantly launched with a free run take-off. Having no arrestor wires or barrier, each landing aircraft would have to be struck below on the cruciform lifts to provide a clear deck before the next could land. Doors opened from the lower hangar onto the quarterdeck to allow seaplanes to be lowered and recovered by cranes.

Glorious had 45 aircraft embarked from Malta whilst Victor was onboard. Still five months from the Fleet Air Arm adopting squadron numbers, *Glorious* carried seven flights of Hawker Nimrod and Fairey Flycatcher fighters, Blackburn Ripon torpedo bombers and Fairey IIIF spotter reconnaissance aircraft. All aircraft had the distinctive broad yellow band around their aft fuselage indicating *Glorious* was their parent carrier. It was an impressive and colourful

A torpedo armed Ripon of No. 462 Flight takes off from Glorious, circa 1932. In October of that year Victor had his first flight in one of these aircraft.

assemblage when ranged on the flight deck ready for launch or packed tightly in the hangar.

The previous year another RAN officer, Lieutenant-Commander Jefferson Walker (1915 class), had been aboard the carrier *Eagle* as assistant navigator when they spent similar days steaming around the numerous land-locked bays of the Greek islands, flying off aircraft to practice defending the Battle Fleet:

> The thrills came when we were roared up by the other side's planes. The way some of these young men fall about the sky in high-powered aircraft astonishes me. The mess is now filled to capacity with the flying personnel from the shore base of Hal Far in Malta … and the wardroom very happy indeed. It is also much married. I understand that young lieutenants go in for marriage and flying because the increased pay for flying helps to finance the marriage.

The bustle, activity and general high spirits aboard *Glorious* with aircraft embarked had a profound impact on the young Victor to whom the carrier seemed "tremendous". There was also the aura of royal patronage as only eight weeks before, the Prince of Wales had landed onboard in a Fairey IIIF of No. 441 Flight.

Glorious left Mudros at 0750 on 10 October with the destroyer *Boreas* in company. At 0830 Fairey IIIFs were ranged up from the hangar and as soon as they were away Flycatchers and

Nimrods emerged and joined them airborne. In the ensuing quiet the opportunity was taken to show the Australian midshipmen over the carrier, or at least those parts of ship that they needed to be familiar with for the next two weeks. Watching the returning aircraft land occupied the remainder of the forenoon watch.

After lunch Victor "went up" for the first time. The exercise was for a force of torpedo armed Blackburn Ripons to strike *Glorious*, attacking through an aircraft generated smokescreen. Naval tactics often called for a ship-generated smokescreen and some aircraft in turn were also fitted with equipment to allow a white stannic chloride smoke screen to be laid. Once the smokescreen had been formed the torpedo armed aircraft, among them a Ripon carrying an excited Victor, burst through the smoke to make their runs against the carrier.

During their two weeks onboard nine lectures, ranging from the history of the Fleet Air Arm ("interesting") to air power in war ("particularly instructive"), were given in the gunroom. Victor was left in no doubt of "how important a part aircraft does and will play" and had no difficulty writing the assigned essay on the effects of naval aviation on naval warfare. He found the whole time aboard absolutely absorbing and, seeing the nature of the additional duties which the aviators undertook, his awakened interest in the Fleet Air Arm quickly turned vocational.

"The most travelled of their generation" - Victor's sketch of his places visited with the Mediterranean Fleet from July 1932 through to August 1933.

A Fairey IIIF taking off from Glorious.

Twice more Victor got airborne. Once it was to experience another torpedo attack on the ship which, this time, was being defended by her fighters. Having had the appropriate lecture, he was also sent up in a Fairey IIIF with a bulky camera and five plates to discover the difficulties of aerial photography. When the plates were developed Victor was modestly satisfied with the images.

Watching night flying for the first time on 22 October two Fairey IIIFs got airborne despite bad wind conditions. The first attempt to land was aborted with red Verey lights. The second attempt never saw the aircraft stabilised on approach and when it touched down the port wingtip caught in the palisade, swinging it violently around and crashing nose first into another palisade. It took an hour to clear the wreckage before the second aircraft could land.

It was not all flying of course as the carrier had other benefits in addition to dining in the wardroom. Divisions on a flight deck meant the marine band could march up and down its length, there was plenty of room for deck hockey (at which the gunroom were beaten badly by the officers) and cinema (using the after lift as a roof was a comfortable affair). The opportunity was also taken to see the sights of Athens. It is notable that before overseas travel was common the junior officers of the RAN were, by some margin, the most travelled of their generation.

Lieutenant George Oldham (1920 class) would probably have been assigned to look after the Australian midshipmen for some of their air course.[13] Oldham had served in *Albatross* as a seaman sub-lieutenant and then took passage to England for the 18th Naval Observer's Course

---

13   Later Acting Rear-Admiral George Oldham CBE DSC MiD* (1906-1974) who commanded *Swan*, *Warramunga* and *Australia*. In 1953 he commanded *Sydney* in her post-armistice Korean deployment.

in 1930. After almost two years in *Glorious* Oldham would have been a mentor for any RAN midshipman showing aviation aspirations.

As all the flights noisily and impressively disembarked *en masse* to Hal Far on 25 October 1932, Victor returned to *London* with his future path now firmly set in his mind. Those two weeks aboard *Glorious* had proved of tremendous consequence for him and the country he served.

HMS *Bulldog* 10 January 1933 to 4 May 1933

After considerable time in cruisers some small-ship time was mandatory, and in early 1933 Victor was transferred to the 1,380-ton destroyer HMS *Bulldog* for four months.[14] Not yet two years old and capable of 35 knots the destroyer had a complement of 134 officers and men under Lieutenant-Commander Charles Churchill. Compared to *London*'s 800 strong crew, top heavy with a flagship's senior officers, this would have been a breath of fresh air to the midshipman. *Bulldog* was one of ten destroyers of the Fourth Destroyer Flotilla in a period when competition among Mediterranean destroyers for "smartness" and ship handling was notoriously intense.

Several days after Victor joined, *Bulldog* sailed for Crete. Over the next few months as they cruised into the spring *Bulldog* steamed as far east as Greece and as far west as the Balearic Islands and to the French St Tropez coast. At times it must have had aspects of a tourist trip for Victor, giving plenty of material to put in his weekly letters back home to Chatswood.

Destroyers normally berthed in Sliema Creek just to the north of Malta's Grand Harbour. There the berths consisted of head and stern buoys. To secure so that they were facing seaward, the destroyers had to make a stern board, that is they had to go up the creek stern

The HMS Bulldog badge.

The destroyer HMS Bulldog, which was less than two years old when Victor went aboard.

---

14 *Bulldog* became famous in 1941 for capturing the Enigma machine and code books of *U-110*.

A biplane flies over neatly moored warships in Sliema Creek, north of Malta's Grand Harbour.

first. There was always intense competition between the destroyer captains to see who could secure to the stern and head buoys in the shortest time. Victor, watching some of the ship handling in performing this manoeuvre, thought it was wonderful to see how very good they were. This dexterity and confidence were something he would later try to emulate in his own ship handling.

While Victor was in *Bulldog* he became a sports casualty playing rugby ashore at Marsa. He had been kicked in the bicep seriously enough to spend time in the hospital ship *Maine*. Meanwhile back in Australia *Albatross* had become a financial casualty of the recession. Still missing a catapult and suitable replacement aircraft for the Seagull IIIs she was paid off into reserve on 26 April 1933. What little naval aviation remained back home would now devolve to the two cruisers and, wasting no time, on 27 April the Naval Board asked the Air Board for a Seagull in each cruiser. The annual bombing and gunnery refresher courses for the handful of naval observers and TAGs would also continue at RAAF Base Richmond.[15]

Returning to *London*, Victor discovered that another Fairey IIIF had been embarked in March. This was the Mk IIIB model strengthened for catapult operations and powered by a

---

15   Captain Cuthbert Pope presented the ships bell of *Albatross* to No. 101 (Fleet Co-operation) Flight at RAAF Base Richmond.

570 horsepower Lion XIA engine. The flight commander was Lieutenant-Commander Edwin Carnduff, commander of No. 447 Flight and, under the strange inter-service compromises of these years, also an RAF flight lieutenant. When Admiralty Fleet Order 1058 was promulgated in 1924 calling for aviation volunteers Carnduff was one of the first, graduating from No. 1 Naval Pilot's Course in 1925.[16] He also would have been most encouraging of Victor's enthusiasm for aviation.

The gunroom now settled down to some serious study when not required for other duties. In August 1933 Victor and his fellow midshipmen sat their seamanship exam before a captain and two commanders. Wearing a midshipman's No. 1 short jacket and dirk they were examined in ten subjects and received marks for their journal and the officer-like qualities they had exhibited throughout their midshipman's time. All five Australians passed: Victor was happy with his "comfortable" second class pass. The short jacket was put away permanently on 1 September 1933, when Victor was promoted acting sub-lieutenant. That single stripe on his sleeve had taken six and a half years to achieve.

On Victor's promotion and discharge to courses Captain Harwood wrote that he was a reliable and trustworthy young officer who was good at taking charge. Although intellectually rather slow he was found well up to the average in common sense. Scoring 8 for reliability and 7 for power of command, any slowness in thinking was no longer held remiss against these most valuable attributes. He was a trusted and dependable subordinate officer whose common sense was more highly prized than intellect.

Royal Naval College Greenwich 1934

The newly promoted officers travelled from Malta to Tilbury docks by liner and then by train to London. After a short leave they reported to the Royal Naval College Greenwich for the next six months. The college's 17th century Wren buildings, on the Thameside site of a Tudor Palace where Henry VIII and Elizabeth I had been born, much impressed Victor. The royal majesty of dining in the Painted Hall or attending service in the chapel had been inspiring surroundings for generations of Royal Navy officers. While there were officers from most of the Dominion navies, the majority of the 30 acting sub-lieutenants in the class that the Australians joined had gone through Dartmouth as the Anson Term while the Flinders Year had been at Jervis Bay.

At Greenwich the various courses were purely academic. English, history, mathematics, physics and French were all taught by eminent instructors. None of the Australians did well at French despite the vocabulary of seamanship terms and warship classes that the French masters back at Jervis Bay had drilled into them. The instructor was an eminent French professor whose favourite method of increasing his students' vocabulary was to get them

---

16   In 1939, aged 37, Edwin Carnduff was too old for most flying appointments. He commanded the gunboat *Cricket* on the China Station in 1941 and the sloop *Scarborough* for three years until the end of 1944. At the Normandy landings *Scarborough* was immediately behind the minesweepers to mark the cleared path for the closely following assault convoys.

The Royal Naval College Greenwich. On the hill behind is the Royal Observatory marking the prime meridian.

doing crossword puzzles. The Australians for the most part could not even write down the French clues, let alone sort out the answers.

History under Professor Geoffrey Callander, whose book *Sea Kings of England* had been a textbook back at Jervis Bay, was more enjoyable.[17] However nothing academic gave Victor greater pleasure that being able to play rugby for Greenwich over a complete season. With London so close, he also took advantage of every opportunity to socialise and see the sights of one of the world's most imposing cities. He later remarked, perhaps with the hindsight of seeing the city after the Blitz, that it was then very clean and orderly.

Promotion to sub-lieutenant required new uniforms which the low pay did not cover. Inevitably that meant the creating of an account with Gieves & Company, who had tailored Royal Navy officers' uniforms for the past century. The firm had a time payment system and so an allotment from one's pay to Gieves was common. With premises in London's Bond Street, Portsmouth and in Malta's Valetta, it was a rare officer who did not source his uniforms from Gieves.

A young officer's pride in uniform was matched by Gieves pride in quality tailoring. Having grown out of a midshipman's short "bum-freezer" jacket Victor required an officer's frock coat. These frock coats were made and delivered while his course was still at Greenwich. To ensure the correct sartorial standard had been reached, each junior officer had to parade in front of the college's captain who would decide if the fit and cut was satisfactory. Victor's midshipman's dirk had been provided by the Australian government, but a sub-lieutenant wore a sword which also needed purchasing from Gieves.

After the general studies at Greenwich there were a series of specialist courses ashore in various of the RN's stone frigates (shore establishments). Gunnery at HMS *Excellent*, Whale Island; torpedoes and electrics at HMS *Vernon* and navigation at HMS *Dryad* in, unsurprisingly, Nav House. The final studies were the signal and divisional courses while accommodated at Portsmouth Barracks.

---

17   Later Sir Geoffrey Callander, Dartmouth's head of history and then the first Professor of History at the Royal Naval College. Lacking sufficient textbooks for the study of naval history he wrote his own. Shortly after instructing Victor, he became the first director of the National Maritime Museum.

The gunnery school had a strict reputation with much spit and polish and no sense of fun, which Victor considered a hindrance to effective training and thus good results. A certain amount of license was usually permitted at the final guest night dinner on completion of examinations. George Knox went down to the small farm they had at Whale Island and borrowed a draft horse and took it into the anteroom after dinner. This example of Australian humour found no appreciation from the staff of the gunnery school.

For daily divisions one of the acting sub-lieutenants under training was detailed each morning as the officer of the guard. When it was Victor's turn, he was getting ready with the guard to march down to the parade ground. Letting his newly purchased sword hang down by his side, touching the deck while putting on his gloves, there boomed out a stentorian voice from one of the gunnery instructors (who subsequently became a full admiral) "Officer of the Guard, what do you think you are, a wretched paymaster?"[18]

Successful completion of these exams was a prerequisite for promotion to lieutenant. Results would be tabulated in each year's Navy List for all to see along with the revised seniority their results gave. None of the five achieved the proverbial "Five Firsts" that would gain approving comment in the college annual magazine and indicate someone clearly destined for the highest ranks. The rugby season and being hopeless at French ensured Victor only achieved a third-class certificate for his Greenwich studies, while a little more application gained him second-class certificates in seamanship, navigation and gunnery. Victor achieved a single first-class certificate in torpedoes. Still solidly average he gained two and a half months seniority compared to Dowson's five months and Langford's half a month.

Returning to Australia at the end of 1934, all five sub-lieutenants enjoyed their socialising aboard the Orient liner RMS *Oronsay* to the full. Victor commenced a month's foreign service leave the week before Christmas 1934. Reflecting that on promotion to sub-lieutenant his seniority was set at 16 March 1934, Victor supposed he could have worked a bit harder and achieved better results.[19] Overall, however, he had loved his rugby season and considered the trade-off to maximise his first experiences of England well considered.

---

18   When telling this story Victor would always apologise to the Supply Branch that it demeaned.
19   On promotion to sub-lieutenant Smith's seniority was set at 16 March 1934. In comparison Dowson's was 1 January, Knox 1 March, Hancox the King's Medalist was also 16 March and Langford was 16 May.

CHAPTER 4

BACKGROUND TO AUSTRALIAN NAVAL AVIATION AND SMITH'S RAN SERVICE 1935 – 1937

A T THE BIRTH OF NAVAL AVIATION within the British Empire there were Australian pioneers. Lieutenant Arthur Longmore RN, born on Yarrara Station near Holbrook and a graduate of *Britannia* Royal Naval College, went from command of his torpedo boat as one of the initial four selected for naval pilot training in 1911. Instructed on borrowed civilian machines, having promised to pay for any damage, Longmore was awarded the Royal Aero Club Aviator's Certificate No.72. Shortly thereafter the British Army's Royal Flying Corps was constituted with naval and military wings until 14 July 1914, when the navy established the Royal Naval Air Service. Longmore, the first British pilot to take off and land on water, took the First Lord of the Admiralty, Winston Churchill, flying in 1913.[1]

Longmore watching Churchill step ashore after their 1913 flight.

It was Churchill who coined the term "seaplane" and at his prompting Longmore made history again with the world's first successful airborne release of a live torpedo on 28 July 1914. Another *Britannia* graduate, Lieutenant Basil Ash RN, had the unsought distinction of being the first Australian naval aviator to die in WWI when he failed to return from an anti-submarine patrol on 29 September 1914. Longmore, having formed No. 1 (Naval) Squadron, first advocated the specialist role of observer and formalised their training. He also nurtured the early career of Flight Sub-Lieutenant Roderic "Stan" Dallas, the second highest scoring Australian ace of the war with 39 victories who was awarded the DSO and DSC* before his death in 1918. Stan was one of hundreds of Australians who volunteered to serve with the RNAS, nine of

---

1   Later Air Chief Marshal Sir Arthur Longmore GCB DSO DL RAF (1885-1970). He recommended Flight Sub-Lieutenant Reginald "Rex" Warneford of his squadron for the Victoria Cross when Rex destroyed Zeppelin LZ 37 on 7 June 1915, the first victory by an aircraft over an airship and the first VC to a naval aviator.

A Sopwith Camel on Sydney's flying-off platform above the forward 6-inch gun, showing the short run required with at least twenty knots of wind over the deck.

whom gained ace status with five or more victories.[2]

As Assistant Superintendent for Design in the Admiralty's Air Department in 1917, and a member of the Admiralty Committee on Deck Landing, Longmore was at the forefront of early carrier "flat-top" designs and the turret-mounted flying off platforms for battleships and cruisers. The Admiralty were vigorously promoting naval aviation given its clear anti-Zeppelin and gunnery-spotting roles in addition to reconnaissance scouting for enemy submarines and warships.

Brisbane, serving in the Indian Ocean, borrowed Sopwith Baby N1014 from the seaplane carrier *Raven II* in May 1917. Stowed on the boat deck, it took only five minutes to hoist out and recover the Baby, which was tasked for several weeks with twice daily reconnaissance. Captain Claude Cumberlidge RN enthusiastically reported back on the usefulness of these flights to the Naval Board in Melbourne.

Australia, *Melbourne* and *Sydney*, serving with the Grand Fleet, participated in early experiments to embark and launch wheeled fighters in late 1917, urged on by *Sydney's* innovative Australian-born Captain John "DQ" Dumaresq CB RN. Having a biplane's low wing loading and stall speed, the Sopwith Pup could be airborne in less than five metres with a wind over the deck of twenty knots, while the later 1½ Strutters and Camels needed only a few metres more. The initial fixed platforms were soon superseded by rotatable turret-mounted ones, avoiding the ship needing to pull out of formation to launch into wind. It was a one-way trip for the aviator, recovery being to ditch near a friendly warship and hope for rescue if not near friendly shores. By war's end the Grand Fleet's battleships, battlecruisers and cruisers embarked over 100 aircraft.

More than 200 ships had winches fitted to tow a kite-balloon observer at altitudes of up to 1,500 feet. With a telephone connection from the balloon's basket direct to the ship's bridge their usefulness in gunnery spotting and surveillance had been obvious since their 1915 deployment by the balloon ship *Monica* in the Dardanelles. Two Australian midshipmen arguably became the first RAN aviators when they volunteered for balloon duties from the gunroom of the battleship *Canada*. George Armitage and John Collins, graduates of the Pioneer 1913 class, did

---

2   Longmore, when he handed over squadron command on posting in early 1916 to the battlecruiser *Tiger* and the Battle of Jutland, recommended the young flight sub-lieutenant for promotion. Dallas went on to command No. 1 (Naval) Squadron from June 1917 until his death.

a three-week course in mid-1917 under the 80,000 cubic foot *Banshee II* at Hurlingham. After five flights they went solo and gained their Free Balloon Licences. The extra five shillings per day when airborne doubled their pay and was much envied by the other midshipmen, who did not have to undergo the stomach-churning bouncing in strong wind conditions or grimly hang on in a high-speed turn with the balloon basket almost scraping the waves.

On 1 April 1918, the 55,000 personnel and 3,000 aircraft of the RNAS merged with the RFC to become the Royal Air Force. Eight weeks later *Sydney* and *Melbourne* launched their Camels against *Kampstaffel* 1's Hansa-Brandenburg W19 twin-seat seaplane fighters on 1 June 1918. These RAN cruisers had initiated the first ship-launched interception of enemy fixed-wing aircraft. Flight Lieutenant Albert "Cyril" Sharwood RAF, newly converted from a flight sub-lieutenant RNAS, failed to find *Sydney* after the action. He ditched his Camel N6783 in front of the destroyer *Sharpshooter* and was recovered, later being mentioned in despatches.

In Australia the Naval Board had recognised the usefulness of the new air branch immediately, proposing as early as 1915 that an Australian Naval Air Service of four seaplanes be formed. Unfortunately, these plans could not be supported by a stretched RNAS. The board had to be content with providing letters of recommendation to suitable volunteer reservists, who would make their own way to Britain and join the RNAS. After the Armistice, with only one military airfield in Australia and no dedicated naval airfields, workshops or depot carrier, the three RAN ships disembarked their aircraft and returned home.

In June 1918 the Council of Defence was told that "The necessity for the establishment of a Naval Air Service is unquestionable". What followed was the first of four cycles of boom and bust for Australian naval aviation, through which Smith would serve from the 1920s until the 1970s.[3] Initially witnessing the end of the first cycle as a junior officer, he was destined to be an active participant and then initiator in the following three.

The decade of reports, committees and inter-service battles from 1918-1928 saw the concept of naval aviation being solely the navy's purview wax and wane as respective rear-admirals fought administrative battles against the Air Board under the intransigent Group Captain Richard Williams DSO RAAF.[4] While control, and therefore budget, was fought over, the commitment to having aircraft at sea, whether naval or pubescent air force, never waned.

Both the battlecruiser *Australia* and the light cruiser *Melbourne* embarked an Avro 504 of the Australian Air Corps in 1920. This aircraft proved dangerously underpowered in the tropics and during five months aboard *Melbourne* the aircraft only flew three times before a strained, warped and waterlogged airframe was gladly offloaded ashore. It was a lesson already learned in the war that these early airframes, once exposed on a warship's deck at sea, had a serviceability often counted only in days.

---

3   Cycle 1: 1921-1935 "Fabric and Fragile", Cycle 2: 1935-1944 "Metal and Catapults", Cycle 3: 1947-1959 "Carrier Force", Cycle 4: 1960-1983 "Decline and Recovery".
4   Later Air Marshal Sir Richard Williams KBE CB DSO RAAF (1890-1980).

In April 1921 the government announced the purchase of Fairey seaplanes for the navy, apparently unconcerned that Fairey had only come third after Vickers and Supermarine in the 1920 Air Ministry competition for seaplanes. ANA-1 (Australian Naval Aircraft Number 1), the first of six Fairey IIID floatplanes, was launched into the River Hamble, naval fashion, on 12 August 1921. In Australia the Air Corps became an Australian Air Force that March, receiving King George V's approval to be the Royal Australian Air Force from 18 August. When the ANA airframes arrived in country at the end of the year, they were immediately subsumed into the forming RAAF and re-registered with serials A10-1 to A10-6.

While the First and Second Naval Members of the Naval Board desired ship-borne aircraft the Third Naval Member, Engineer Rear-Admiral Sir William Clarkson KBE CMG, remained opposed on safety and stability grounds.[5] He would not countenance adding the weight of aircraft, derrick and hangar to any existing light cruiser. By 1923 it was regretfully accepted by the Naval Board that no existing RAN warship would be modified to operate aircraft.

In mid-1923 the secret Memorandum 221 "Empire Naval Policy and Co-Operation" was sent to Australia by the Committee of Imperial Defence. The policy was for consideration and adoption at the forthcoming Imperial Conference in London. Stating that naval forces can make good use of seaborne aircraft, it recommended a distinct Dominion navy operating cruisers built to carry one or more amphibians. Commonality to the RN in all areas of personnel, operations and equipment was vital, and to ensure this was the proposal for "a free interchange, both of individuals and of ships" with the Royal Navy.

The Committee of Imperial Defence recommended that the RAN acquire a seaplane carrier to use as a mobile aerial base and repair shop and that future Australian cruisers be built to carry amphibians. Observers had been trained in the RN since 1921's No. 1 Naval Observer's Course. The Naval Board in Melbourne anticipated the requirement for Australian aircrew and called for volunteers. In 1923 three officers from the naval college's 1915 class commenced training at RAAF Base Point Cook on the shores of Port Phillip Bay near Melbourne. Lieutenant Joseph "Joe" Hewitt joined Pilots Course No. 1 with five Army and six Air Force colleagues while Lieutenants Henry Chesterman and Vincent Kennedy passed an *ad hoc* short observers course.

The presumptive head of the RAN, Rear-Admiral Percival Hall-Thompson CB CMG RN, had been seated at the Australian table with Prime Minister Bruce during the October 1923 Imperial Conference. Hall-Thompson arrived at Melbourne's Navy Office on 25 February 1924, as First Naval Member of the Commonwealth Naval Board. To institute the proposal agreed by the prime minister he commenced the first five-year construction programme of those aviation-capable cruisers and, later, a seaplane carrier while advancing, against considerable resistance, the scheme to train naval pilots and observers. It was his Commonwealth Naval Order 37 of 1925 that proclaimed the establishment of a Fleet Air Arm of the Royal Australian Navy. With

---

5   The Third Naval Member of the Commonwealth Naval Board controlled naval dockyards and bases and was responsible for the construction and engineering of ships and their repair and modification.

The Fairey IIID aboard Geranium for the 1924 Barrier Reef survey.

these efforts Hall-Thompson, and his successor Rear-Admiral William Napier CB CMG DSO RN, can lay fair claim to being the great-grandfathers of the Australian Fleet Air Arm.

For 1924's Barrier Reef survey a Fairey IIID was flown from Point Cook to Townsville where it was precariously embarked on the sloop *Geranium*. The aircraft was secured for passage on the ship's wartime balloon platform although open waters were avoided. Flight Lieutenant Ernest Mustard and Lieutenant Vincent Kennedy operated the seaplane from protected moorings and surveyed some 2,000 square kilometres of uncharted waters.[6]

The RAAF formed No. 101 (Fleet Co-Operation) Flight on 1 July 1925, at Point Cook and the Air Board ordered Supermarine Seagull III amphibians to replace the Fairey floatplanes. The first Australian Seagull, registration A9-1, was launched with champagne by Dame Mary Cook on 26 February 1926. No novice at such events, having launched the Orient liner *Orama* in 1924, Dame Mary as she swung the champagne bottle declared "I name you Australian Seagull No. 1. Good luck to all who fly in you and God bless you".

Hall-Thompson in 1925 thought the future of the Fleet Air Arm had secure ministerial approval. The RAAF, however, seeing the threat to their basic concept of a single independent air service, thought differently. The Naval Board were not strategic philosophers but valued aircraft at sea for reconnaissance and gunnery/torpedo spotting, considering that anything on, under or over the water was self-evidently in their purview to control. The respective boards continued their administrative battles. On 18 January 1928, cabinet finally decided against a dedicated Fleet Air Arm. The RAAF would provide pilots, aircraft and maintainers embarked on navy ships while the navy would appoint and train observers and telegraphist/air gunners.

Albatross, constructed at Cockatoo Island dockyard, entered service in January 1929. Fortuitously, since she had not been designed with the Seagull in mind, the amphibian did fit through the hatch down to the seaplane carrier's hangar deck. A shortage of trained observers was covered by RN loan officers. Naval aviators embarked with No. 101 Flight did so dual ranked as RAAF flight lieutenants and flying officers. *Australia* had arrived in Sydney in October 1928, joined by *Canberra* in February 1929. Neither *Australia*, *Albatross* nor *Canberra* had catapults fitted although the cruisers did have a catapult platform aft of the funnels - in later nomenclature they were "fitted for but not with".

---

6   Later Group Captain Ernest Mustard DFC (1893-2002), a pioneer of commercial aviation in New Guinea and managing director from 1935 of Australian Transcontinental Airways.

The increasing weight and wing loading of the latest aircraft types meant catapult experiments were still ongoing in the UK. Lieutenant Colonel Harry Busteed RAF, an Australian test pilot commanding the Marine Aircraft Experimental Establishment had flown the first successful compressed air catapult launch from *Slinger* on 18 June 1918.[7] By 1929 the default power for catapult experiments was a cordite explosive charge, many of these trials being undertaken by Flying Officer Frank Whittle RAF before he went on to design the turbojet engine.[8]

A Seagull III embarked on the catapult platform of Canberra, during the first "Fabric and Fragile" cycle of Australian naval aviation.

A catapult, crane, aviation fuel and aircraft stores created many problems for naval architects, but until the 1936 London Treaty permitted new aircraft carriers, the only way to get enough aircraft to sea was with catapult-equipped cruisers and capital ships. The early 1930s saw the Home and Mediterranean Fleets with steadily increasing numbers of embarked ship's flights.

Prior to the arrival in Australia of an operational catapult, and also an airframe capable of withstanding the stresses of a catapult launch, the RAN made do with trial embarkations of the RAAF Seagulls. Midshipman Smith had seen the first of these embarkations aboard *Canberra* in 1931 before joining the Mediterranean Fleet. Decades later as an admiral he would comment that there had been a certain amount of lethargy on the part of senior officers towards a well-organised Fleet Air Arm. However, those skirmishes between Naval Board and Air Board in the 1920s and 1930s would never have been apparent to a junior officer. Likewise, his supposition that there never seemed to be great enthusiasm for naval aviation from the Naval Board of the 1920s and 1930s was equally ill-founded.[9]

HMAS *Canberra* 23 January 1935 to 3 April 1936

On 23 January 1935, Sub-Lieutenant Victor Smith joined *Canberra* for the second time. In this appointment, and his next in *Australia*, Victor watched the first cycle of Australian

---

7   Later Air Commodore Harry Busteed OBE AFC RAF (1887-1965). Holder of Aviator's Certificate No. 94, Busteed had been aboard the first experimental seaplane carrier *Hermes* when she was sunk by *U-27* in 1914. In 1917 he served with Longmore and demonstrated landing using arrester cables on the converted battlecruiser *Furious*. In 1925 Busteed served as Senior Officer Commanding Flying aboard *Furious*.

8   Later Air Commodore Sir Frank Whittle OM KBE CB FRS (1907-1996).

9   Rear-Admiral Percival Hall-Thompson's wife Helen wrote in her journal that Val "was always having rows with the government over the navy affairs and I thought he might resign". A century later family lore maintains these arguments centred over the establishment of a Fleet Air Arm.

naval aviation end and the second begin, as fragile canvas-covered aircraft hoisted overboard gave way to robust metal-skinned aircraft catapulted into the air. Seeing this evolving capability, Victor also saw the detrimental effect a cyclical stuttering towards a viable Fleet Air Arm could have on those who committed their careers, and in some cases their health and their lives, to naval aviation.

The HMAS Canberra badge used in the 1930s and featuring the coat of arms of the city of Canberra. The Latin phrase "Pro Rege, Lege et Grege" translates as "For the King, the law and the people".

Victor's senior watchkeeper onboard the flagship was the RAN's original observer, Lieutenant-Commander Henry "Chesters" Chesterman (1915 class). Commencing a short RAAF course in 1923 with his classmate Vincent Kennedy, Chesters went to England in 1927 for the 11th Naval Observer's Course. Surviving several ditchings and flying off the carriers *Eagle* and *Furious*, Chesters returned to Australia aboard *Canberra* on her delivery voyage in February 1929. In Port Melbourne he found a newly commissioned *Albatross* awaiting aircraft and aircrew. For three years Chesters laboured with his RAN, RN and RAAF colleagues to entrench that seaplane carrier's aviation capability into the RAN. When *Albatross* joined the eight ships already in reserve in 1933 there was an instant surplus of observers.

Naval careers begin early and most end early with few officers remaining on the active list beyond their mid-40s. Lieutenant-commanders retired at 45, commanders at 50 and captains at 55. Age combined with a shortage of specialist postings meant Chesters, after manning a desk in Navy Office, considered himself lucky to be posted to the flagship as Squadron Training Officer. Seniority and staff duties ensured he did not fly again.

Canberra's designated ship's observer was Lieutenant George Oldham, whom Victor had last seen aboard *Glorious*. Also aboard was Lieutenant Palgrave "Pally" Carr (1922 class) who had completed his three permitted years with the RAAF as a pilot. Informed by senior air force officers that no navy pilots would ever be posted to No. 101 Flight for either cruiser, Pally passed this information on to the Naval Board.[10] The board quietly ended naval pilot training in June 1934.[11] George Clarke (1921 class) had just resigned from the navy given the lack of pilot career progression while Pally himself, after executive seaman duties aboard *Canberra*, took passage for an observers course in May 1936.[12] The Air Board had so comprehensively won the campaign for control that there was no (P) against Pally's name in the Navy List, the only aviation specialist qualification now allowed being the (O) for Observer.

The 1923 Imperial Conference had enunciated the principle of "interoperability" whereby

---

10 On the outbreak of war Pally Carr was the observer in *Orion*'s Supermarine Seafox. Disembarking from *Hermes* he commanded a Swordfish detachment ashore in Ceylon. In May 1942 he joined *Australia* for squadron observer duties.

11 Even observers who were also pilots were no longer permitted to undergo refresher flying as pilots since "their services will be required exclusively in their present specialist rank of observer".

12 Later Flight Lieutenant George Clarke (1907-1940) joined the RAAF Reserve on leaving the RAN in 1934. Called up at the outbreak of war Flight Lieutenant Clarke embarked a Walrus in *Australia*.

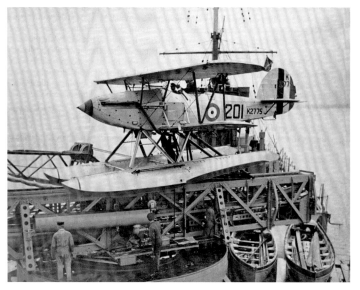

A Hawker Osprey, arguably the most elegant floatplane of the 1930s, mounted on a EIIIH catapult.

any RAN officer or ship was able to seamlessly integrate with their RN counterparts. Officers flowed between the RAN and RN for training and service as did the ships. When Victor rejoined *Canberra* in Sydney Harbour it was to find her new squadron consort was the exchange RN heavy cruiser *Sussex* (Captain Stuart Bonham-Carter CVO DSO RN), *Australia* having sailed the previous month for the UK. *Sussex* was sporting on her catapult perhaps the most elegant floatplane of the era, a Hawker Osprey flown by Lieutenant Charles "Crash" Evans RN and his observer Lieutenant George Duncan RN. George had been on the 18th Naval Observer's Course of 1930 with *Canberra's* George Oldham.

Victor's immediate focus was to be awarded his Bridge Watchkeeping Certificate. Granted at the captain's sole discretion, it required more than just the requisite knowledge and ability. With the Officer of the Watch often in complete operational charge, responsible for the safety of 700 men and £2,000,000 of warship, Victor had to have the captain's complete trust. Captain Harold Walker RN could only sleep soundly knowing his ship was being watched by a competent officer able to react correctly to any contingency and confident he would be called immediately when required. Six months after joining, the 22-year-old Victor had the requisite trust of Captain Walker. On 30 July Victor gained his BWC and was "competent to take charge of a watch at sea as a lieutenant, and to perform efficiently the duties of that rank". Appropriately this occurred during two weeks of evolutions with *Sussex* operating out of Jervis Bay in sight of the old college buildings.

In a great number of Victor's OOW duties running the ship's underway routine from the bridge, or as Officer of the Day in harbour, he had flying stations piped. Two weeks after he joined, *Canberra* hoisted onboard Seagull A9-8 flown by Flying Officer Charles Pearce RAAF, the assigned pilot from No. 101 (Fleet Co-operation) Flight.[13] The cruiser then sailed with *Sussex* for a pre-summer cruise work-up. On twelve of the next eighteen days there were flying evolutions, from torpedo spotting to shadowing exercises. With a practice torpedo

---

13   Later Air Commodore Charles Pearce DFC MiD (1910-1980) was awarded the first RAAF DFC of WWII for an attack on a U-Boat with No. 10 Squadron RAAF. He later commanded No. 11 Squadron RAAF from Port Moresby.

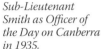

Sub-Lieutenant Smith as Officer of the Day on Canberra in 1935.

RAAF Seagull A9-6 taking off from alongside a cruiser in Sydney Harbour. Another of these seaplanes, A9-8, was embarked on Canberra in early 1935.

costing the same as a suburban house, recovery was a prime concern of both the torpedo officer and the ship's paymaster, with its rapid location at the end of a practice run by the ship's flight always lauded. Victor was getting comprehensive exposure to the effects on the ship of operating an embarked aircraft.

Along with general ship duties and watch keeping, Victor was the navigator's assistant and sub of the gunroom. The traditional *Canberra* rivalry that had always existed with *Australia* between the two gunrooms and ships transposed to *Sussex*. Victor found that the cadet-midshipmen and midshipmen (eighteen in January 1936) gave him no trouble and his gunroom ran on an even keel. Most of these "snotties" were from the 1932 class, the first to have no experience of Jervis Bay.[14] When they proceeded on to RN cruisers and destroyers, much of their sea time was spent patrolling the Iberian coast during the Spanish Civil War.

Life onboard was busy; from being present when hands turned to at 0600 in harbour until liberty men was piped. When Officer of the Day in harbour, overseeing the ship's routine, Victor would wear his Gieves frock coat with sword belt, as would all the officers gathered in front of their men at Sunday Divisions. Victor was now a member of the wardroom whose formal dinners each weeknight would see him changing into his mess undress uniform with stiff shirt and collar.

While relations between officers and lower deck were necessarily more formal than Victor had experienced as a midshipman, he always enjoyed the levelling of the sports field. There were numerous opportunities for games, with a make-and-mend practically every Wednesday afternoon to go ashore and compete against other ship's teams and locals.

---

14   Included among their number was Hugh David Stevenson, the smallest of his college year at 4'10" when he arrived at Flinders Naval Depot in 1932, and the most junior cadet-midshipman of *Canberra*'s gunroom in January 1936. Thirty-seven years later Vice-Admiral Sir David Stevenson, Chief of Naval Staff 1973-1975, would serve under Admiral Sir Victor Smith, Chairman of the Chiefs of Staff.

The previous August *Australia*'s Seagull A9-6 was torn from its mounting in a squall off Western Australia. The vulnerability of the Seagull airframe on the catapult platform was demonstrated yet again ten weeks after Victor joined, when *Canberra* was returning from the squadron's summer cruise to New Zealand. On passage between Port Lyttelton and Hobart A9-8 was damaged beyond repair in a vicious Tasman Sea gale. Only two serviceable Seagulls now remained in the RAAF.

Lacking an airworthy aircraft, Flying Officer Charles Pearce left *Canberra*. He took passage to the UK in the briefly recommissioned *Brisbane*, whose crew would man the new light cruiser *Sydney* when *Brisbane* paid off for the scrapyard in September 1935. *Sydney*'s executive officer was the WWI qualified balloon pilot, now Commander John Collins. The 1913 pioneer graduates of the college were rapidly approaching seniority for cruiser commands with a consequent decrease in the number of RN officers needed on Australian loan for senior appointments. *Sydney* was already fitted with a catapult, and Pearce would be the cruiser's pilot under her observer Lieutenant (O) Francis Fogarty, just off the carrier *Furious*.

Meanwhile *Canberra*'s spring cruise encompassed waters as far north as Rabaul in New Britain, familiarising Victor with areas he would get to know only too well in 1942. And, of course, the Melbourne Cup in November by long tradition required a naval presence. For the summer cruise south to Hobart at the start of 1936, Flying Officer Athol Richards embarked the last airworthy Seagull.[15] A9-5 was then disembarked to the technical squadron at Point Cook while *Canberra* was alongside at Port Melbourne on 3 March 1936. Richards

The gale damaged Seagull A9-8 aboard Canberra on 5 April 1935.

15   Later Group Captain Athol Richards (1912-1984) he commanded No. 10 (Sunderland) Squadron, RAAF, during the war.

then proceeded to No. 1 Flying Training School for conversion training to the new Seagull V aircraft. Several years before the RAAF had sent out specifications for an amphibian that could be catapulted with a full military load. Supermarine accepted the challenge, designing and building 24 Seagull Mark Vs for a project cost of £345,000.

Victor regarded Captain Walker as a fine commanding officer with high standards.[16] In naval tradition men with the surname Walker are nicknamed "Hooky", which here proved particularly apropos. Walker had lost his lower right arm when part of *Vindictive*'s storming party during the Zebrugge Raid of 1918. Fitted with a hook and being naturally right-handed made his writing almost indecipherable. Walker had his secretary type that Victor was a first-rate young lieutenant who set a very good example as president of the gunroom and was eminently conscientious and sound. Finding Victor pleasant and cheerful with a sense of humour, he was still considered rather shy. Unsurprisingly Victor was noted as very strong physically, who played a good game of rugby and pulled a good oar.

Having been awarded his watchkeeping certificate Victor was now able to specialise. When entering on Victor's confidential report in what capacity he would be considered suitable, Walker had his secretary type "Observer". As *Canberra* was the flagship, Victor was also under the immediate eye of Rear-Admiral Wilbraham Ford CB RN, commanding His Majesties Australian Squadron, who concurred in all that Captain Walker had reported.[17]

Newly promoted Lieutenant Victor Smith, seniority 16 March 1936, left *Canberra* on 3 April as an EIIIH rotating catapult was finally being fitted at Garden Island Dockyard. He would have slightly begrudged missing out on the next exciting weeks when naval personnel were given air experience on the new aircraft type at RAAF Base Richmond. No. 101 Flight was re-designated as No. 5 (Fleet Co-operation) Squadron and on 21 April 1936, Richards embarked Walrus A2-5 aboard *Canberra* in Port Jackson for three days of catapult trials.

---

16   Later Admiral Sir Harold Walker KCB MiD*** (1891-1975). Reverting to the RN Walker commanded the battlecruiser *Hood* in 1938 and the battleship *Barham* in 1939. After wartime service he became Second-in-Command of the East Indies Fleet in 1945.
17   Later Admiral Sir Wilbraham Ford KCB KBE (1880-1964) was Vice-Admiral-in-Charge during the Siege of Malta and then Commander-in-Chief Rosyth.

Australia passing through the Panama Canal in March 1935, en route to the UK where a catapult was fitted.

HMAS *Australia* 9 May 1936 to 5 March 1937

The HMAS Australia badge.

Australia had arrived in the UK in March 1935 via the Panama Canal. Her crane was immediately modified to lift the heavier Walrus amphibian and a catapult, the cordite powered EIIIH, was fitted in Portsmouth Naval Dockyard.[18] After a short spell in the Mediterranean, she returned to the UK with the First Cruiser Squadron to participate in the King's Silver Jubilee Naval Review at Spithead on 16 July 1935. King George V, who had served in eleven ships of his father's navy, now reviewed 157 ships of his own.

In 1935 Germany reintroduced conscription. The so-called Peace Ballot occurred in Britain, supporting pacifism while endorsing collective security through the League of Nations. Italian aggression against Abyssinia led to a partial mobilisation of the RN from the end of August and 40,000 tons of destroyers about to be disposed of under the terms of the London Naval Treaty were retained.

When *Australia* sailed for the Mediterranean in that gathering naval response to Mussolini's invasion of the Ethiopian Empire on 12 September 1935, she did so with the first delivery Walrus A2-1 embarked. Lieutenant-Commander (O) Vincent Kennedy was observer, and the pilot was Flight Lieutenant James Alexander RAAF, who had stood by the aircraft during assembly.[19] The First Cruiser Squadron moved to Alexandria and the Walrus became integral to the cruiser's routine. *Sydney*, commissioned the same month, immediately had an EIIIH

---

18   A Fairey IIID weighed 5,050 pounds. The Supermarine Seagull V, soon renamed the Walrus in British service and universally nicknamed the "Shagbat" or "Pussers Duck", weighed 8,050 pounds.

19   Later Group Captain James Alexander OBE MiD** (1903-2006). During WWII commanded Nos. 9, 10 and 11 Squadrons, flying seaplanes and flying boats.

catapult fitted, before joining the Second Cruiser Squadron at Gibraltar in November with *Walrus* A2-2 embarked.[20]

As naval forces concentrated in the Mediterranean from as far afield as the China Station, *Sussex* cut short her Australian exchange and made a high-speed passage to Alexandria where she arrived in October. With her arrival the First Cruiser Squadron comprised the flagship *London* with *Devonshire*, *Shropshire*, *Sussex*, *Exeter*, *Berwick* and *Australia*. Whilst the Italians fought in Abyssinia the squadron, under Rear-Admiral Max Horton CB DSO**, undertook months of hard training in semi-warlike conditions.[21] A WWI submarine ace, Horton had initiated the tradition of hoisting the *Jolly Roger* on his submarine *E9* when returning from a successful patrol. His squadron knew he cared little for spit and polish as long as the guns worked.

As well as working hard, the squadron played hard. Winning the Cruiser Pulling Regatta and being "Cock of the Fleet" was every ship's desire and it was *Australia*, not the expected favourite *London*, that won the 1935 Regatta. Whether in cricket, rugby, boxing or water polo, teams from *Australia* proved dominant.

By the end of 1935 League sanctions against Italy were taking effect and the threat of an enlarged conflict receded. In January 1936 King George V died and the fleet was put in mourning. The squadron spent endless hours to improve their air defences and the catapult was often used to launch the Queen Bee, a radio-controlled Tiger Moth used for gunnery tracking and practice. These exercises showed all the cruisers to be woefully deficient in accurate anti-aircraft gunnery. On 6 March 1936, Hitler marched into the Rhineland and *Sydney* joined the First Cruiser Squadron in Alexandria several days later.

Victor, now increasingly called VAT after his initials, had been appointed to *Australia* and was placed in charge of a draft of twenty sailors of various branches also posted to the cruiser. Embarking his draft in the liner SS *Esperence Bay* they sailed from Sydney via the Indian Ocean and Suez Canal to Port Said. The sailors become very popular onboard with their fellow passengers, and it proved a happy voyage both for the officer and his men. Catching a train from Port Said to Alexandria the draft joined *Australia*, just returned from Anzac Cove ceremonies in Turkey.

VAT was made a Divisional Officer in addition to his watchkeeping duties and immediately settled into his new ship. Commanding *Australia* was Captain Herbert Forster MVO RN, a familiar face to VAT as Forster had first been loaned to the RAN in April 1927 as captain of the naval college. Just as he had marvelled as a midshipman at the number of warships in Malta, he now found watching the assembled fleet operating in company at sea thoroughly impressive.

---

20   As the remaining A2 series came off the production line they were shipped direct to Australia for No. 1 Seaplane Training Flight and No. 101 Flight. Twelve were taken on RAAF charge in 1936, with the rest following in 1937.

21   Later Admiral Sir Max Horton GCB DSO** SGM (1883-1951). During WWII Horton was Flag Officer Submarines and then Commander-in-Chief Western Approaches where, more than any other individual, he was responsible for victory in the Battle of the Atlantic.

"Cock of the Fleet" – a smart looking Australia with a Walrus embarked.

Anxious preparations for the July 1936 Regatta followed a visit to Athens. In the pulling competitions VAT, who had first struggled with pulling the heavy oar of a whaler as a boy in Jervis Bay was now well recognised as "a good oar" and was a welcome addition to the wardroom crew. For 60 years no ship had been "Cock of the Fleet" two years running and there was much jubilation when *Australia* managed the feat by winning consecutive regattas. Victor's well-developed sporting instincts regarded pulling regattas as something intrinsically worthwhile, an attitude shared with the whole fleet, who felt that winning a regatta signified a ship that was rather special. Certainly, VAT would always hold that *Australia* had been a very fine ship indeed.

Australia and *Sydney* headed south through the Suez Canal for home on 15 July 1936. There they resumed the normal routine of the Australia Station. Although Rear-Admiral George Hyde had slowly built up the annual monies allocated for the navy, now almost doubled from the depths of the depression, much of that was funding for new light cruisers and destroyers. Days at sea for the ships in commission were reduced to save money. This increased harbour time meant many man-hours were dedicated to keeping the ship very smart. At one point both *Australia* and *Canberra* painted their ships' sides in gloss enamel rather than the normal matte finish. In the bright Sydney sunshine the result was dazzling and much admired by VAT, who maintained a lifetime's obsession with having a "smart" ship or establishment.

Captain Forster was also finding much to admire about his most junior lieutenant. Marked very highly for reliability VAT was keen, hardworking, loyal and tactful. If he only showed average initiative that was well outweighed by his common-sense. Smart in appearance with a good manner to his subordinates, VAT got on well with everyone. Now not seen as shy, but rather he was considered on the quiet side while still showing good social and physical qualities.

VAT wished to be a pilot but, that specialisation not being available to a RAN officer in 1936, he repeated his desire to do an observer's course. Also anxious to specialise as an observer was Harrie Gerrett (1926 class) aboard *Canberra*, who had been a team-mate in that winning 1929 college rugby XV. *Albatross*, still in reserve in Sydney Harbour but often used by the ship's flights as a refuelling point and overnight base, was fitted with a catapult in September. The Second Naval Member wrote that "if it transpires that *Albatross* is to commission in January 1938 … we shall want every observer we can raise".[22] Harrie was considered "barely above average" so VAT, considerably better reported, was selected ahead of his senior and informed that he would be going to England in early 1937 for his specialist course. Harrie followed six months later, the first of many to find that VAT's career would outdistance their own.

A Naval Observer's course was expensive and required those selected to be bonded for a return of service. On a document signed and sealed on 4 December 1936, Victor Alfred Smith of *Bomera*, Help Street, Chatswood, an officer in the Permanent Naval Forces of the Commonwealth was:

> Held and firmly bound unto His majesty the King his heirs and successors in the sum of five hundred pounds (£500) of lawful British money.

On 3 March 1937 VAT once again found himself on a passenger liner leaving Sydney Harbour and sailing west for the UK via Suez. Many onboard were travelling to celebrate the coronation of the new king, the newspapers reporting a gay farewell, with many cabin cocktail parties before the RMS *Maloja* cast off at noon.

---

22 *Albatross* commissioned in April 1938 and sailed for the UK, having been accepted by the Admiralty as part-payment for the light cruiser *Hobart* (ex-*Apollo*). She proved a useful vessel in the coming conflict until torpedoed off the Normandy beaches in 1944 with more than 100 casualties.

CHAPTER 5

OBSERVER 1937 – 1939

IN THE '30S, IF YOU WANTED TO SPECIALISE IN NAVAL FLYING,
YOU BECAME AN OBSERVER.

VAT SMITH, 1992.

Although the wartime role of observer between 1915 and 1918 had been well entrenched in both the RFC and the RNAS, the RAF pursued a post-war policy of commissioned general duties pilots fulfilling all airborne roles. This "pilots only" club mentality was adopted in turn by the RAAF in 1921, and lasted well into the 1930s, despite navigation standards being demonstrably inadequate.

Whether navy or air force was to win the struggle for control of maritime air the Admiralty committed to needing aircrew observers, a need firmly established by Longmore and his No. 1 (Naval) Squadron who had spotted for warships firing off the Belgian coast in 1915. They had moved from visual Aldis lamp to W/T Morse code signalling under the drive of another Australian, Acting Flight Commander Douglas Evill.[1] Well aware of the lack of accuracy with their big guns during the war, many admirals felt that "the future of gunnery depends to a large extent on the efficiency of observation from the air" and the 1st Naval Observer's Course began in November 1921.

The naval attitude, fundamentally different from that of the air force, was that an efficient observer was as valuable as a competent pilot. Reflecting the importance of observers, it was decided that their specialist status would be recognised with an (O) annotation in the Navy List to accord equality with their gunnery, navigation, torpedo and signals qualified brother officers. This started with the RN Navy List in January 1924, while (P) first appeared in the RAN Navy List of July 1926, and the first (O) in October 1927.

Under pressure from the Naval Board in Melbourne, the RAAF had offered a short observer's course to two RAN officers in 1923, based on information received from the RN about aerial "naval co-operation". While Kennedy of this course then volunteered for the RAAF pilot's course in 1925, Chesterman eventually joined the RN's 11th Naval Observer's Course in 1927 to fully qualify as a naval observer. A trickle of RAN officers to the UK for observer courses over the next ten years meant VAT was only the eighth when he joined the 31st Naval

---

1   Later Air Chief Marshal Sir Douglas Evill GBE KCB DSC AFC DL RAF (1892-1971). Travelling from Broken Hill he joined the RN as a cadet in 1905. Persuaded by his cousin Longmore to specialise in aviation, Evill qualified privately while serving in destroyers and commanded No. 2 (Naval) Squadron in 1916.

Observer's Course on 3 May 1937.[2] Serendipitously, due to his age and seniority, this placed him in a position to successfully straddle both pre- and post-war naval aviation. In the coming war itself VAT was to experience a range of wartime appointments he was lucky to survive.

The *Maloja* arrived in England at the start of May, just ten days before the coronation of King George VI in Westminster Abbey on 12 May 1937. While VAT reported to Australia House on London's Strand, and then to Portsmouth, the focus of the Empire was on the coming celebrations. VAT made sure he did not miss out on the spectacle.

It was a buoyant time for the Australian navy, steadily expanding from the core of ships and men preserved in the depths of the Great Depression by Rear-Admiral Munro Kerr RN. When VAT first went to sea in 1931 there were only four warships in commission: the two new County-class 8-inch heavy cruisers *Canberra* and *Australia*, the seaplane carrier *Albatross* and the destroyer *Anzac*. Under the steady, if autocratic, hand of Rear-Admiral George Hyde RAN, the annual naval estimates were steadily increasing despite ongoing Treasury department scrutiny.

International events had assisted Hyde in arguing for increased naval expenditure. Germany had withdrawn from the League of Nations in 1933 and announced, in 1935, that it would expand its army to six times the size permitted by the Treaty of Versailles, with concomitant increases in her *Kriegsmarine* and *Luftwaffe*. Italy invaded Abyssinia in June 1935 and Mussolini was increasingly bellicose in his speeches. Germany reoccupied the demilitarised Rhineland in March 1936 and supported, with Italy, General Franco's Nationalists in the Spanish Civil War. In the Pacific Japan continued her aggressive expansionist policies and her *Kaigun* (naval forces) were deploying for the second Sino-Japanese war - commencing two months after the coronation and held by some to be the actual start of WWII.

In this coronation month the RAN now mustered three cruisers, the new light cruiser *Sydney* joining the two heavy cruisers. Instead of a single destroyer there was now a destroyer flotilla, transferred from the RN in October 1933, comprising the elderly *Stuart* (originally commissioned in December 1918), *Waterhen* (July 1918) and *Vendetta* (October 1917). In addition, there were two new sloops *Yarra* (January 1936) and *Swan* (January 1937). Vital surveying had started again from *Moresby* in April 1935 after a five-year hiatus. Two more light cruisers, *Hobart* (ex-*Apollo*, January 1936) and *Perth* (ex-*Amphion*, June 1936) would commission into the RAN in September 1938 and June 1939 respectively. All these vessels, plus the recommissioned out of reserve light cruiser *Adelaide* (August 1922), would see the RAN enter the coming war with reasonable, if sometimes antiquated, tonnage. Projecting five cruisers fitted with catapults, VAT knew his immediate career prospects on return to Australia were bright. Many felt that the sun was shining again on the navy after a long spell of inclement grey, although there were

---

2   VAT was the RAN's 8th observer and its 13th naval aviator. RAN observer graduates prior to WWII (year of college entry) were H Chesterman 1927 (1915), C Brooks 1928 (1917), G Hall 1930 (1915), G Oldham 1930 (1920), P Bailhache 1931 (1918), F Fogarty 1933 (1923) and P Carr 1936 (1922). VAT Smith 1937 (1927) was followed by H Gerrett in 1938 (1926). Hall, Bailhache and Carr qualified as pilots and were seconded to the RAAF before returning to naval service and an observer's course.

The coronation procession through Admiralty Arch on 12 May 1937 with sailors lining the route. VAT was watching from the other side of the arch in Hyde Park.

clearly storm clouds on the horizon.

The King's reply to the loyal addresses from the assembled Dominion Prime Ministers on 11 May talked of a world "harassed by perplexity and fears". Certainly, Germany was pursuing a policy of revanche, the Italians were determined on an empire, and the naval limitation treaties had lapsed in December 1936. Only nine months before, Hitler had ordered a four-year plan to be equipped for war by 1940. The government in the UK was, by necessity, pursuing a policy of deterrent rearmament in parallel with political appeasement. The Australian Prime Minister, Joseph "Honest Joe" Lyons, seated next to the Queen at Buckingham Palace, would have agreed with King George's statement that they had "... inherited a great tradition of liberty and service ... which we shall work together to preserve".

The next day, Coronation Day, VAT and a friend were lucky enough to get good seats on a temporary stand in Hyde Park to watch the procession pass in the drizzling rain. From the raised stand VAT would have been able to see the Emotion television cameras set up on Apsley Gate at the park's entrance.[3] Linked by cable to their control vans and thence to Broadcasting House and the transmitting aerials at Alexandra Palace, this was the UK's first major outside TV broadcast. The pictures were seen on the 12 x 9 inch screens at up to 50 miles, double the advertised range.

---

3   A television cost GBP £75 in 1937, the equivalent of GBP £6,500 (AUD $12,000) today.

"The Fleet's lit up!" Illumination of ships on the night of the Coronation Naval Review.

In the procession to Westminster Abbey were a long line of coaches for the dominion prime ministers, Joe Lyons's coach being escorted by mounted Australian troopers with emu feathers in their slouch hats, immediately behind the Canadian prime minister's coach with his accompanying Mounties. There was also an Australian military troop marching among the dozens of uniformed contingents from around the Empire. Preceding the King's escort of mounted empire troops were the highest ranking naval, military and air officers. VAT's unforgettable memory was seeing the Lord Commissioners of the Admiralty, in naval full-dress uniform, riding on horseback. To his prejudiced eye this proved the versatility of the naval service.

The culmination of the celebrations was when the Home and Reserve Fleets, painted in their dark warship grey, gathered at Spithead with the Mediterranean Fleet, attractive in light grey, for the Coronation Naval Review of 20 May. Ten British battleships and battlecruisers proudly led the review but, in a sign of evolving force structure, there were four carriers in the eight long columns of 134 warships. The evening's BBC Radio broadcast became famous for the commentary of Lieutenant-Commander (retired) Thomas "Tommy" Woodrooffe. Having imbibed generously with old comrades in the wardroom of the battleship *Nelson*, as the fleet illuminated at 2245, he repeatedly exclaimed "The fleet's lit up … it's fairyland … the fleet's lit up … fairy lamps". Then, as *Nelson* swung in the current, a "tired and emotional" Tommy confusedly cried "There's no fleet! It's disappeared! …the fleet's gone … there's nothing between us and heaven". It took an amusing four minutes before the technicians were able to cut the power to his microphone.[4]

Among the foreign warships in G Line was the new Deutschland-class cruiser *Admiral Graf Spee* with an embarked Heinkel He 60 floatplane. Although it was labelled a treaty busting warship Germany had not been a signatory to the tonnage limits agreed in 1922 and 1930. The *Graf Spee*, at 16,000 tons and armed with six 11-inch guns, well earned the sobriquet "pocket battleship". She was only two and a half years away from her demise off Montevideo. Also present in G Line was the French battleship *Dunkerque*, beached in 1940 to prevent her sinking after being badly damaged by the 15-inch guns of *Hood* over in F Line. Further down F Line was the destroyer *Encounter*, fated to be sunk in 1942 by the Japanese cruiser *Ashigara*, several cable lengths down from *Graf Spee* in G Line. The carriers *Glorious*, *Courageous*,

---

4   Later Acting Commander Thomas Woodrooffe (1899-1978) was suspended by the BBC for a week. Forgiven, he was recalled to duty and commanded *Coventry City* in 1940 before serving with the Admiralty Press Division.

Furious and *Hermes* were in E Line. *Hermes,* based on a cruiser hull, was half the size of the other three which were all conversions from battlecruisers. The revolutionary *Ark Royal* had been launched but was still eighteen months from being commissioned.

After the excitement of the coronation, VAT settled down to his specialist studies. Part 1 of the course was eight weeks of instruction at the Signals School in Portsmouth and the Gunnery School at Whale Island. At the Signals School the theory of W/T was covered in a few lectures, but the practical training occupied many hours. The students worked up to a speed of 22 words per minute to be able to easily read 15 per minute airborne. Having practised visual Morse from a signalling lamp on the quarterdeck at the naval college when a teenager VAT easily got up to speed. The Gunnery School, keen to have corrections to their fall of shot by airborne observers, treated the lieutenants as "disciples of the art" rather than VAT's previous experience as junior course-fodder needing close watching and discipline.

Part 2 of the course was twenty weeks ground instruction and practical training in the air with B (Naval Observers) Training Flight at the RAF School of Naval Co-operation. Based at RAF Lee-on-Solent in Hampshire, the main training airframe was the Blackburn Shark in both its floatplane and wheeled variants. Half the working days were spent in the classroom learning theory, with the other half airborne over land as well as sea.

There were eight RN lieutenants on the course with VAT and, in the normal nature of things, they became close friends. Being an aviation course there were ups and downs, with several of the downs being unplanned. All the early training flights from Lee-on-Solent were in the Blackburn Shark biplane which was notorious for its unreliable Tiger engine. When the first training wave of five Sharks took off from Lee-on-Solent at the course's commencement, almost immediately three of the five had to do forced landings. Of VAT's first three flights two ended in similar forced landings owing to oil pressure problems. Inevitably reviving memories of his father's cantankerous Model T Ford, it did not imbue VAT with great confidence in the aircraft of the Fleet Air Arm of the RAF. Later, flying in the Swordfish and then the Walrus, with their reliable Pegasus engines, VAT expressed no such doubts.

Once able to successfully stay airborne long enough to practice the lessons of ground school it proved a comprehensive course with VAT finding it all "most interesting". Navigation, air-to-air firing, spotting for gun and torpedo, bombing, photography, reconnaissance and yet more navigation, all while sending and receiving signals on the W/T equipment. VAT's most valuable navigation tool was his Bigsworth chart board.[5] A square wooden board with pivoting parallel ruler and protractor attached, it was invaluable for plotting courses and determining position in the cramped open cockpit.

Completing the course in December, VAT was posted as an acting observer to *Glorious.*

5   Air Commodore Arthur Bigsworth CMG DSO* AFC MiD (1885-1961) served with the RNAS and carried out the first night attack on a Zeppelin in May 1915. WE Johns, author of the *Biggles* books, had worked at the Air Ministry with Bigsworth.

There he would complete consolidation training at sea before formal confirmation as a naval observer. In stark contrast to naval officers who qualified as pilots, VAT and his course mates were not awarded any wings to wear on their uniforms. The prevailing attitude was that observers wished to preserve their identity as Executive Branch officers and feared that specialist insignia could be perceived as a shift in allegiance to the very junior Air Branch, which might damage their career prospects. As it eventuated this was not something VAT needed to worry about.

The front view of a Blackburn Shark, showing the foldable upper and lower wings allowing for efficient stowage in cramped aircraft carrier hangars.

A Blackburn Shark during the Coronation Fleet Review flypast in May 1937.

Blackburn Shark

Powerplant: 760 hp Armstrong Siddeley Tiger VI (Shark Mk II). A 14-cylinder air cooled radial.

Speed: Max 130 knots, cruise 103 knots

Range: 543 nautical miles (almost five hours airborne)

Max Weight: 8,111 pounds

Crew: Three

Armament: One fixed Vickers machine gun and one flexible Vickers or Lewis machine gun.

Bomb Load: one 18-inch torpedo or 1,600 pounds of bombs

The Blackburn Shark, a biplane TSR (Torpedo Spotter Reconnaissance) carrier aircraft, began production in 1934 after deck landing trials. The metal fuselage was strengthened for catapult launches and contained watertight compartments to aid flotation if the aircraft ditched. Using distinctive slanted struts instead of bracing wires, the Shark had foldable upper and lower wings. With fabric flying surfaces, there was a hydraulic wing-locking mechanism, arrester hook and pneumatic brakes.

Sharks entered service with No. 820 Naval Air Squadron aboard *Courageous* in 1935 and later equipped Nos. 810 and 821 Squadrons. In its seaplane configuration Sharks served aboard battlecruisers. Rapidly replaced as a front-line aircraft from 1937 by the Fairey Swordfish it saw most use as a training aircraft and in secondary roles such as target towing. A total of 238 Sharks in three models were produced, with export sales to Portugal and Canada. The type proved relatively unreliable but did see active service during the desperate days of the Dunkirk evacuations and during the Japanese invasion of Malaya.

HMS *Victory* 11 December 1937 to 3 January 1938

With *Glorious* still undergoing a refit in Portsmouth Dockyard, VAT was appointed to a holding billet for three weeks during which he took leave. Thus, he found himself borne briefly on the books of *Victory*, Nelson's famous 1805 flagship at the Battle of Trafalgar. Still in commission after 160 years, *Victory* was flying the flag of the Commander-in-Chief Portsmouth.

HMS *Glorious* 4 January 1938 to 23 May 1938

Joining *Glorious*, VAT had two weeks onboard to become familiar with his ship's duties before the carrier sailed. He would have been intrigued to see that after her last major refit the carrier now had arrestor wires fitted and the upper hangar doors forrard had been welded shut after a storm had breached them and destroyed six aircraft. The flight deck and round-down had also been extended aft over the quarterdeck. At 27,560 tons and with a crew of 1,260, *Glorious* had an operational range of 3,000 nautical miles at 24 knots.

On 16 January 1938 *Glorious* sailed for Weymouth Bay where she embarked No. 802 Squadron (Nimrods and Ospreys) and No. 825 Squadron (Swordfish) from RAF Abingdon in Oxfordshire. There the other change that VAT would have noticed from 1932 was that a batsman, or Deck Landing Control Officer, had been introduced to carrier operations in 1937, guiding the pilot in his curving final approach. *Glorious* then headed for Malta via Gibraltar where she had left her other two Swordfish squadrons, Nos. 812 and 823, ashore at RAF Hal Far. These were embarked on 7 February as she left Malta for Alexandria, Egypt. These four squadrons would alternate between *Glorious* and Hal Far, with occasional disembarkations to Dekheila near Alexandria.

Over the next eighteen months, as he had in 1932-33, VAT saw much of the Mediterranean and its contiguous countries, but this time it was mainly from the air. Ports in Corsica, Yugoslavia, Greece and Cyprus were visited where time alongside could often be a week or more. Longer periods were spent in her homeport of Malta (nine weeks from November 1938 to January 1939) and in Alexandria.

Glorious, having disembarked all squadrons to Hal Far, entering Grand Harbour, Malta. Her aft flight deck extension is prominent, with the "GL" identifying letters just visible near the lift well.

Glorious's hangars extended to both sides of the ship so to go forward or aft on the upper deck meant walking through the hangar space. With an open stern below the flight deck more than one pilot, dipping too low on finals, found himself on the quarterdeck amidst wreckage, much to the commander's displeasure. Overall VAT found life aboard *Glorious* reasonably comfortable.

While consolidating, VAT would fly with any squadron that needed an extra body. No. 802 Squadron's Hawker Nimrod fighters were single seaters, but her Ospreys had a reconnaissance role in addition to their fighter capabilities and carried an observer. Smith would operate the radio and do the navigation but since the Osprey, even without the drag of the large floats fitted to the seaplane version, had a limited range, he never found the navigation very complicated. The Osprey's Rolls-Royce Kestrel II engine was the first cast-block V-12 from Rolls-Royce and established the basic pattern for most of their future designs. It was certainly reliable enough to gain no adverse comment from VAT. Most often, however, VAT would fly with the other three squadrons onboard whose Swordfish I aircraft rapidly became a favourite. He would always recall them as "those wonderful aircraft".

In a Swordfish the air gunner fired a Lewis gun covering from each beam through the stern, but his principal duty was operating the radio set, so he was designated a TAG or Telegraphist Air Gunner. The observer was the jack of all other trades except the actual flying. He was the navigator and later, when radar sets were fitted, he was also the radar operator. The Swordfish could stagger up to 10,000 feet for high level bombing in which instance the observer was the bomb aimer. When long range tanks became available this filled the space normally seating the observer so the TAG would be left out of the crew and the observer would operate the radio as well. He was kept very busy.

With an impressive final score of 81% for his course and consolidation training, VAT officially qualified as an observer on 7 May 1938. On 16 May all four squadrons embarked for several weeks of exercises. While they were at sea on 24 May 1938, VAT was attached to No. 825 Squadron for "O" duties.[6]

Hitler had annexed Austria in March and the Sea Lords were well aware of the need to prepare for the looming conflict, while the government was equally aware of the need for appeasement to allow for continued rearmament. The Admiralty tripled student numbers on each Naval Observer's Course to 30 from July and Prime Minister Neville Chamberlain co-signed away Czechoslovakian sovereignty with the *Münchner Abkommen* or Munich Agreement of 30 September 1938. The Czechs called it the *Mnichovská Zrada* - the Munich Betrayal - but while it did not lead to "peace for our time" it did "buy time".

---

6   Incorrectly noted as "O" duties with No. 812 Squadron in his personal file.

Swordfish V4431 of No. 825 Squadron as flown by Eugene Esmond and VAT Smith, CO and SOBS of No. 825 Squadron, from the Ark Royal in October 1941.

FAIREY SWORDFISH MARK I
Powerplant: Bristol Pegasus 775 hp nine-cylinder radial air-cooled supercharged engine.
Speed: Max 132 knots, cruise 90 knots
Range: 770 nautical miles (546 nm with 1,500-pound bomb load)
Max Weight: 8,700 pounds
Crew: Three - Pilot, Observer and Telegraphist/Air Gunner.
Armament: One fixed Vickers machine gun and one flexible Lewis machine gun.
Bomb Load: One 18-inch torpedo or 1,500 pounds of sea mine, depth charges or bombs.

Powered by the reliable "Peggy" engine, the Swordfish was considered a lucky aircraft by those who flew it. The fabric-covered wings and fuselage were often too flimsy to trigger a cannon shell's contact fuse. With a very low stalling speed and docile if heavy controls, the type ensured a relatively safe return to a night landing on even the narrow pitching deck of an escort carrier. The biplanes fixed undercarriage and open cockpits gave it an old-fashioned look. In action several cylinders of the engine could be shot out and it would keep running.

Given the lack of funding for fleet aircraft the design consciously combined as many functions as possible into a single airframe. The Swordfish became known for its outstanding reliability and as an excellent, if slow, torpedo dropping platform. Updated with modern weaponry and radar, the Swordfish had a unique career, and was still in front line service in the anti-submarine role in 1945.

A Swordfish TSR (Torpedo Spotter Reconnaissance) three-crew Mark I could extend its operational range by adding an extra fuel tank in the observer position when required. To cope with the stress of firing eight 60-pound high-explosive or 25-pound armour-piercing rocket projectiles, the lower mainplane of the Mark II was strengthened with a metal undersurface. Losing a crewman and gaining the latest Air-to-Surface Vessel radar the Mark III, even with the more powerful Pegasus 30 engine, needed to be fitted with rocket-assisted take-off gear to enable escort carrier operations at maximum weight in low wind conditions.

The "Stringbag" nickname reflected the all-purpose nature of a housewife's string shopping bag. Whatever was deemed useful for the mission - bombs, depth charges, torpedo, rocket projectiles, flares, sonobuoys, mines, searchlight or radar - was attached to the forgiving airframe and sent out on operations.

Reliable, lucky and successful in action, the type outlived its planned successor, the Albacore. An initial order for 86 Swordfish saw deliveries commence in February 1936 with No. 825 Squadron being the first front-line unit to receive Swordfish at Hal Far that July. Albacores commenced their delivery flights in 1939 with production ceasing 800 aircraft later in 1943. After 2,392 production aircraft the final Swordfish Mark III was delivered in August 1944.

A Swordfish about to catch the arrestor wire on a RN carrier.

No. 825 Squadron 24 May 1938 to 19 August 1939

These were halcyon days for VAT. He was serving aboard a smart and happy carrier in the specialisation he had aspired to since his two-week air course in 1932. In Malta cheap and serviceable second-hand cars were readily available and petrol was only a shilling a gallon. The weather in the eastern Mediterranean was almost invariably sunny and fine for flying and games, both of which were available in abundance. Altogether his life both ashore and embarked was very pleasant.

The badge of No. 825 Squadron which had the motto "Nihil Obstat" (Nothing Stops Us).

Observers were appointed to the carrier and attached to a squadron. This meant that observers were available for ship's duties except when required for flying or squadron ground training. VAT's secondary duties were as an assistant divisional officer and the carrier's sports officer. Given the importance placed on sport by the naval hierarchy coupled with a ship's company of over 1,000 men, VAT was kept very busy indeed. Captain Lumley Lyster RN, well aware of the magnitude of this particular secondary duty, considered VAT did valuable work in running the ship's company's games and noted that he was very good in his dealings with the men.[7]

One evening in Alexandria VAT was with a group of officers on the quarterdeck talking to the captain who remarked that if he had his time over again, he would join the Fleet Air Arm. Someone commented that it seemed an unusual remark coming from a gunnery officer. Captain Lyster's reply was "Yes, but I mean it!" From an officer who had commanded the Gunnery School in 1935, taking charge of the gun carriage carrying the body of King George V

---

7   Later Vice-Admiral Sir Lumley Lyster KCB CVO CBE DSO RN (1881-1972). Lyster had drafted the attack plan for Taranto in 1935. When Rear-Admiral, Mediterranean Aircraft Carriers, aboard *Illustrious* in November 1940, he executed it. Afterwards he was appointed Fifth Sea Lord and Chief of Naval Air Services.

at his state funeral, this was a profound statement which showed a depth of enthusiasm for his ship and the role of her aircraft.

In early 1939 VAT was also made fleet water polo officer. Daily routine meant that unless he had a specific ship's duty to undertake, he would go ashore most afternoons to watch or participate in games he had organised. Shipboard etiquette required VAT to ask permission of Commander Edward Evans-Lombe before going ashore early, but so frequent were his requests that the commander soon told VAT that unless he was on duty the commander would not expect to see him onboard in the afternoon.[8] This freedom suited VAT very well and he was not of the character to abuse it, as the commander well knew.

When the squadrons were disembarked to Hal Far, normally the case when the ship arrived at Malta, the observers remained onboard and visited Hal Far as required according to the squadron training programme. The system worked satisfactorily in the circumstances and enabled observers to remain familiar with their normal professional duties as opposed to specialist aviation duties. The RN pilots of the time held both naval and air force commissions, necessary as the squadron maintenance personnel were all RAF. VAT's first squadron commander, Lieutenant-Commander Alan Brock RN, also held the RAF rank of squadron leader.[9] VAT remembered one case where an RN pilot was a lieutenant-commander who had commanded a squadron, but the Air Board had not seen fit to promote him beyond flying officer.

VAT recognised that the arrangements for naval aviation at this time were not entirely satisfactory. The RAF provided the majority of pilots for ship-borne flights and the RN the remainder. Given the special nature of work involving naval ships and operations over the sea the navy provided all the observers and TAGs. The RAF provided the maintenance personnel who fitted in quite well and VAT particularly remembered one flight sergeant in No. 825 Squadron aboard *Glorious* "He was a magnificent chap … a great leader of men and a very knowledgeable rigger and fitter".

In the case of the RAF pilots, there were a few who had gone through the RAF College Cranwell, but the majority were short service commission officers. All the RN pilots were permanent commission. On the whole VAT saw it working smoothly. Occasionally there would be an RAF pilot who was a bit unhappy with his lot, saying that if he had wanted to fly from ships, he would have joined the FAA and not the RAF, but that seldom happened.

On 1 May 1939, with all in the British services well aware that war was likely, VAT remarked on a general feeling of unease and disquiet as No. 825 Squadron disembarked from *Glorious* as she went to her assigned mooring in Alexandria's outer harbour. At Dekheila airfield, about ten miles outside of Alexandria, they flew the normal training programme ashore and

---

8   Later Vice-Admiral Sir Edward Evans-Lombe KCB CB (1901-1974), he commanded *Glasgow* before becoming Chief of Staff for the British Pacific Fleet from December 1944.
9   Alan Brock (b. 1903) was a graduate of No. 4 Naval Pilot's Course 1925-26 who had survived when his curiously named (and ugliest of the inter-war naval aircraft) Blackburn Blackburn N9987 crashed off the deck of *Furious* into the Firth of Forth.

appreciated the many bonuses of their situation over the next seven weeks. It was not far from the airfield to the sporting club at Alexandria where swimming, squash and tennis were all readily available. VAT also flew one of the most beautiful flights he ever experienced, a dawn sortie from Alexandria following the Nile to Cairo. It was to be his last peaceful interlude for many years.

The Admiralty regained full control of the Fleet Air Arm on 24 May 1939. The inherited shore bases were promptly given ship's names while training and support units were assigned unused second-line squadron numbers from No. 750 upwards.[10] In August the newly appointed Fifth Sea Lord and Chief of Naval Air Services - a position last occupied in 1918 - having studied the staff papers left by the RAF, projected that it would take until 1943 to overcome the inherited shortcomings of the Fleet Air Arm. He grimly forecasted that in the event of war the position would be very serious in 1940 and 1941.[11] It is sobering to read that the assumptions made by the naval staff for a front-line squadron was 20% "wastage" of aircraft and 10% "wastage" of aircrew per month.

Current RAN practice saw observers as natural selections for the three-month meteorology course, as were hydrographers and instructors. Lieutenant Pally Carr (O) had just completed the course in March after two years in *Furious* and *Courageous*. With only five qualified meteorology officers in the RAN in 1939, three of whom were observers, VAT was selected in August to attend the course before his return to Australia. Captain Lyster, when handing over command of *Glorious* to Captain Guy D'Oyly-Hughes DSO* DSC that June, had written that VAT was an efficient observer and a very promising young officer of strong character who was keen and hardworking. With no hint of shyness now evident, VAT was seen as possessing a charming personality. He was a good messmate who exhibited very good social qualities.

Taking passage from Port Said to London in a P&O ship, VAT arrived at Essex's Tilbury Docks two days after the Germans had invaded Poland. It was 3 September 1939, the day the UK and France declared war on Germany.

---

10   RAF Ford commissioned as HMS *Peregrine*/Naval Air Station Ford housing No. 1 Observers School (Nos. 750, 751 and 752 Squadrons) and RAF Lee-on-Solent commissioned as HMS *Daedalus*/Naval Air Station Lee-on-Solent housing No. 2 Observers School (Nos. 753 and 754 Squadrons).

11   Memorandum dated 4 August 1939 by Vice-Admiral Sir Alexander Ramsay GCVO KCB DSO (1881-1972), who had commanded *Furious* in 1929 and flew his flag in *Courageous* as Rear-Admiral Aircraft Carriers from 1933 to 1936. He was Fifth Sea Lord and Chief of Naval Air Services in 1938-39.

CHAPTER 6

TO WAR IN THE ARK 1939 – 1941

The Atlantic Star.

THE BATTLE OF THE ATLANTIC, the longest and most critical campaign of WWII, began when the passenger liner *Athenia* was sunk by *U-30* on 3 September 1939. This battle was not to finish until 8 May 1945. Those who took part in operations against the enemy at sea in this ocean were awarded the Atlantic Star.

On arriving in London from Tilbury Docks, VAT immediately reported to the naval liaison officer at Australia House. At 1115 the BBC Home Service broadcast Prime Minister Neville Chamberlain's announcement that, as Hitler had not responded to demands to leave Poland "This country is at war with Germany". A distraught Chamberlain declared it "a bitter blow" whereas a bellicose Winston Churchill, newly returned as First Lord of the Admiralty after an absence of 24 years, was "fighting the pestilence of Nazi tyranny". Churchill adjourned his first board meeting with the sea lords saying "Gentlemen, to your tasks and duties".

In Australia the warning telegram "Australia Prepare" had been received days before by the Acting Chief of Naval Staff Captain John Collins, our intrepid balloon pilot of 1917. The War Book was consulted, and mobilisation started on 29 August. As RAN ships proceeded to their war stations, with the possibility of immediate action, Collins gained the prime minister's approval to make the Naval Board war signal "Australia Total" immediately on receipt of the Admiralty war telegram "All Ships Total Germany". Sending this before any formal Cabinet or Parliamentary announcement meant, in effect, the RAN declared war on Germany before Australia did.[1]

At Australia House VAT was told to walk the twenty minutes to the Admiralty and report to the RN Officers' Appointments section. Several floors above him the Fifth Sea Lord was drafting a memorandum reporting a shortage of 100 pilots and 78 observers. Even allowing for the 50 RAF pilots on loan, there was no pool of aircrew and no surplus for training or to form new squadrons. With this critical shortage of observers in the RN (but not in the RAN) there was to be no meteorology course or return to Australia, instead VAT was off to war in the carrier *Ark Royal*. By 1830 he was on the "Jellicoe Express" leaving London's Euston

---

1   In a post-war interview Collins remarked "We in the navy liked to be a little ahead of things!"

station heading north to Thurso in Scotland, arriving at 1530 the following afternoon.[2] From Thurso it was across the water to Scapa Flow in the Orkney Islands where the Home Fleet had concentrated on mobilisation. This large body of sheltered water provided ready access to both the North Sea and the Atlantic.

Ark Royal, known simply as the *Ark* to her crew, was a built-for-purpose aircraft carrier commissioned in December 1938. Her design incorporated numerous improvements over the preceding carrier conversions whose hangars and flightdeck were superstructure additions. She was twice the size of *Hermes*, the first ship designed from the keel up as an aircraft carrier. The *Ark*'s double hangars, armour protected, were integral within the welded hull, whose steel flight deck was the "strength-deck" of the many decks. Her 27,000 tons encompassed a full-length flight deck of 800 feet with improved arrester gear and serviced by three lifts. The carrier's complement was 1,600 and she could make up to 31 knots. The *Ark* was poised to become the most famous British carrier of WWII and her armoured design became the basis for the following *Illustrious* class.

The HMS Ark Royal badge.

The FAA had only 30 poorly performing two-seater Blackburn Roc and Skua fighters at the war's commencement. These were embarked on *Ark Royal* and *Glorious*. With none available for *Courageous*, *Furious*, *Eagle* or *Hermes*, those carriers were compelled to sortie initially without a single fighter embarked. Such desperate times cannot have failed to have an impact

The modern built-for-purpose carrier, Ark Royal.

---

2   This 717-mile journey was so named in WWI after Admiral Sir John Jellicoe GCB OM GCVO SGM (1859-1935), commander of the British Grand Fleet based at Scapa Flow, and Governor-General of New Zealand 1920-24.

on VAT's future outlook. Critically short of aircrew with understrength squadrons flying antiquated aircraft - such was the price of having naval aviation subservient to Air Board priorities throughout the preceding years.

No. 821 Squadron   5 September 1939 – 12 August 1940

When VAT reported aboard the *Ark* there were four Swordfish squadrons, Nos. 810, 818, 820 and VAT's 821 plus two fighter squadrons, Nos. 800 and 803. Harrie Gerrett, who had finished his observer's course six months after VAT, was an observer in No. 820 Squadron with the inevitable nickname "Digger". However, Harrie had been struggling, his confidential report from his previous carrier *Courageous* declaring him slow and not showing "much indication of being an efficient observer".

It was with these understrength squadrons of Fairey Swordfish Mark I aircraft that VAT and Harrie would face the rigours of that first year of hostilities. *Ark Royal* sailed with four destroyers on 11 September to form an anti-submarine hunting group into the western Atlantic where

The No. 821 Squadron badge. The squadron motto was "À Coup Sûr" meaning "With A Sure Blow".

eighteen U-boats were operating. Although taking the offensive, this anti-submarine role was a misuse of an inadequately screened fleet carrier in those early days before the carrier strike mentality had been codified. It would take just a week to discover how costly that misuse could be.

As the fleet passed through the defensive nets and mine barriers protecting the Scapa Flow anchorage, Commander David "Darbo" Harries RAN (1921 class) commanding *Seagull*, one of the ships of the First Minesweeping Flotilla, ensured their safe passage. VAT would later be Harrie's executive officer in another war on another carrier. Helping ensure the *Ark*'s accurate navigation past those mine barriers was the Assistant Navigator, Lieutenant Robert Kerruish RAN (1929 class), who VAT remembered from naval college.[3]

The *Ark*'s Swordfish in waves of up to twelve aircraft could patrol out to distances of 120 miles in diverging searches. The first U-boat was sighted and attacked with 100-pound bombs on the second day of the patrol. As destroyers were detached in pairs to hunt this and subsequent sightings, *Ark Royal* would continue with a screen of the remaining destroyers. As the *Ark* would turn into wind for aircraft launch and recovery, worryingly the screening destroyers would often continue along the group's base course and would not be adequately protecting the carrier.

On the fourth day of the patrol, 14 September, *Ark Royal* was making 26 knots to catch up with her screen, having launched three Skuas against *U-30* reported 180 miles away. Undetected,

---

3   Later Commander Robert Kerruish (1915-1967) was navigator of *Coventry* and survived her sinking in September 1942. He returned to the Pacific for service in *Adelaide* and *Shropshire* before he was invalided ashore with defective eyesight.

the stalking *U-39* fired three of the new electric G7a torpedoes. Spotting the torpedo tracks, the desperately turning carrier was saved when faulty magnetic pistols exploded the torpedoes prematurely 80 metres astern. *U-39* was subsequently depth charged to the surface and abandoned. Two of the Skua's attacking the distant *U-30* ditched when hit by fragments from their own ill-designed bombs skipping off the surface. When six slower Swordfish arrived, including three from No. 821 Squadron with VAT almost certainly one of the observers, they bombed the submerged shadow of the submarine without success.[4]

Three days later, further to the west the 27,000 ton *Courageous*, with only two screening destroyers, turned into the wind and into the path of *U-29*. The carrier sank fifteen minutes after being hit by two torpedoes and 519 men of her 1,260 crew were lost along with 25 Swordfish. Surviving the next four hours of depth charge attacks before silently escaping, every member of *U-29*'s crew was awarded the Iron Cross. The Admiralty faced the stark fact that it was too costly to risk their precious remaining fleet carriers using existing anti-submarine tactics and weapons with inadequate numbers of available destroyers.

Vice-Admiral Aircraft Carriers Sir Lionel Wells KCB DSO, flying his flag in *Ark Royal*, reported that successful reconnaissance flights in conditions too bad for peacetime "have given me increased confidence in the Observers" while warning that "The shortage of Observers in *Ark Royal* was felt in this operation and there is no doubt until it can be remedied, the ship will be working much below her operational capacity." He also maintained that a minimum of six destroyers were needed on anti-submarine work with four destroyers always to remain in his carrier's screen. Wells further strongly urged the immediate modifications and testing to be able to load depth charges onto a Swordfish.

Towards the end of September *Ark Royal* sailed with the Home Fleet towards the Skagerrak between Denmark and Norway in an unsuccessful attempt to draw out the German fleet. Sortieing again on 25 September the *Ark*'s Skuas intercepted three Dornier Do 18D flying boats. They shot down one in the first FAA kill of the war. The Luftwaffe responded to the broadcast sighting report by launching a force of nine He 111H and four Ju 88A-1 bombers. The *Ark* recovered all her aircraft which were struck below and awaited the first concentrated aerial bombing attack upon a carrier. The concept of an "umbrella" or combat air patrol (CAP) over a fleet was not yet fully current, the standard procedure in the face of air attack being for all aircraft to be de-fuelled and sheltered in the protected hangar. Supposedly the high-angle weapons of the fleet would deal with the bombers. None of the attacking Heinkels or Junkers were shot down and a 1,000-kilogram bomb landed within six metres of the bow causing the whole ship to rear up and heel, leading the *Luftwaffe* to claim they had sunk the carrier. This was a period VAT later described as "relatively quiet".

---

4   The 100-pound WWI era anti-submarine bomb used at this stage of the war was ineffective. This was proven months later when an RAF Anson, whose crew's aim was better than their recognition, scored a direct hit on the submarine HMS *Snapper* but inflicted no damage. Even a 500-pound bomb would have to explode within a few metres of a U-Boat hull to cause fatal damage.

In response to the threat from commerce raiders including *Admiral Graf Spee*, trade protection became the new focus for *Ark Royal*. Leaving behind one Skua squadron, *Ark Royal* and the battlecruiser *Renown* formed the hunting group Force K, one of nine groups deployed, and headed for the South Atlantic. Arriving off Freetown on 12 October, VAT commented that their base, the capital of Sierra Leone and headquarters of the Commander-in-Chief South Atlantic, had very little to recommend it. Two days later back at Scapa Flow, with superb daring and skill, *U-47* penetrated the defences and sank the battleship *Royal Oak*. Among the 835 dead were 134 boy seamen under the age of eighteen.

The Swordfish squadrons were kept busy with long-range patrols as the carrier initially operated between Dakar and Ascension Island, then further into the South Atlantic to the Cape, and briefly into the Indian Ocean. Patrolling along the 20° east meridian between 38° and 40° south the weather was so bad flying was only possible on one day in five. Heading west to Brazil they were a disappointing day's sailing away when the Battle of the River Plate against *Graf Spee* was fought on 13 December. The three Force G cruisers of *Ajax*, *Achilles* and *Exeter* engaging the German pocket-battleship had their fall-of-shot corrections provided by *Ajax*'s Fairey Seafox.

Again sailing the breadth of the South Atlantic, *Ark Royal* arrived at Freetown for a week over New Year before heading for Dakar in Senegal to search for enemy merchant ships. Her Swordfish had now flown almost five million miles, being able to search an area of 20,000 square miles a day. Approaching Portsmouth early on 15 February 1940, No. 821 Squadron disembarked

A formation of Swordfish over Ark Royal.

to *Daedalus*/Naval Air Station Lee-on-Solent for a month while the ship had a much-needed refit. It had been a monotonous time for the squadron although those faithful Pegasus engines, coupled with the observer's good navigation, meant there had not been a single ditching.

While both *Ark Royal* and *Furious* were undergoing refits, the Home Fleet briefly had no operational carrier. No. 821 Squadron embarked back aboard on 20 March, along with Nos. 810 and 820 Squadrons, and *Ark Royal* sailed for the eastern Mediterranean to conduct flying training with *Glorious* in what was, with Italy still a peaceful belligerent, then a quiet area. On 2 April No. 821 Squadron disembarked for night flying training ashore at the Egyptian Air Force base at Dekheila. Vice-Admiral Wells received a signal from the Admiralty on 9 April for the immediate return to the UK of the two carriers and No. 821 Squadron hurriedly re-embarked. The Germans had invaded Norway and the elderly *Furious* was being sent to hold the line as the lone available carrier.

Lacking any available fighter aircraft, *Furious*, hurried out of refit, embarked two squadrons of Swordfish and set course for a flying-off position to attack enemy ships in Trondheim Fjord on 11 April. All eighteen aircraft of Nos. 816 and 818 Squadrons were committed to the first carrier-launched large scale torpedo attack ever made. Not finding the expected heavy cruiser *Admiral Hipper*, the torpedoes grounded in the shallow water attempting to reach a small destroyer anchored well inshore. Two weeks later *Furious*, damaged by a near-miss and unable to make more than 20 knots, withdrew, having lost half her Swordfish and with every surviving airframe flak-damaged. The "wastage" rate had been high and the need for fighters over the fleet, over the strike formations and over the army ashore could not have been starker.

As *Ark Royal* approached home waters Captain Arthur Power CVO, a *Britannia* King's Medallist and gunnery officer at the Dardanelles in 1915, wrote confidentially that Harrie Gerrett, while now an able enough observer, needed to put more energy into his general duties and was marked well below average for his lack of zeal and energy.[5] VAT, in contrast, was felt by Power to be an observer of well above average ability who was most useful in general ship duties and developing into a first-class officer. In zeal, energy, leadership and reliability VAT was consistently marked considerably above average.

When *Ark Royal* arrived in Scotland's Pentland Firth on 23 April, No. 821 Squadron was flown off to *Fieldfare*/Naval Air Station Evanton to make room for more fighters. Eighteen Skuas and five Rocs were embarked to join the 21 Swordfish remaining on board. *Glorious* embarked eighteen biplane Sea Gladiators, eleven Skuas and eighteen RAF Gladiators (landed aboard by navy pilots). As this first RN carrier force sailed to relieve *Furious* on station off Norway, VAT, to his certain disappointment, remained ashore with his squadron. In the carrier's screen was the anti-aircraft cruiser *Curlew* whose Type 79 early-warning radar could range out to

---

5   Later Admiral of the Fleet Sir Arthur John Power GCB GBE CVO (1889-1960). Power had a central role in planning the invasions of Sicily and Italy. As Commander-in-Chief of the East Indies Fleet, he conducted operations against the Japanese in Borneo and Malaya, before taking their surrender in Singapore.

80 nautical miles and direct "umbrella" (CAP) aircraft towards a threat. A CAP would be maintained by the Sea Gladiators while the Skuas were tasked as both fighters and bombers with the Swordfish committed to bombing and torpedo strike. The ferried RAF Gladiators of No. 263 Squadron were guided ashore by two Skuas to the improvised landing strip on the frozen Lake Lesjaskogsvatnet where they suffered high losses.

Over the following weeks *Ark Royal* sortied regularly from Scapa Flow to provide air cover for both the army and the navy over Norway. Bombing targets at Narvik and Trondheim, in between anti-submarine patrols and surface searches, her squadrons had a demanding time. After the Norwegian Campaign was lost the carrier joined Force H out of Gibraltar and, on 3 July, conducted torpedo attacks against French battleships, then going on to bomb the Italian airbase at Cagliari. In No. 820 Squadron that August Harrie was still reported as lacking zeal in his ship duties but "cometh the hour, cometh the man" and having "led a squadron against the enemy with courage and ability" Harrie was Mentioned-in-Despatches for "continued gallantry and devotion to duty."[6]

In Australia most of the 1927 Flinders year class who had not graduated, or returned to civilian life because of the manpower reductions of the early 1930s, once again donned uniform. Patrick George-Kennedy was prevented from re-joining being considered more valuable to the war effort as a pastoralist on his Yelma Station, a circumstance he felt bitterly about for the rest of his life.

Back ashore No. 821 Squadron spent a week at Evanton before flying on 1 June to *Sparrowhawk/* Naval Air Station Hatston, the rapidly expanding airfield just to the north of Scapa Flow in the Orkneys. Their main task was anti-submarine patrols day and night to force the U-Boats further north in the North Sea to hinder their course west into the Atlantic, and to protect the waters around the north of Scotland, the Orkneys and the Shetlands.

Hatston was no backwater, however, as the fleet anchorage was in range of *Luftwaffe* bombers and subject to many air attacks. It was from here that disembarked Skuas sank the light cruiser *Königsberg* alongside in Bergen harbour in April and carried out further strikes in May. The air station became, by default, a shore-based reconnaissance and air-striking force deputising as a carrier in the forward area. All squadrons, whether Walrus, Skua or Swordfish, front-line disembarked or training ashore, were committed as required.

June 1940 proved a sobering month for VAT. On 8 June during the withdrawal from Norway *Glorious* was returning to Scapa Flow with only two screening destroyers and no aircraft airborne or at alert when they were intercepted and sunk by the battlecruisers *Scharnhorst* and *Gneisenau*. Despite the hopeless gallantry and sacrifice of the destroyers *Acasta* and *Ardent* all three ships were sunk, but not before *Acasta* burst through the covering smokescreen she had laid in the line of fire between the battlecruisers and her carrier, scoring a torpedo hit abreast

---

6   *London Gazette*, 4 October 1940, Lieutenant Harrie Gerrett (O) RAN, MiD "for continued gallantry and devotion to duty and good service whilst serving in HMS *Ark Royal* in operations in the Mediterranean."

The German battlecruiser Scharnhorst, which helped sink the carrier Glorious on 8 June 1940.

Scharnhorst's rear turret which killed 48 sailors. Among the 1,519 allied losses was VAT's observer course-mate Lieutenant-Commander John Watson. The damaged *Scharnhorst*, with a hole 12 x 4 metres through which 2,500 tons of water flooded the adjacent compartments, withdrew into Trondheim Harbour for a temporary hull patch from the repair ship *Huascaran*. While there she topped up her ammunition supplies from the supply ship *Alstertor*.

The final French troops had been evacuated from Dunkirk on 4 June and then on 10 June, as German troops approached Paris, Italy declared war. Mussolini's desire to turn the Mediterranean into the ancient Roman Empire's *Mare Nostrum* or "Our Sea" would have significant consequences for both the *Ark* and VAT. With trade routes to the Empire through the Suez Canal threatened, the see-sawing North African campaign commenced in the Libyan desert as the Mediterranean became a major focus for the FAA. The British Empire was now standing alone against the Axis, never having expected to be fighting German, Italian and Vichy French forces all at once.

The *Scharnhorst* under *Kapitän zur See* Kurt Hoffmann was already a nemesis for the Royal Navy. The previous November she had sunk the armed merchant cruiser *Rawalpindi* of the Northern Patrol, enforcing the blockade on Germany. Captain Edward Kennedy, placed on the retired list in the post-war retrenchments of 1921, had returned at age 60, proudly appointed to his new command. Despite being hopelessly outgunned he would not surrender and there were few survivors.

Unscathed by several RAF attacks in April, *Scharnhorst* had outpaced the battleship *Renown* after an inconclusive engagement. *Scharnhorst's* gunnery was such that her first hit on *Glorious* was at an incredible 25,600 metres range. Alongside in Trondheim Fjord on 11 June, twelve Hudsons dropped 36 bombs, but all missed the battlecruiser. Two days later *Ark Royal* mounted a strike against the same target. Fifteen was the maximum that could be launched in one range given the light winds and the fact that there were only fifteen Skua pilots with previous dive-bombing experience.[7] Leading two flights of three from No. 800 Squadron in Skua 6A was Lieutenant (O) Robert Bostock, a graduate of VAT's observer course, with the squadron's commanding officer Captain Richard Partridge (P) DSO Royal Marines. Diving at 60 degrees from 7,000-feet they released their 500-pound bomb at 2,000-feet and the following aircraft reported a bright flash from just aft of the funnel but this, the only bomb that hit, did not explode.

In brilliant sunshine, with the defences alerted by coast-watchers and a mistimed RAF Beaufort attack on Vaernes aerodrome, the Bf 109s of II./JG77 and Bf 110s of I./ZG76 had scrambled. Only seven of the fifteen Skuas, desperately evading in the morning surface mist, made it back to the carrier, with the promised Blenheim long-range fighter support not materialising until the survivors were departing. Among the missing was Skua 6A; VAT had lost another observer course-mate while the *Ark* mourned the loss of half their remaining fighters and experienced aircrew in a single mission.

With temporary repairs complete, *Scharnhorst* sailed for her home-port Kiel on 20 June escorted by the destroyers *Hans Lady*, *Hermann Schoemann* and *Erich Steinbrinck* plus the torpedo boats *Greif* and *Kondor*. The next morning the torpedo boats *Falke* and *Jaguar* also joined the screen making for a formidable force.[8] It was now VAT's turn to face the 65 guns of the battlecruiser and the 57 guns of her *Kriegsmarine* escort.

Scharnhorst Strike 21 June 1940

When the operations officer at Hatston received a reconnaissance Hudson's report that *Scharnhorst* was at sea off Sognefjordan, sailing south down the Norwegian coast with a heavy escort, he quickly calculated that their closest point of approach to Hatston, at 240 miles, would briefly be at the extreme maximum range of a torpedo armed Swordfish. Exceptional navigation would be vital, so VAT, now No. 821 Squadron's senior observer, was tasked with command of a daylight strike against the battlecruiser.

There were only six aircraft available with internal long-range tanks fitted, three each from Nos. 821 and 823 Squadrons, and these were each "torpedoed up" with the hefty 1,610-pound weapon. The 69-gallon long-range tank occupied the mid-cockpit position, so only two crew could man each aircraft. This gave VAT even more work as he also had to do the W/T communications and fire the gun if necessary. For the crews manning No. 823 Squadron's Swordfish, the strike was particularly personal as half of their unit had gone down with *Glorious*. They would press home the attack to the 1,000 yard release point whatever the odds.

Leading the formation was VAT flying with the squadron's senior pilot, Lieutenant John Stenning.[9] Cleverly offsetting a degree or two east to avoid missing the enemy force VAT

---

7   Armed and manned aircraft were close packed in a "range" on the aft flight deck ready to launch.

8   These destroyers were 50 percent bigger than the RAN's ageing "Scrap Iron Flotilla" of *Stuart*, *Vampire*, *Vendetta*, *Voyager* and *Waterhen* who had been with the Mediterranean Fleet since November 1939.

9   Later Commander John Stenning (1914-2001) had joined *Britannia* as a cadet in 1927 and qualified as a pilot in 1937. After No. 821 Squadron he was senior pilot of No. 832 Squadron (Albacores) aboard *Victorious* and survived the 9 March 1942 attack on *Tirpitz*. As Lieutenant-Commander (Flying) in the escort carrier *Striker* John saw further service in the Atlantic and Arctic.

The painting "A Gallant Failure" by artist Drew Harrison, depicting the No. 821 Squadron Swordfish crewed by observer VAT Smith and pilot Lieutenant John Stenning attacking the Scharnhorst on 21 June 1940.

ensured the six Swordfish flew across the North Sea at an economical 85 knots, constantly updating his drift calculations as the wind shifted. Once in sight of the Norwegian coast VAT turned them north at 1600 and shortly sighted the wakes of the German force off Utsyvire in a perfect example of intercept navigation.

At 1604 the escorting *Erich Steinbrinck* reported sighting six attacking torpedo aircraft. Stenning nosed over the lead Swordfish, making almost 130 knots "going downhill", and the small strike force commenced their attack runs in the clear visibility against an awesome anti-aircraft barrage from the battlecruiser and her screen. *Scharnhorst* commenced firing at 1607 and recorded a torpedo exploding in her wake at 1611. At 1620 the escorting *Kondor* reported two aircraft down as the attackers, several with flak damage, withdrew. Only two minutes later *Luftwaffe* fighters arrived over the ships, any earlier and the entire Swordfish force would probably have been lost. VAT was proving to have that prized aircrew attribute - good luck.

After the event, ever reticent, VAT wrote only that it had been "a rather frightening experience". Perhaps the comments of a No. 818 Squadron observer he later knew, following the attack on a lone *Bismarck* in May 1941, provide a better description:[10]

---

10   Sub-Lieutenant (O) "Terry" Goddard flying with Lieutenant (P) Stan Keane of No. 818 Squadron.

… We had found her. So, down we went … the altimeter is spinning, spinning, spinning … she was a fire-spitting monster. Everything was coming at us and she was illuminated … awesome. This ship was just magnificent. It looked exactly like a battleship should, I mean scary and everything but just a beautiful ship.

Once the attack has started it's all about the pilot … the observer just stands by and gets really excited watching what is going on. You are not thinking you are going to be killed, you're thinking you are going to hit the bastard and that's it … the more you frig around, the more chance they get to hit you, so we just went straight in. We got as low on the deck as we could and went straight in … she just got bigger and bigger. The flak is bursting over our heads … the small arms fire is pretty well all around us - and hitting us every once in a while - but we get in to drop the torpedo … do a quick turn away.

The disappointment all felt at not achieving any hits as *Scharnhorst* combed the torpedo tracks was reflected in some carping criticism by several desk-bound senior officers. VAT, as the leader in the air, knew the good visibility precluded any element of surprise and the best tactic was an immediate full-strength attack. He would also have calculated that there was no adequate reserve of fuel and any manoeuvring to attempt a coordinated attack from different sectors would have meant the loss of the entire force while returning to base. Thirty minutes after VAT's strike six Beauforts bombed unsuccessfully from altitude, losing several of their number to the now present fighters. When the four surviving Swordfish withdrew, they were 265 miles from Hatston. VAT quickly recalculated and led them on a direct diversion to RAF Scatsta, a forward base in the Shetland Islands 44 miles closer than Hatston. After well over five hours flying one aircraft landed with only ten minutes of fuel remaining. While refuelling temporary repairs were made to some of the flak damaged airframes before taking off again.

It is worth reflecting that in the May 1941 strikes against *Bismarck* nine Swordfish were launched at a range of 120 miles from *Victorious*. Attacking at dusk, aided by low cloud and the new ASV radar, one hit was achieved. When *Ark Royal* launched fifteen aircraft into a gloomy evening of foul weather with *Bismarck* only 40 miles distant, they were able to remain hidden in low cloud until committing to the final miles of an attack run and scored two hits. Neither strike had to slowly manoeuvre past a screen of hostile destroyers to attack their target at extreme range in bright daylight. By September 1942 RN tactical notes were recommending a minimum of sixteen aircraft to ensure a torpedo hit, confirming VAT's decision of two years previous to attack immediately, in full strength and with no sector manoeuvring.

VAT led his six Swordfish straight at the enemy despite feeling like "a sitting duck" heading for a battlecruiser and her powerful screen trying to make his life unpleasantly short. Imbued with duty and instructed from a young age in the cherished fighting tradition of Nelson, VAT did not hesitate – "in a situation like that there is no option, and you have to press on".[11] All

---

11   "No captain can do very wrong if he places his ship alongside that of an enemy" – Vice-Admiral Horatio Nelson aboard the *Victory* off Cadiz, 9 October 1805, on the eve of the Battle of Trafalgar.

six aircraft pressed on and two, both from No. 823 Squadron, went down.[12]

Although the Swordfish had a magnificent war, it was too frequently demonstrated by the loss of aircrew lives that the faithful biplane was suicidally slow and vulnerable in daylight attacks against alert targets with good visibility. This was proved time and again, and ignored *in extremis* by planners and aircrew alike, just as VAT and his fellow aircrew ignored it that day in June 1940 when he led the historic first mass torpedo attack against a capital ship at sea. Rear-Admiral Naval Air Stations described the strike as a gallant failure with inadequate force, but it was far from being the last in those desperate years![13]

The 1939-1945 British War Medal with a bronze oak leaf emblem signifying a Mention in Despatches, as awarded to VAT Smith for the attack on the Scharnhorst.

A Mention in Despatches is awarded to a person whose name appears in an official report by a superior officer, describing their gallant or meritorious service in the presence of the enemy, which is then sent on to higher command. When the 1939-1945 British War Medal was issued VAT wore the bronze oak leaf emblem on the medal ribbon to signify that he had been so mentioned:

For bravery when attacking the German battlecruiser *Scharnhorst*.[14]

No. 760 Squadron 13 August 1940 to 14 September 1940

On 19 July at the Battle of Cape Spada Captain John Collins, escaped from his duties at Melbourne's Navy Office, commanded an Allied force of five destroyers from his light cruiser *Sydney*. After engaging the Italian Second Cruiser Division, the *Bartolomeo Colleoni* was sunk. After months of tedious patrols from Hatston, VAT decided a more active role would also suit him and applied for transfer to a Fulmar fighter squadron. Captain WHM Marin, Royal Marines, the commanding officer of No. 821 Squadron farewelled his senior observer who had taken the greatest interest in the squadron and "shown himself to be resourceful and capable" with "plenty of fighting spirit and has conducted himself well as the senior officer of a torpedo striking force in action". Perspicuously, given VAT's later career, he mooted his suitability to further specialise as a staff officer.

The No. 760 Squadron badge.

Sent to *Raven*/Naval Air Station Eastleigh, a short distance from Southampton, VAT joined the second-line No. 760 Squadron. This fleet fighter pool unit was equipped with four Skuas,

---

12   Killed in action were Sub-Lieutenant (P) Leonard Cater (21 years) with Petty Officer (A) Frederick Davis (23) and Sub-Lieutenant (A)(P) Maurice White (23) with Naval Airman First Class Charles Hull (20).

13   The first ship-launched strike against a capital ship at sea was twelve days later on 3 July 1940. Six Swordfish from *Ark Royal*'s No. 818 Squadron attacked twenty minutes after sunset in a thick haze against the fleeing French battleship *Strasbourg* screened by six destroyers. No hits were obtained.

14   *London Gazette* 25 Oct 1940. Mention in Despatches: For bravery when attacking the German Battle-Cruiser *Scharnhorst* - Lieutenant Victor Smith RAN, Lieutenant John Stenning and Naval Airman First Class Edwin Milsom.

two Rocs and a single Sea Gladiator. Here VAT would keep his hand in at flying while awaiting appointment to a front-line squadron.

Admiral of the Fleet Sir Charles Forbes GCB DSO, Commander-in-Chief Home Fleet, reflecting on his Norwegian losses described the Skua, Swordfish and Walrus as "the slowest aircraft of their respective types in the world" and urged urgent acquisition of high-performance fighters. The quickest way to get sufficient modern fighters to sea was to be allocated deliveries from the existing RAF production lines of single seat types and to source Grumman Wildcats under Lend-Lease. With the Battle of Britain then being fought in the skies above the Air Ministry building, the navy's needs would have to wait.[15] The stop-gap solution was to continue their existing order of Fairey Fulmar two-seater fighters, although they were painfully aware that a Fulmar's 230 knots was inadequate to attack a 260 knot Ju 88. Fighting under such conditions would surely invite further "wastage".

Because of the shortage of RAF fighter pilots during the battle, the FAA was called on to help. At *Raven* all the naval pilots under instruction at the Fighter School volunteered and some 23 joined Fighter Command where they at least flew the latest aircraft. The two naval air squadrons thrown into the battle, Nos. 804 and 808, flew Sea Gladiators and Fulmars. Some 57 FAA aviators flew in the Battle of Britain and became known as "The Few of the Few".[16]

When the *Adlerangriff* (Eagle Attack) phase, which had begun in mid-August against RAF airfields, morphed into the heavy bombing of *Unternehmen Loge* (Operation London) on Saturday 7 September, VAT was on weekend leave in the city. On this first day of the London Blitz the *Luftwaffe* sent 348 bombers and 617 fighters during daylight and 247 bombers that night. When he returned to his hotel, the manager told VAT he had been ordered to report to his station immediately. The invasion code-name "Cromwell" had been issued at 2007 with fears that German landings were imminent. The bombing had stopped any Southampton bound trains, but VAT managed to find a taxi driver willing to drive the 85 miles despite the hazards.

Although it was alerted for dockyard defence over Southampton and Portsmouth, No. 760 Squadron was not used in the Battle of Britain. When VAT later submitted a traveling claim for the taxi fare, he was informed that it was an officer's responsibility to provide his own means of transport when returning from leave, invasion emergency notwithstanding.

---

15   The Battle of Britain is usually dated 10 July 1940 to 31 October 1940 and the London Blitz commenced on 7 September 1940.
16   Winston Churchill in the House of Commons, 20 August 1940 "Never in the field of human conflict was so much owed by so many to so few".

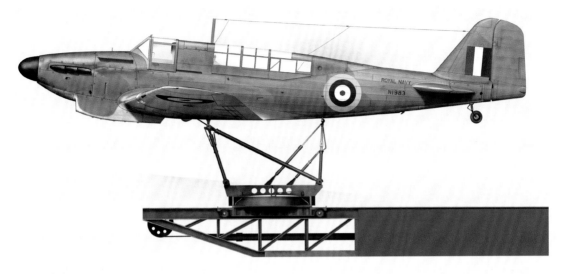

Fairey Fulmar two-seat fighter of No. 807 Squadron in which VAT Smith saw service launching from the catapult aboard HMS Pegasus.

FAIREY FULMAR MK I

Powerplant: 1,035 Rolls-Royce Merlin VIII

Speed: 236 knots at 9,000 feet

Range: 780 nautical miles

Max Weight: 10,200 pounds

Crew: Two

Armament: 8 x 0.303-inch calibre Browning Mk II machine guns, 1 x hand-held Thompson 0.45-inch calibre sub-machine gun

Considered too large, too heavy and too slow the Fulmar nevertheless had several positive attributes. Its weight meant it rapidly accelerated to 390 knots in a dive allowing for one good firing pass before "mixing it". It could fly CAP over the fleet for four hours, double that of a Hurricane, and carried an impressive 750 rounds per machine gun compared to the Hurricane's 334 rounds. Excellent visibility allowed for easier carrier approaches and the huge rear cockpit was appreciated by the observer. Light and responsive on the controls, the Fulmar had no handling vices.

Critical operational deficiencies were lack of speed and a woeful rate of climb, taking fifteen minutes to climb to 15,000 feet. The main fuel tank between the two crew positions was armoured and the pilot had an armoured windscreen, but the observer was unprotected. The first operational unit was No. 806 Squadron which embarked aboard *Illustrious* in September 1940. By the end of that year there were four front-line squadrons including No. 807.

With no aircraft mounted weapon for the rear seat, the desperate stop-gap nature of the type and time was reflected in the Admiralty order that all observers were to be issued a Thompson sub-machine gun. A total of 250 Mk I and 350 Mk II variants were produced. Considerably better than the Skua or the Roc, the Fulmar, inadequate against the latest Italian and German land-based fighters and bombers, nevertheless held the line until Hurricanes and Spitfires could be converted and finally sent to sea from July 1941 and August 1942 respectively. They joined increasing numbers of American-built Grumman F4F Martlets/Wildcats.

A Fairey Fulmar fighter which entered operational service in late 1940. Note the large "glasshouse" style rear cockpit for the observer.

No. 807 Squadron 15 September 1940 to 14 November 1941

The No. 807 Squadron badge. The squadron motto was "Quoquo Versus Veriti", meaning "Ready to Strike in All Directions".

On 15 September 1940 No. 807 Squadron formed at *Kestrel*/Naval Air Station Worthy Down near Winchester. Initially the unit had nine Fulmar Mk Is increasing to twelve aircraft on charge by November. The commanding officer was Lieutenant-Commander James Sholto Douglas who had commissioned in the RAF in 1928 and seen active service on the Indian North-West Frontier during the early 1930s. As a flight lieutenant he had transferred to the FAA and joined No. 822 (Swordfish) Squadron. VAT was SOBS or Senior Observer, and the remaining aircrew were a mix of regular Navy (A) and Volunteer Reserve (A).

As the squadron worked up without major incident, VAT's rugby mentor from Jervis Bay days, Edward Fogarty Fegen, now captain of an armed merchant cruiser coincidentally named *Jervis Bay*, won acclaim for his actions on 5 November 1940. The sole escort of 38 merchant ships in Convoy HX.84, when the heavy cruiser *Admiral Scheer* appeared he signalled the convoy to scatter while immediately engaging the enemy head-on, an engagement he and 188 of his crew did not survive.[17] Buying time for the majority of the merchantmen in his charge to escape, it was an exploit recognised with a posthumous VC gazetted less than three weeks later. VAT was not surprised to hear of Fegen's heroism and took pride in having known such a fine officer whose attacking spirit he was already emulating. Fegen's sacrifice highlighted how stretched the navy was to ensure protection of Britain's vital trade routes.

The German occupation of northern France meant that the four-engine Focke-Wulf 200

---

17   The 15,420-ton Deutschland-class heavy cruiser *Admiral Scheer*, was half as big again as *Canberra*. Mounting 6 x 11-inch guns she also embarked two Arado Ar 196 seaplanes.

The 7,000-ton catapult trials and training ship HMS Pegasus.Laid down prior to WWI, it was so slow it was restricted to escorting eight knot convoys.

The HMS Pegasus badge.

Condors of *Kampfgeschwader* 40, relocated from Norway, could range 1,000 miles along the convoy routes from their Bordeaux-Merignac base and exact a deadly toll untroubled by Allied fighters. In ten weeks, attacking from masthead height to ensure accuracy, they sank almost 90,000 tons of shipping. With losses to surface raiders and U-boats as well, Britain's lifeline was critically threatened. Calling Condors "the scourge of the Atlantic" Churchill, by 27 December, was demanding from his First Sea Lord "What have you done about catapulting expendable aircraft from ships?" The answer was three Fulmars from No. 807 Squadron!

At a conference on 12 November, attended by Admiral Sir Tom Phillips, Deputy Chief of Naval Staff, the proposed countermeasures to get expendable fighters to sea protecting convoys started to take form. Before spare RAF Hurricanes were available, Fulmars would be used although they only had a ten-knot speed advantage against a Condor. Phillips thought little of their chances, but it was the only option available at short notice to provide defensive air cover for the valuable convoys.

Audacity, the initial escort carrier being converted from the captured German freighter *Hannover*, would not be available until September the following year. The first of an eventual 35 catapult armed merchantmen, supplied with pilots from the RAF's merchant ship fighter unit, did not sail with a convoy until June 1941. The navy had started fitting out four auxiliary vessels as fighter catapult ships, but these would not sail until May 1941, manned with fighter direction officers and radar operators plus aviators from No. 804 Squadron. However, Churchill

A Fulmar showing its precarious looking mounting on the catapult ship HMS Springbank.

and the Admiralty wanted immediate action and orders went out to the still working up No. 807 Squadron, now at *Vulture/* Naval Air Station St Merryn in Cornwall, for Operation *Specimen*.

The commanding officer and VAT, with other aircrew and maintenance sailors, proceeded to Portland to embark three Fulmars by lighter on *Pegasus* to protect Convoy OG.47. One aircraft was secured in the hangar with the overhead hatch closed, one on the hangar hatch itself and one on the catapult. Having sortied into action aboard the newest and fastest aircraft carrier, VAT now sortied on the oldest and slowest. Originally named *Ark Royal* and converted on slips into a seaplane carrier in 1914, the vessel had seen service at Gallipoli. In 1934, renamed *Pegasus*, she became a catapult trials and training ship.

Pegasus was refitted with a tripod mast to carry the early Type 286M radar, accurate to 70 degrees either side of the bow with a range of 25 miles. The plan was for the ship to trial sailing with a westbound Atlantic convoy then changing to an eastbound convoy, maximising its time in the danger zone to protect against the Condors. *Pegasus* had no radio set to communicate with the fighter after catapulting, which was a one-way trip. Survival for the crew was dependent on making the nearest landfall if in range, or recovery by a ship upon ditching or baling out. For ten days no inspection or maintenance of the aircraft on the catapult was possible due to spray and ship's motion with the winds gusting to 65 knots. The heavy swell restricted the convoy's average speed to only three knots.

The Commodore of the Convoy in the merchantman *Egyptian Prince* was Vice-Admiral Bernard Fairbairn CBE, a naval cadet in 1894 who had volunteered from retirement for this demanding role. Of *Pegasus* with her embarked Fulmars, he reported that:

> The presence of this ship provided tangible evidence of action being taken to protect ships and did more to hearten and encourage the convoy than any other measure so far taken.

Before RAF volunteer pilots manned their precariously mounted one-shot Hurricat fighters aboard a CAM (Catapult Armed Merchantman) ship protecting a convoy, there were the naval aviators of No. 804 Squadron aboard FCS (Fighter Catapult Ship) auxiliaries, where volunteering was not considered. And before them all was VAT Smith, SOBS of No. 807 Squadron, his commanding officer James Sholto Douglas and their maintainers aboard the FCS *Pegasus*. They first protected the 30 merchantmen of outbound Convoy OG.47 which sailed on 9 December 1940, and the 21 ships of inbound Convoy SL.57, which safely arrived in Liverpool on 19 December.[18] No enemy aircraft had come within striking range of the Fulmars which were catapulted ashore once in Belfast Lough. VAT's laconic summary of these events merely noted "We did the first sortie and all was quiet".

Another pilot and observer took over in the New Year, and while Convoy OG.49 was at sea a Condor did appear. The Fulmar was quickly manned, engines started and the aircraft was run back on the catapult. When the order to fire was given, nothing happened. In the excitement no one had put a cordite charge in the catapult firing chamber. There was no repeat of this mistake on 11 January 1941, when Petty Officer Fred Shaw was catapulted from *Pegasus*. Unable to close with the Condor, he did drive it off before diverting 250 miles to Belfast. By February 1941 85 ships had been sunk by Condors and No. 804 Squadron aircrew were now manning *Pegasus*, and later the *Ariguani*, *Springbank* and *Maplin*. It was from *Maplin*, escorting Convoy SL.81, that the Australian-born Lieutenant Robert "Bob" Everett catapulted off in a Hurricat and downed the first Condor. After being safely picked up by the destroyer *Wanderer* he was subsequently awarded a DSO.

While VAT was at sea No. 807 Squadron had moved on to *Heron*/Naval Air Station Yeovilton in Somerset, where he and the commanding officer rejoined. On 2 January 1941 the only fatality of their work-up occurred when two aircraft collided during an air firing practice. Midshipman (A) Joseph Rainford's wing folded too close to the ground for him to bale out and he was killed. The other aircraft, missing a wing tip, managed to land safely. This single loss was a testament to the squadron's seniors at a time when training and working-up would normally consume more aircrew than actual operations.[19] No. 807 Squadron continued its training at *Gannet*/Naval Air Station Prestwick and *Sanderling*/Naval Air Station Abbotsinch at Paisley in Scotland. Sometimes it seemed to VAT his main task was to get the temperamental R/T set to work, often requiring "a blend of curses, kicks and aerobatics (with the pilot's assistance)".

Finally ready for front-line service, No. 807 Squadron embarked on *Furious* in March. This enabled VAT to get reacquainted with his old No. 825 (Swordfish) Squadron, now under the command of Lieutenant-Commander (A)(P) Eugene "Winkle" Esmonde, which was also embarked. VAT's squadron was ferried to Lagos and carried out patrols searching for German surface raiders. For three weeks no raiders were seen. The need for accurate navigation was harshly demonstrated on 27 March when Acting Observer Sub-Lieutenant (A) Roger Hodgetts was unable to direct his pilot back to "mother" after a reconnaissance flight. Low on fuel Sub-Lieutenant (A)(P) Oscar Wheatley landed in Vichy French Dakar and they became prisoners of war.[20]

---

18   OG convoys were Outbound Gibraltar from Liverpool and SL convoys were inbound Sierra Leone to Liverpool.

19   For Royal New Zealand Navy Volunteer Reserve aircrew in the FAA the statistics were: 52 killed in flying training/second-line squadrons/delivery flights; 41 killed in front-line squadrons working-up and exercises; 42 killed on convoy patrols and operations.

20   Repatriated in 1943, acting Lieutenant-Commander Oscar Wheatley MiD RNVR (1918-1945), was commanding officer of No. 808 (Hellcat) Squadron aboard *Ameer* and was killed in strikes against Sumatran airfields on 20 June 1945.

In this malarious country, despite taking quinine precautions, VAT became infected. Perhaps, in common with most aircrew, he was fearful of losing his flying medical so did not consult the naval doctors for suppressive treatment. The disease was to seriously trouble him with recurrent bouts of fever and general malaise for many years.

A Fulmar catches a wire while landing.

The squadron now re-equipped with ten Fulmar II's powered by the 1,300 hp Rolls-Royce Merlin 30 engines. The marginal improvements in rate of climb (twelve minutes to 15,000 feet) and 1,000 rounds per gun were welcome, as was the endurance with an external drop tank of five and a half hours. Ferried north in *Furious*, along with six Swordfish of No. 825 Squadron, four of which were equipped with the secret ASV radar, they rendezvoused in the Atlantic with Force H from Gibraltar. On 5 April 1941, *Ark Royal* swapped her nine Skuas for the Fulmars of No. 807 Squadron and four old Swordfish for the new ASV equipped aircraft.[21]

A frontal view of the Ark Royal, whose carrier tactics including the use of CAPs quickly evolved during the hectic 1940-41 Mediterranean operations.

This was a different carrier from the one VAT had disembarked twelve months before. She was now world famous after many months as the prime striking force in the western Mediterranean. Her carrier tactics had evolved with each operational success and were quickly incorporated into standard procedure. Reconnaissance would now reach out as far as 170 miles and the ASV Swordfish became of significant tactical advantage in shadowing enemy surface units and on anti-submarine patrols day and night. Strategic bombing had expanded from airfields to include a torpedo "Dambusters" type raid against the Tirso dam in Sardinia, and a successful strike against the Leghorn oil refinery. No longer were *Ark Royal's* fighters defueled and awaiting the inbound enemy hunkered in the hangar decks, instead they would form a CAP over the force and be vectored towards any threat.

With no air warning radar, directing the fighters relied on the Type 79 equipped anti-aircraft cruiser *Sheffield*, positioned close to the carrier, passing radar reports to the *Ark's* fighter

---

21   Force H on this day being the battleship *Renown*, flying the flag of Vice-Admiral Sir James Somerville KCB DSO (1882-1949), in company with *Ark Royal*, the cruiser *Sheffield* and five destroyers.

direction officer, initially Lieutenant-Commander (O) Charles Coke.[22] With amazing spatial awareness Coke, balancing an observers' Bigsworth board on his knee in the operations room, would accurately vector the fighters to close with the enemy giving a recommended height and an estimate of the enemy's course and speed. Meticulous as always, VAT realised the room for error and would keep his own plot in the aircraft while he was airborne.

To protect the Italian and German supply lines to their North Africa troops, and cut those of the Allies to Egypt, the Luftwaffe's X *Fliegerkorps* moved to Sicily in January 1941 and added their 230 plus aircraft to the *Regia Aeronautica* squadrons already in action. *Illustrious* in the eastern Mediterranean was fitted with a Type 79 radar. Heavily damaged by Ju 87 dive bombers on 10 January, the carrier withdrew to Norfolk, Virginia, for repairs. It was 21 of her Swordfish that had crippled half the *Regia Marina*'s capital ships at Taranto on the night of 11-12 November 1940.[23] In the vanguard of the second-strike force that night was another of VAT's course mates, Lieutenant George Carline, SOBS of No. 819 Squadron, flying with his commanding officer. VAT had arrived in a theatre of operations that would provide him with all the action he desired.

Force H, after ranging the Bay of Biscay looking for *Scharnhorst* and *Gneisenau* had just completed a "club run", an operation steaming close enough to the under-siege island of Malta to fly off Hurricanes to reinforce their beleaguered RAF units.[24] With the German invasion of Greece in April and then Crete in May, the Mediterranean was effectively divided in two. Force H from Gibraltar would operate to the west of Sicily and the hard-pressed Mediterranean Fleet, with the new carrier *Formidable* and attached RAN units, would operate in the east from Alexandria. The commander of submarines Karl Dönitz was now ordered to move U-boats into the area. When the Italian army was driven back in North Africa *Generalleutnant* Erwin Rommel was placed in charge of the *Deutsche Africa Korps*.

At the end of April, after helping blockade *Scharnhorst* in Brest, another club run saw 23 Hurricanes flown off south of Sardinia. They were led to Malta by three Fulmars to avoid navigation errors. Back in Gibraltar, Force H sailed on 5 May to rendezvous with "Tiger" convoy as it approached the straits. Carrying troops, 295 tanks and 53 crated Hurricanes for the desert forces in Egypt, in the escorting warships were Mediterranean Fleet reinforcements. It was critical to get the convoy past the Sardinian straits and through to Alexandria. *Ark Royal* and her escorts initially provided a covering force on 6 May to the north-east of the convoy in case the *Regia Marina* sortied. When her ASV-equipped Swordfish, searching out to 140 miles south

---

22   Later Captain (O) Charles Coke DSO (1909-2003), a 1935 graduate of the 26th Naval Observer's Course credited with inventing modern maritime fighter direction off Norway in April 1940. After *Ark Royal* Coke joined *Victorious*, a carrier he commanded in 1958 before retiring early to paint and travel.
23   "Taranto … should be remembered forever as having shown once and for all that in the Fleet Air Arm the navy has its most devastating weapon" - Admiral Sir Andrew "ABC" Cunningham KCB DSO**. Among the attackers was West Australian Lieutenant (P) Charles "Sprog" Lea DSC RNVR.
24   The colloquial morale-enhancing term "club run" showed that they considered Force H the best in the navy and thus members of an exclusive club.

and west of Sardinia before dawn on 7 May found no sign of Italian warships, the covering force rejoined the convoy as close escorts and prepared for the inevitable air attacks. Late that morning an enemy signal stating that the convoy had been sighted was intercepted.

Pre-war the navy had not expected its carriers to operate within range of land-based fighters, or indeed to fight the armed forces of three nations in Europe instead of just the one. Now operating in waters that the *Regia Aeronautica* and the *Luftwaffe* were attempting to dominate, every fighter onboard was needed. The maintainers worked through the night, but 8 May dawned with only twelve out of the eighteen Fulmars of Nos. 807 and 808 Squadrons serviceable.

Damaged and Ditched 8 May 1941

Ark Royal flew off reconnaissance Swordfish from 0500 with orders to break radio silence only if any enemy units detected were a threat to the fleet. An hour later dawn broke with poor visibility, low cloud and rain with gusting winds. Recovering her search aircraft, the *Ark* then launched the first CAP of two No. 807 Squadron Fulmars, Red Section, led by the commanding officer and VAT at 0830, landing back on two hours later as another two No. 807 Squadron Fulmars launched.

When the light cruiser *Naiad* in the advance screen opened fire and radar reported contacts bearing 080 degrees at twenty miles distance, two more No. 807 Squadron Fulmars were launched at 1143. This included VAT, only seventy minutes since landing on, now flying with Lieutenant (P) Nigel "Buster" Hallett leading White Section. Joining the already airborne Blue Section, they drove off the enemy. At 1207 the radar screen was clear, and they were recalled to patrol overhead the carrier. *Ark Royal* now commenced a rolling CAP, launching fighters every hour to ensure there was always a section airborne with more than 90 minutes endurance. Each section would have an observer in the leader's aircraft and a TAG in the wingman's. Buster and VAT landed back on at 1334.

A No. 807 Squadron Fulmar fighter taking off from Ark Royal. The cruiser Sheffield is on the carrier's port quarter.

At 1338 enemy aircraft were reported at low level on a bearing of 064 degrees and a distance of 32 nautical miles. This was a force of eight S.79 bombers of 38 *Gruppo* escorted by twelve Fiat CR.42s of 3 *Gruppo* based in Sardinia. The Fulmar had a slight speed advantage over the CR.42 but the small Fiat biplane was much more manoeuvrable and the instruction to the Fulmar pilots was not to "mix it" with the Fiats. Today there was no choice and Black Section commenced a head-on attack against three fighters. Black One was seen to break away to the left in a vertical dive and flattened out at 500 feet. The commanding officer and SOBS of No. 808 Squadron were not seen again and went down with their aircraft. Black Two took evasive action into cloud and dived towards the fleet where the pursuers broke away when approaching the ship's barrage range. As Black Two circled *Fearless* he was fired at.

Green One's observer had his leg shattered by an explosive bullet and they landed on at 1405. Green Two, engaged and damaged by three CR.42s, joined up with Black Two. Green Three, hit in the tailplane by a CR.42, went into a spin but while recovering attacked an S.79. During this melee radar reported enemy aircraft bearing 096 degrees at 25 miles distance. These were five S.79 torpedo bombers who released their torpedoes from amongst the destroyer screen. Captain Loben Maund conned *Ark Royal* to comb the tracks, two torpedoes passing down his port side and two to starboard. One bomber was shot down during the attack and two while withdrawing to the south.

Black Two with Green Two and Three landed on between 1437 and 1439 just after VAT and Buster launched again in White One to join the already airborne Blue Section of No. 807 Squadron. *Sheffield* reported a snooper at 1510 and both White and Blue Sections bounced an S.79 being flown by Captain Armando Boetto. White Section attacked, followed by Blue, with the bomber catching fire and breaking up. It was the squadron's first kill, but all four Fulmars had been hit by determined return fire.[25] Meanwhile fleet anti-aircraft guns had shot down another two S.79s. White Two, Petty Officer (P) Johnson and Leading Airman (AG) Shave, reported that their leader's damaged fighter, hit in the radiator, was emitting white vapour with the engine just ticking over. VAT in White One fired three red Verey flares to indicate they were ditching.

Buster and VAT, tightening their harnesses until they could hardly breathe and busy working out the best direction to ditch having regard to the swell and wind direction, ignored the ship's firing at them as they came down. VAT, with typical restraint, later described this friendly fire as a "nuisance". Approaching as close to a stall as he dared while keeping positive control of the aircraft, Buster let the Fulmar settle gently into the chop with nose-up. It was still like hitting a brick wall that would have left bruises where their harnesses crossed their torsos. The theory was then to release the dinghy, climb in and wait for rescue.

The Fulmar was seen by their White Two wingman to sink within 30 seconds and no

---

25   The S.79 was shot down 95 miles south southeast of Sardinia at 1525. It was shared between the four Fulmars crewed as follows: White One: Lieutenant (P) Hallett/Lieutenant (O) Smith; White Two: Petty Officer (P) Johnson/Leading Airman (AG) Shave; Blue One: Lieutenant (P) Gardner/Petty Officer (O) Carlyle; and Blue Two: Lieutenant (P) Firth/ Leading Airman (AG) Godfrey.

A very welcome sight, the destroyer HMS Foresight which rescued VAT and Buster after their 8 May 1941 ditching.

dinghy appeared, but the green fluorescine in the water around the swimming pilot and observer was visible from ten miles at 2,000 feet. White Two flew towards the nearest destroyer and the TAG signalled the downed aircrew's position. Buster, after the adrenalin of combat, was badly shocked by the ditching, escape and cold-water immersion. Not a strong swimmer, he started to lose heart as they struggled in the swell, saying he did not think he could go on much longer. VAT, recalling his lifesaving lessons at Flinders, rallied his pilot.[26] Telling Buster to never give up and that his life was valuable VAT kept his head above water until *Foresight* hove into view after 20 minutes and rescued them. It is a certainty that as they were revived by Surgeon Lieutenant John Foxton a tot of naval rum was prescribed.

When the damaged Blue Section landed back on at 1546 and White 2 at 1658 *Ark Royal* was down to only seven serviceable Fulmars. Over the next several hours small formations were chased off by Fulmars or beaten off by anti-aircraft fire, although a stick of bombs at 1621 straddled the carrier, drenching the flight deck from the near misses. At dusk a large *Luftwaffe* force of 28 Ju 87s and six Bf 110s were detected ahead closing from Sicily. Three No. 807 Squadron Fulmars, including the commanding officer in Red One, were already airborne and the remaining four serviceable fighters were launched at 1923. All seven intercepted, and the running battle scattered the attacking formations who jettisoned their bombs. Five Fulmars, four with battle damage, landed on between 1945 and 2000 with the first crashing on deck. Half an hour later there was a grimly determined torpedo attack by three S.79s in close formation, undetected by radar at their wave-top height, and again Captain Maund conned the *Ark* to comb the tracks, with two torpedoes passing down the starboard side only 50 yards away.

The final CAP landed on at 2138 as *Ark Royal*, with only three serviceable Fulmars remaining, sped west at 25 knots leaving the convoy and close escorts entering the Sicilian Narrows. This escort group included VAT and Buster aboard *Foresight*, now minesweeping ahead of the convoy with the rest of the Eighth Destroyer Flotilla.

Just after midnight the merchantman *Empire Song* hit a mine. *Foresight* and *Fortune* went to give assistance, taking off crew and passengers. When she eventually blew up 57 tanks and ten

---

26   Later Captain Nigel "Buster" Hallett DSC* (1913-1993). A 1926 Dartmouth Cadet Buster graduated from No. 32 Naval Pilot's Course in 1935. Grounded for low-flying and sent to sea in *Malaya* he was court-martialled and dismissed from the service in 1937 for disobeying the battleship's captain. Reactivated on the emergency list at the start of the war he became one of the RN's leading aces and fighter wing leaders. Buster left No. 807 Squadron to command No. 884 (Spitfire) Squadron aboard *Victorious*.

Seen from Sheffield the Ark Royal is drenched by near misses while under air attack south of Sardinia.

Hurricanes were lost. *Foresight*, with 130 survivors in addition to VAT and Buster, was ordered into Malta as Tiger convoy was handed over to Alexandria-based escorts. In Egypt, the tanks and Hurricanes were quickly thrown into attempts to relieve the 9th Australian Division and other units besieged at Tobruk.

Sailing to rejoin Force H, *Foresight* was damaged and lost crew in an air attack, so it returned to Malta for repairs. At a loose end onboard, VAT and Buster spent their days ashore at Hal Far airfield despite continual heavy bombing. Meanwhile *Furious*, escorted by the dummy battleship *Anson* (the old battleship *Centurion* with wooden guns), joined *Ark Royal* for a club run delivery of 47 Hurricanes to Malta during which *Foresight* was finally able to rejoin Force H.[27] Reaching Gibraltar on 23 May, VAT and Buster reported aboard the *Ark* at 1300, two weeks after their ditching.

Two days later the battlecruiser *Hood* was lost along with 1,415 of her crew at the Battle of Denmark Strait against *Bismarck* and *Prinz Eugen*. The Home Fleet gathered all its forces and VAT's old No. 825 Squadron, launching from *Victorious* at midnight on 24 May, managed a single torpedo hit on the 50,000-ton *Bismarck*. Force H was ordered the next day to "Steer so as to intercept BISMARCK". In 50+ knot gale conditions the flight deck was pitching 60 feet and rolling 20 degrees, which was outside even wartime operating limits for Fulmars and extremely hazardous for Swordfish, several of which crashed as they attempted to land. When VAT's great friend from their 31st Observer's Course Lieutenant-Commander (O) James "Jim" Stewart-Moore, the commanding officer of No. 820 Squadron, mistakenly led a strike on *Sheffield*, it proved fortuitous, as the premature explosions caused by the new duplex magnetic pistols meant only dependable contact pistols were fitted to the torpedoes for the final desperate strike by fifteen Swordfish of Nos. 810, 818 and 820 Squadrons that evening. The observer to the strike leader was another course mate, Lieutenant Edmund Carver. The vital hit damaging *Bismarck*'s rudder allowed the battleships, cruisers and destroyers to finally close.

These momentous events VAT watched, no doubt assisting where possible, but no Fulmars

---

27   After doubling for the new 46,000-ton *Anson* the 1913 era 26,000-ton dreadnought's final role was to be scuttled as a breakwater off Omaha beach on 9 June 1944, to protect Mulberry harbour.

A No. 807 Squadron Fulmar patrols over a convoy in 1941.

got airborne. Neither did Harrie Gerrett, now flight commander of a Walrus aboard the Home Fleet flagship *King George V*, who was similarly deck-bound by the weather and sea state as the battleship helped batter *Bismarck* into a hulk. In the early evening the surfaced *U-556* saw *Renown* and *Ark Royal* appear out of the mist head-on, with activity on the *Ark*'s flight deck visible as she prepared that final strike. There were no escorting destroyers, as they had been detached running low on fuel. Empty of torpedoes at the end of a patrol, *U-556*, unseen, impotently submerged. The *Ark*'s famous good luck had held once more.

For the next five months the *Ark* continued to live up to her motto: *Desire n'a pas repos* - zeal does not rest. There was an intensity of consecutive operations that is now hard to envisage and little rest for VAT. Between operations ships would sail to exercise in company if not undergoing maintenance, and Fulmars would sometimes disembark to North Front to provide air defence over the Gibraltar base. Cheerfully enduring the hard slog and continuous attrition with little respite, VAT's later memory understandably blurred and sometimes transposed events. There were to be many more days of intense air battle like that of 8 May as Force H sortied again and again into that dangerous breach of the Axis's *Mare Nostrum*, west of Sicily and south of Sardinia, leading on to Malta.

In Gibraltar the *Ark*'s Royal Marine band would greet the latest carrier ferrying aircraft from Britain with *Ferryboat Serenade*. The two carriers would then go stern to stern and transfer Hurricanes over a timber bridge before a night departure on a club run. There were four runs in June alone including joint runs with *Furious* and *Victorious* which saw 149 Hurricanes flown off. These were always fraught, as often a CAP could not be flown until the crowded deck was cleared of the RAF aircraft. The unremittingly hazardous nature of flight deck operations was demonstrated at the end of the month with a tragedy for No. 807 Squadron when aircrew were cross decked to *Furious*. As the tenth Hurricane began its take-off run from that carrier, it hit the island, rupturing the external fuel tank. Among those killed in the subsequent conflagration was Acting Sub-Lieutenant (A)(P) Owen Wightman RN (20) who had been with the squadron since its formation.

In addition to the delivery runs of aircraft, there were vital Malta convoys in July and September to re-supply the island. The first of these, Operation *Substance*, delivered 65,000 tons of food, ammunition, fuel and troops. It was while protecting this convoy on 23 July that VAT went for his second swim south of Sardinia. Flying with his commanding officer Sholto Douglas and with Buster as wingman they intercepted two formations of S.79s at 12,000 feet at a distance of 22 miles from the convoy. Their separate head-on attacks against both formations disrupted the bombing runs. Sholto Douglas and VAT repeatedly attacked alone the larger formation of five, shooting down one and damaging another, which dropped out of formation where it was finished off by Buster. They made seven attacks in total, causing several of the enemy to jettison their bombs, before being so damaged by return fire they ditched, in flames, as did two other Fulmars. Meanwhile a coordinated and unseen low-level torpedo strike by seven S.79s killed 26 aboard the destroyer *Fearless* and 39 aboard the cruiser *Manchester*.

This time the Fulmar's dingy worked as advertised and VAT qualified for membership of the Goldfish Club.[28] When they were picked up by the destroyer *Cossack*, recently arrived from home waters, their Mediterranean suntans had them initially mistaken for Italians and several of the crew were keen to deal harshly with the "prisoners", although the atmosphere improved with an unexpected reunion when William Wheeler (1929 class), the flotilla's torpedo officer, appeared.[29] VAT's "driver" James Sholto Douglas was awarded an immediate DSO for his aggressive flying against such odds. The flyers were transferred promptly back to the *Ark*, and the air battles continued with No. 807 Squadron losing Sub-Lieutenant (A)(P) Kenneth Grant RNVR (23) and Leading Airman Hugh McCleod (20) two days later. Kenneth had shot down a shadowing Cant Z.506B and was in turn shot down, the four aircrew of the Cant being rescued by the destroyer *Foxhound*. Driving off twelve bombers, two No. 808 Squadron Fulmars were shot down and Lieutenant (P) Alistair Kindersley RN, a Battle of Britain veteran, was recommended for a posthumous Victoria Cross, but received a mention in despatches instead. The second crew survived and the TAG, Petty Officer William Cuttriss, who had damaged an S.79 with his Thompson sub-machine gun as they dove under it at 50 metres range, was awarded a DSM. VAT never recorded using his own Thompson.

After Operation *Substance* VAT was recommended by the captain of *Ark Royal* for command of a squadron in due course. Captain Maund saw him as "capable, conscientious and hardworking … with a thorough knowledge of his work and who can be relied upon at all times". It was also noted that, despite all else occupying his waking hours, he would still take part in ship and divisional games whenever possible to keep fit.

The siege of Malta had commenced in June 1940 with only six Gloster Sea Gladiators for air defence of the island Churchill called an "unsinkable aircraft carrier". In May 1941 General Rommel warned that "without Malta the Axis will end by losing control of North Africa" and the RN and RAF committed not just to its defence under siege but to turn it into a base for offensive operations. Club runs continued, often with strikes ashore by aircraft and shore bombardments by ships escorting to and from the flying-off positions. Steering close inshore

---

28   Members of the Goldfish Club were aircrew whose lives were saved by life jacket or dinghy and numbered 9,000 by war's end. The Caterpillar Club was for those who had survived by parachute.

29   Lieutenant William Wheeler DSC MiD (1915-1941) was decorated for his actions when *Cossack*, *Maori* and *Zulu* attacked *Bismarck* at night with torpedoes. He was among the 159 lost when *Cossack* was torpedoed by *U-563* west of Gibraltar several months later.

off neutral Valencia on 24 August, returning from a mining decoy operation, the *Ark* had fifteen Fulmars and ten Swordfish circling Force H, countering enemy propaganda which claimed to have sunk her yet again.

Two club runs in early September saw another 45 aircraft launched for Malta. Alongside at Gibraltar on 20 September three *Maiale* (pig) *Siluro a Lenta Corsa* human torpedoes from the *Decimal Flottiglia* MAS courageously attacked Gibraltar harbour. Active patrols prevented them approaching *Nelson* or *Ark Royal* and they could only attack merchant ships. The following day *U-371*, the first *Kriegsmarine* submarine to enter the Mediterranean, passed through the Straits of Gibraltar.

Operation *Halberd* in late September, with home fleet units heavily reinforcing Force H, brought in an additional 85,000 tons of supplies and 2,000 troops to Malta.[30] On 25 September the *Ark* flew off 24 of her 27 Fulmars for air interception exercises and the opportunity was taken for six fighters to fly around all ships for recognition purposes. At 1327 on 27 September, with tension high after a morning of air attacks, the *Ark* had 14 Fulmars airborne when another torpedo attack by SM.84s developed which saw *Nelson* hit. *Rodney*, while protecting the *Ark*, shot down a No. 807 Squadron Fulmar whose crew were picked up by *Duncan*. A few minutes later another No. 807 Squadron Fulmar was shot down, again by *Rodney* and again the crew were picked up by *Duncan*. However, a Fulmar of No. 808 Squadron shot down by *Prince of Wales* was not so lucky, with both aircrew being killed.

The next club run saw VAT catch up with Lieutenant (O) Gerald "Gerry" Haynes (1925 class) who was now SOBS of No. 828 (Albacore) Squadron. Eleven Albacores of No. 828 Squadron and two Swordfish launched to Hal Far on 18 October where they joined the shore-based No. 830 (Swordfish) Squadron in their hazardous night strikes against enemy shipping and aerodromes in Sicily and Libya. Haynes was the only one of No. 828 Squadron's nine original observers to survive.[31]

On return from this run, Vice-Admiral Sir James Somerville KCB DSO was made a Knight of the British Empire for his command of Force H. As he was already a Knight of the Bath, *Ark Royal* signalled "Fancy twice a knight, and at your age, too". This rapport had been built up with the admiral, an 1897 *Britannia* cadet recalled from retirement, often coming over from his flagship to fly in the back seat of a Swordfish or Fulmar to better understand the "trade" of the young men who carried out his strike orders and protected his ships.

On 1 October VAT was appointed SOBS of No. 825 (Swordfish) Squadron, which had been aboard the *Ark* since June after their strike against *Bismarck* from *Victorious*, thus returning to the squadron he had served in when he joined *Glorious* in 1938. The squadron had lost eight

---

30   Group 1: Battleship *Nelson*, *Ark Royal*, cruiser *Hermione* and five destroyers. Group 2: Battleships *Prince of Wales* and *Rodney*, cruisers *Kenya*, *Edinburgh*, *Sheffield*, *Euryalus* and twelve destroyers.
31   Later Lieutenant-Commander Gerry Haynes DSO RAN (1911-1999). Gerry had transferred to the Emergency List in 1933. Reappointed in 1939 he qualified as an observer and was the first RAN aviator to command a squadron in December 1941, stepping-up when Lieutenant-Commander (O) David Langmore DSC failed to return from a strike.

aircraft in English Channel operations under the RAF's Coastal Command during the Calais and Dunkirk evacuations where five, including the commanding officer, were shot down by Bf 109s during a single bombing raid on 29 May 1940. The replacement commanding officer, "Winkle" Esmonde, afterwards prophetically commenting on the futility of sending out slow biplanes from shore bases during daylight without fighter escort. As VAT mastered the use of ASV radar he and Winkle quickly fell into the usual habit of commanding officer and SOBS flying together.

A further 26 Hurricanes for Malta were launched from *Ark Royal* and eleven from *Argus* on 12 November and Force H turned back west towards Gibraltar.

Kapitänleutnant Guggenberger, the commander of U-81.

Ark Royal lost 13/14 November 1941

Two U-boats, *U-81* (*Kptlt* Friedrich Guggenberger) and *U-205* (*Kptlt* Franz-Georg Reschke) had just forced the Straits of Gibraltar and were about to put an end to the *Ark's* extraordinary run of luck. Admiral Somerville, flying his flag in the battleship *Malaya*, had received intelligence reports of submarine activity east of Gibraltar and had six Swordfish sweeping ahead of Force H in addition to aircraft out from North Front. *Malaya*, *Ark Royal*, *Argus* and the radar fitted cruiser *Hermione* were being screened by seven destroyers. Italian aerial reconnaissance reports that Force H was returning were passed on to the U-boats and Dönitz signalled "Return of English group expected north of Qu.CG9593. Guggenberger to occupy same attack area as Reschke".

At dawn on 13 November *U-205* fired three torpedoes at *Ark Royal* but the only detonation was in the wake of the destroyer *Legion*. On surfacing Reschke sent a sighting report and Guggenberger raced to intercept some 25 miles off Gibraltar. Stalking Force H with its circling aircraft and screening destroyers, *U-81* fired a spread of four torpedoes in the calm seas from

The Ark Royal listing after being hit by a torpedo fired by U-81 on 13 November 1941.

between the distant and close escorts at the battleship. On firing the sudden loss of weight forward threatened a surface breach so Guggenberger ordered all spare men to the bow and *U-81* dived deep. Over the following hours he counted 162 depth charge explosions as they slowly withdrew to the northeast.

As *U-81* fired at *Malaya* the *Ark* turned starboard into wind at 22 knots to land a Swordfish, passing across *Malaya's* quarter and at 1541, just as the Swordfish landed, the torpedo struck on the starboard side abreast the bridge, whipping the ship violently. VAT was in the Air Intelligence Office 24 metres above the water and still felt a "terrific smack". The 341-kilogram charge ripped a hole 40 x 9 metres which was made larger as hull plates peeled back under the carrier's 22,000 tons of forward momentum, until she stopped in the water ten minutes later. He didn't think for the moment that it was a torpedo hit, because of the carrier's speed and a good screen of destroyers and aircraft, but Guggenberger had just earned the *Ritterkreuz*.[32]

As the *Ark* quickly took on a significant list from major flooding in the starboard boiler room, the four Fulmars of No. 807 Squadron flying CAP, along with the airborne Swordfish from No. 805 Squadron, flew to North Front. With the loss of steam was the loss of electrical power and communications since *Ark Royal* had not been designed with diesel back-up generators. There was no power for the pumps, but the battery powered emergency lighting worked.

With the list at 18 degrees Captain Maund ordered the evacuation of all surplus crew and *Legion* put her bow against the *Ark's* port quarter. A bed of hammocks was laid on *Legion's* forecastle onto which most of the crew swarmed down by rope from the flight deck or jumped from the lower hangar deck. For VAT "there was nothing dramatic about leaving the Ark" as he went down a rope hand-over-hand and found no problem getting aboard *Legion*.

With many mistakes and much bravery, the damage-control parties laboured against flood and fire before finally conceding defeat twelve hours later at 0430 on 14 November when they abandoned a ship now listing 35 degrees. In her demise were many lessons for future carrier design and effective damage control training. The *Ark's* final vestige of her well-used-up luck had ensured just a single fatality amongst the crew. The very gallant *Ark Royal*, first to effectively demonstrate a carrier's offensive strike capability and the most famous carrier of her era, rolled over and sank at 0613 on 14 November 1941.

Awarded a CBE only four weeks before for the *Bismarck* action, Captain Loben Maund was court-martialled and found guilty of negligence for damage control failings.[33] VAT had obvious professional pride in the carrier, held by all serving in her, but also regarded the ship with great affection. He had reached a stage where he thought the *Ark* would go on forever, so felt her sinking as "a very great personal loss".

---

32 *Ritterkreuz des Eisernen Kreuzes* - Knight's Cross of the Iron Cross - Germany's highest award.
33 Later Rear-Admiral Loben Maund CBE (1892-1957). He went on to serve in Combined Operations and helped develop RN landing craft. Mentioned in Despatches for his part in the July 1943 invasion of Sicily and appointed Rear-Admiral, Landing Ships and Craft, in October 1944.

Several days later Winkle Esmonde had found time to hurriedly report that VAT was "keen and very reliable … an above average leader capable of commanding a squadron". Back in the UK on survivors' leave, VAT visited Gieves for new uniforms. It would take another year, and another sinking, before the naval accountants approved compensation for the loss of his uniforms and personal effects.

VAT was subsequently awarded the Distinguished Service Cross for his *Ark Royal* service, as promulgated in the *London Gazette* on 1 January 1942. The citation read:

The Distinguished Service Cross.

> Distinguished Service Cross
>
> Smith, Victor Alfred Trumper, Lieutenant, RAN
>
> For outstanding zeal, patience and cheerfulness and for setting an example of wholehearted devotion to duty. This officer, serving in HMS ARK ROYAL, Force "H", as Senior Observer of 807 Squadron, has set a high standard of courage and a fine example. He has been shot down into the sea by enemy aircraft on two occasions and having been picked up by a destroyer on each occasion, he has returned making light of his experience and showing unabated keenness to engage the enemy.

The Africa Star.

The operational area of North Africa included the Mediterranean Sea between the Suez Canal and the Straits of Gibraltar. All who served with Force H were awarded the Africa Star.

Reformed at Lee-on-Solent in the New Year, No. 825 Squadron continued under Lieutenant-Commander Winkle Esmonde DSO. Winkle, loath to lose VAT, had requested him to continue as Senior Observer; however, Australia House had received instructions for VAT to return home. This proved fortuitous as six weeks later, on 12 February 1942, the six disembarked Swordfish of No. 825 Squadron at a snowbound RAF Manston were ordered to attack *Scharnhorst*, *Gneisenau* and *Prinz Eugen*. Heavily escorted by over 30 destroyers, flak ships and E-boats they were making their "channel dash" with 252 Luftwaffe fighters swarming overhead.

When Vice-Admiral Dover Sir Bertram Ramsay rang the First Sea Lord expressing his reluctance to order the Swordfish into a daylight attack Admiral Sir Dudley Pound unequivocally replied that "the Navy will attack the enemy whenever and wherever he is to be found!" Despite the almost complete lack of RAF fighter cover No. 825 Squadron commenced their forlorn strike with *Kapitän* Kurt Hoffmann of the *Scharnhorst* immediately exclaiming that "… it is nothing but suicide for them." All six Swordfish were shot down, killing thirteen of the eighteen aircrew including VAT's successor as SOBS Lieutenant (A) "Bill" Williams RN, flying with the CO and Petty Officer (A) William Clinton. Esmonde received a posthumous VC.

CHAPTER 7

THE PACIFIC 1942

The 1939-1945 War Medal.

VAT's 1939-1945 WAR MEDAL had on the reverse a lion standing on the body of a double-headed dragon. Those two heads of an eagle and a dragon signified the principal occidental and oriental enemies of WWII. VAT had faced the occidental for 26 months; he was now about to confront the oriental. The American Joint Chiefs of Staff declared that in 1942 allied forces "would constantly be on the verge of ultimate defeat".

Taking passage for Australia, VAT was at sea in a merchantman on 7 December 1941, when aircraft from six Imperial Japanese Navy carriers attacked the United States Pacific Fleet at their moorings in Pearl Harbor, Hawaii. Having studied the FAA Taranto raid, the Japanese daylight strike was devastating, and the war became truly global.

With passage longer than usual due to shipping disruption, VAT had nine weeks to ruminate on his war so far. Recalling naval actions in the Atlantic and Mediterranean he felt that the shock loss of the famous *Hood*, which had greatly affected morale at the time, had come to be accepted as the price to pay when a ship commissioned in 1920, whose upgrades had been delayed due to inter-war economies, was pitted against a 1940 battleship. Subsequently, hunting down the *Bismarck* had balanced the score to some degree. With the demise of the *Ark* so recently experienced, the need for improved design and damage control also occupied his thoughts.

VAT considered the significance of carrier strikes becoming the main weapon of the fleet. While *Ark Royal* had ranged the western Mediterranean from Gibraltar, *Illustrious* had ranged the eastern from Alexandria, where it had been a very courageous and astute move, to attack the Italian fleet at Taranto. The defence was formidable. Taranto, as a fleet base, had many ship-borne guns in addition to the shore mounted anti-aircraft guns defending the harbour. There were also barrage balloons adding to the hazardous task as the Swordfish dived low in the flare-lit harbour to release their weapons and then get out of the maelstrom as best they could. VAT realised that Taranto had, more than anything else, established the real value of a Fleet Air Arm.

There were the sad losses of friends and classmates to reflect on. When the inaugural RN escort carrier *Audacity* was sunk by *U-751* on 21 December 1941, George Carline, a veteran of the Taranto strike, went down with her. One third of VAT's Naval Observer's Course of 1937 were now names to be inscribed on later memorials. From that winning 1929 College

Rugby XV, three had already perished. William Anderson, who on failing to graduate in 1930 joined the RAF and won a DFC on the North West Frontier in 1933, had been shot down and killed in June 1941. Bill Langford, slow in mathematics at the college, was one of 138 lost when *Parramatta* was torpedoed by *U-559* off the Libyan coast a fortnight after the *Ark* went down.[1] Also lost that November was Eric Mayo, torpedo officer in *Sydney*, which was surprised and sunk by the German raider *Kormoran* off Western Australia. There were no survivors from *Sydney's* crew of 645 and the Australian Prime Minister, John Curtin, had wept.

VAT had personally experienced the losses steadily accumulating in the two Fulmar fighter squadrons aboard *Ark Royal*. On a single Malta resupply convoy, Operation *Substance*, the intensity of the running air battles saw Nos. 807 and 808 Squadrons lose twelve of their 24 Fulmars in six days with two crews lost and four crews, including VAT and Sholto Douglas, rescued from the sea. Now, with the Japanese advances, the war was reaching a nadir and VAT, having been shot down twice and knowing the 12 February 1942 fate of his late No. 825 Squadron, would have been in no doubt of his vulnerable mortality.

When Admiral Sir Tom Phillips KCB, commander of Force Z, sortied from Singapore without defensive air cover and went down with the *Prince of Wales* and *Repulse* off Malaya on 10 December 1941, the losses had a significant effect on the Australian public.[2] Schooled in the impregnability of both that island bastion and the RN there was disbelief coupled with a natural feeling of being let down. VAT could not help conjecturing what would have been the result if *Ark Royal* had been in company. Overall, he felt that up until then the navy had had a hard but fairly successful war, in the main remaining on top despite heavy losses.

In the 1920s the RN view was that only the British Empire would be in a position to restrain an aggressive Japan. They had reassured an isolated Australia with the Singapore strategy, sending a major fleet to that base within four to six weeks of hostilities. This policy had been officially, but quietly, abandoned just before the outbreak of the European war. VAT recognised that there was a question of priorities, with Britain desperately pressed in home waters, the Atlantic and North Africa at the end of 1941. The possibility of Japan beginning a Pacific war naturally did not hold the same sway in Britain as it did in Australia. Unwilling to see Australia's danger as subordinate to other theatres of war the New Year's message from Prime Minister John Curtin looked uninhibitedly to America as the keystone to "hold out until the tide of battle swings against the enemy".[3]

When he reached Sydney in early February 1942, it had been almost five years since VAT

---

1   George "Bill" Langford had been mentioned-in-despatches as first lieutenant of the sloop *Parramatta* during the May 1941 Battle of Crete. When the sloop was torpedoed while escorting a desperately needed ammunition ship to the besieged Tobruk garrison on 27 November 1941, 138 were lost including Bill. There were only 24 survivors.
2   *Prince of Wales* was a modern 40,000-ton battleship while *Repulse* was a 32,000-ton battlecruiser of WWI vintage. This was the same Admiral Tom Phillips who had thought little of VAT and his commanding officer's chances of protecting a convoy with a single catapult-launched Fulmar fighter in November 1940.
3   A policy decision by the First Sea Lord, Admiral of the Fleet Sir Roger Backhouse GCB GCVO CMG, survivor of a Walrus ditching in 1935 (see the Walrus profile on page 120).

had last stepped ashore in Australia. Leaving a bombed, blacked out, rationed country and arriving to a bright Australian summer the "business as usual" attitude of Sydney was a shock. Despite the Japanese advances to their immediate north the war still seemed remote to many Australians unless they had a son or husband serving overseas. This included VAT's parents and sister-in-law Enid, since his older brother Bill had left the public service to join the army in July 1940, embarking for the Middle East that December. Corporal Smith was still months away from his own return home, followed by later service in New Guinea. VAT had accumulated a month's foreign service leave and, surprised but appreciative of the standard of life in Sydney compared to war-time London, welcomed the needed rest from active service.

During the weeks of his voyage and while he was on leave, Japanese forces had achieved a sweep of conquest unparalleled, with the IJN at its zenith of professional prowess and power. Seizing territory rich in natural resources from Malaya to the Netherlands East Indies they had inflicted heavy losses on Allied naval, air and ground forces. Singapore had surrendered on 15 February and fierce fighting was continuing in the Philippines.[4] After the IJN carriers had finished with Pearl Harbor they had turned and fought west and south and now focused their attention on Darwin. There the RAN's original observer, Commander (O) Henry Chesterman, was operations officer in the territory's naval headquarters. An unexpected linchpin in Australia's new defensive perimeter, the IJN carriers attacked Darwin on 19 February. Eleven ships were sunk and 263 people killed. The war was no longer so remote.

On 1 March 1942, the light cruiser *Perth*, the heavy cruiser USS *Houston* and the Netherlands destroyer HNLMS *Evertsen* were lost at the Battle of Sunda Strait. Lieutenant (G) Peter Hancox, Rugby teammate and King's Medalist from VAT's 1927 college year, was *Perth*'s Gunnery Officer. VAT considered him an outstanding officer as well as a friend. Towards the end of that desperate action Peter had been reduced to shooting practice rounds at the IJN cruisers and destroyers. *Perth*'s observer, Lieutenant (O) Neville McWilliam, was also known to VAT having been a member of the 1929 class. Both Peter and Neville were among the 353 who went down with the ship.[5] It was time for VAT to re-enter the war.

Lieutenant (O) Neville McWilliam, who was lost when HMAS Perth was sunk on 1 March 1942.

On 8 March VAT was appointed to *Australia*, the flagship of the ANZAC Squadron formed on 12 February.[6] To date *Australia*'s war had been hard on her embarked Walrus flights. Off Dakar,

---

4   Australian casualties in the defence of Singapore were 1,789 killed, 1,306 wounded and 15,395 prisoners of war from the 8th Division. One in three died in captivity.

5   Midshipman Neville McWilliam had his appointment terminated in 1933 and joined the New Guinea Patrol Service. Called up on the outbreak of war, he qualified as an observer and first served in *Hobart*. Of the 324 from *Perth* taken prisoner by the Japanese only 218 survived captivity, among them Neville's pilot, Flying Officer Allen McDonough RAAF.

6   The squadron was commanded by the Australian born Rear-Admiral John "Jack" Crace CB later Vice-Admiral Sir John Crace KBE CB (1887-1968).

in September 1940, Walrus L2247 had been shot down by Vichy French fighters. Those killed included Lieutenant-Commander (O) Francis Fogarty (30), sub of *Canberra*'s 1931 gunroom containing Cadet-Midshipman Smith. In April 1941 a catapult failure had seen the replacement pilot Lieutenant (P) John Hoath RN, on loan until a RAAF officer became available, killed in Walrus A2-24 and the other two crew seriously injured.[7] Only a week after the ANZAC Squadron formed Hoath's replacement, Flying Officer Edward Rowan RAAF (20), had hit the ship's side, landing off Noumea on 19 February. When Walrus L2327 broke up and burst into flames Rowan was killed. *Chicago*'s motor whaler rescued the injured TAG and the observer, Sub-Lieutenant (A)(O) George Jackson RN.

VAT was not to be the flagship's observer, however. Harrie Gerrett, back in Australia since November, had been transferred from *Canberra* to replace the burned and lacerated Jackson. Also aboard *Australia* was Lieutenant-Commander (O) George Oldham as Staff Officer (Operations) to the admiral and for squadron (O) duties. VAT was instead posted for liaison officer duties in the American heavy cruiser *Chicago*, the USN equivalent of the RN 10,000-ton treaty cruisers. At sea when Pearl Harbor was attacked, *Chicago* had left Pearl on 2 February for Suva, then joined the ANZAC Squadron based in Noumea. It was to New Caledonia that VAT now travelled to take up his appointment.

The composition of the ANZAC Squadron on 9 March 1942 was the RAN heavy cruiser *Australia*, USN heavy cruisers *Astoria* and *Chicago*, together with the New Zealand light cruisers *Achilles* and *Leander*. Bolstered by other US cruisers and destroyers, now designated

Task Group 11.7, they covered the right flank of carrier Task Forces 17 and 11 centred on the *Yorktown* and *Lexington* respectively. The Japanese, having overwhelmed the small Australian garrison in Rabaul, New Britain, were pushing on to invade Lae and Salamaua on the north-east coast of New Guinea. Remaining south in the Gulf of Papua to avoid being land-locked, the carriers

The USN heavy cruiser USS Chicago, which was part of the ANZAC Squadron in the early months of 1942.

---

7   The two injured crewmen were rescued when *Hobart*'s Walrus alighted on the water.

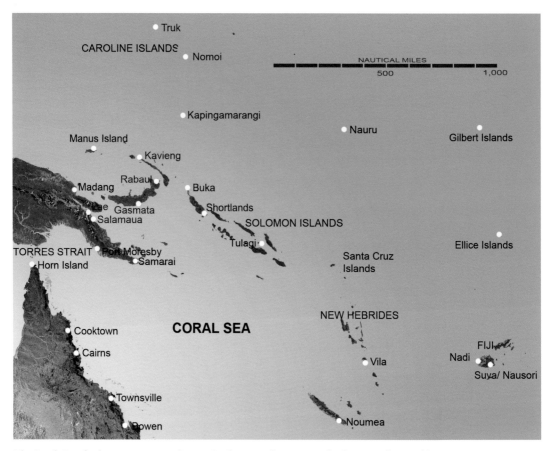

The South Pacific theatre, circa April 1942. By this time the Japanese had occupied several locations in New Guinea including their key base of Rabaul. Allied forces were consolidating far to the south at Noumea in the French territory of New Caledonia. It was at this location that VAT joined Chicago on 20 March. In early May the Japanese would advance into Tulagi in the Solomons and attempt to capture Port Moresby.

launched 104 aircraft over the Owen Stanley Ranges on 10 March to strike the Japanese troop transports; 103 aircraft returned. In the following five days, however, the cruiser force lost six floatplanes and five crews.[8] When the ANZAC Squadron arrived off Noumea on 16 March, to cover the arrival of 15,000 American troops in Convoy ZK.7, VAT was waiting.

The *Chicago*, anchored in Great Road, Noumea, recorded in her war diary for 20 March that at 0900 Lieutenant VA Smith RAN reported aboard from *Australia* for temporary duty. He found his time as a liaison officer an interesting and very enjoyable experience. VAT's opinion of the truculent Captain Howard Bode, universally disliked by his officers and men, is not on record, diplomatically recalling only how he was made very welcome by *Chicago's* ship's company.[9] With a multitude of differences between USN and RN/RAN operational

---

8   One from *Astoria* on 10 March, another two from *Astoria* and two from *Louisville* on 12 March, and one from *Chicago* on 15 March. Only the *Chicago* crew were recovered.

9   Captain Howard Bode USN, had just assumed command of the battleship *Oklahoma* when she was sunk at Pearl Harbor. Ashore that Sunday morning he rushed back to his ship which lost 429 of her crew.

procedures, signals and tactics it was a position that called for sound professional knowledge tinged with diplomacy. VAT relished the opportunity to become familiar with the different American approach to many professional matters and would have envied the fact that *Chicago*, with two catapults, routinely embarked up to four Curtiss SOC Seagull floatplanes.

Back in Sydney normal life for the Smith family continued, VAT's sister Bess marrying Private John Hall on 2 April. The Hall's were also a grazier family - from Stockinbingal in the Riverina - who had moved to Chatswood where John had been a warehouse manager. In uniform for only eight months, he was an orderly clerk in the Australian Army Medical Corps. John's brother Donald, who had also enlisted in the army, was best man.

Admiral Yamamoto Isoroku, aware that time and oil limited his options, supported Stage 2 of *Mo Sakusen* (Operation *Mo*) to consolidate the *Dai-to-a Kyoeiken* or Greater East Asia Co-Prosperity Sphere. This would push the Japanese defensive perimeter further south and east, establishing bases from which to seize the Australian territory of Papua, French New Caledonia, the British Crown Colony of Fiji and New Zealand-mandated Western Samoa. If successful they would disrupt air and sea communications between Australia, New Zealand and the United States. The joint RAN/USN cryptanalysis unit later designated FRUMEL, the Fleet Radio Unit in Melbourne, had partially broken Japanese naval codes and Allied command was forewarned.

Pre-war the USN had envisaged Plan Orange and then Rainbow 5, which involved naval thrusts across the Central Pacific to force a decisive naval engagement with the Japanese. There had been no consideration for a South Pacific action. Even as many USN units withdrew from Hawaii to the west coast of the US, the newly appointed Chief of Naval Operations, Admiral Ernest King, ordered his Pacific commander Admiral Chester Nimitz to keep open the sea lanes to Australia. Nimitz, with rare strategic vision, sought action and committed his precious fleet carriers as the Japanese moved on the Solomon Islands and Port Moresby. The *Enterprise* and *Hornet*, just returned from their B-25 Doolittle Raid against Tokyo, could not reach the area in time, leaving the *Yorktown* and *Lexington* task forces to contest, over several confused days, what became known as the Battle of the Coral Sea.

Chicago supported *Yorktown* in her 4 May strike against an IJN convoy, unloading troops at Tulagi in the Solomon Islands. Meanwhile Task Force 44, the renamed ANZAC Squadron, joined *Lexington*.[10] All forces merged into Task Force 17 on 6 May. The following day Rear-Admiral Frank Fletcher dispatched Jack Crace aboard *Australia* with a cruiser and destroyer force designated TG 17.3 that included *Chicago*.[11] Crace, without air cover, was to intercept a Japanese Port Moresby invasion force of eleven troop transports whose heavy screen could call on land-based and carrier aircraft.

---

10   On 22 April the squadron, now designated Task Force 44, was absorbed by the South West Pacific Area command's Allied naval forces still under Vice-Admiral Herbert Leary USN, who had held the ANZAC area naval command from Melbourne since February. The newly appointed SWPA Supreme Commander was General Douglas MacArthur who had arrived in Australia on 17 March.

11   Heavy cruisers *Australia* and *Chicago*, light cruiser *Hobart* with destroyers *Farragut*, *Perkins* and *Walke*.

On 7 May *Lexington* and then *Yorktown*'s aircraft found and sank the light carrier *Shoho*, famously signalling "Scratch one flat-top". As a result Admiral Inoue Shigeyoshi, commanding the IJN Fourth Fleet, ordered the Port Moresby invasion force to reverse course and not transit the Jomard passage off the eastern tip of New Guinea. Meanwhile Japanese seaplanes were shadowing the lurking TG 17.3 and erroneously reported that it included two carriers. When *Chicago*'s early model CXAM radar detected inbound strikes that afternoon her baptism of fire was rapidly approaching.[12]

VAT's liaison officer duties would have placed him on the bridge near Captain Bode during action stations where he could observe closely as the officers and men carried out their duties for the first time under attack. Fourteen Mitsubishi G3M Betty torpedo bombers were tracked by radar from over 70 nautical miles inbound. Breaking into three groups, eight from ahead where *Australia* was leading, four from the port bow and two from starboard, those on *Chicago* watched as they dove down from 5,000 feet to just 100 feet when five miles away. All guns opened fire including her 8-inch main batteries in barrage fire, raising waterspouts ahead of the low-flying bombers. Most aircraft released their torpedoes from only 50 feet at 1,000 metres distance with six aircraft pressing on through the barrage with reckless courage to within 100 metres of *Chicago* for strafing runs which killed two and wounded seven. Skilful handling by both cruisers saw *Australia* avoid two torpedoes and *Chicago* four. From first to last round was just 180 seconds, with

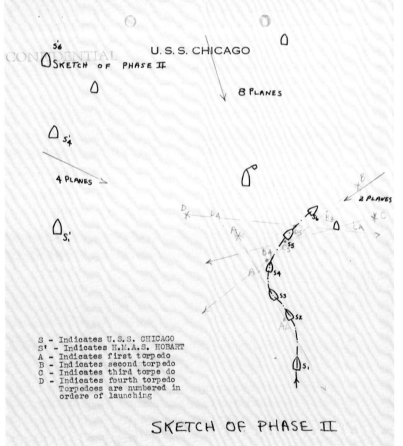

An extract from Chicago's war diary in respect to the air attacks fought off on 7 May 1942.

12   *Chicago* was among the first six USN ships to be radar equipped. CXAM had an expected range of 50 miles for aircraft and 14 miles for ships. At the Battle of the Coral Sea *Lexington*'s improved CXAM-1 detected Japanese aircraft at 68 miles.

five Bettys shot down. VAT, the battle-hardened veteran, had found nothing wanting in his new American allies!

Ten minutes later the next attack was medium level bombing from 18,000 feet which concentrated on *Australia*. From *Chicago* they watched as numerous bombs from nineteen aircraft straddled the flagship, drenching her upper decks. While the enemy withdrew three USAAF B-17s out of Townsville then mistakenly attacked Crace's force from 25,000 feet with what he considered a "disgraceful" lack of accuracy. Informed that the enemy invasion force included one carrier, eight cruisers, eighteen destroyers and two submarines Crace's force remained on station tasked to "destroy enemy units proceeding through the Jomard Passage".

On 8 May multiple hits left *Lexington* so critically damaged that she was later scuttled while the *Yorktown* and *Shokaku* were also hit. When the opposing forces disengaged, the US had lost 69 carrier aircraft and the Japanese perhaps 97. Crace, with no reports or orders from Fletcher, remained on patrol to intercept any invasion forces until low fuel required withdrawal at 0100 on 10 May towards a secret refuelling point in the reefs off the Queensland coast. Crucially neither *Shokaku* or *Zuikaku*, because of battle damage and loss of aircrew, were able to participate in the Battle of Midway a month later, where the Japanese lost four fleet carriers along with the initiative in the Pacific.

Despite the loss of the *Lexington*, strategically the Battle of the Coral Sea was soon apparent as an Allied victory. The Port Moresby invasion force had been turned back, which effectively checked further Japanese expansion. VAT had played a minor role in a battle he regarded as "the first ray of brightness" in the Pacific and which could only reinforce his now settled belief in the primacy of naval air power. This did not prevent him recognising much that needed improving before things would approach the highly professional manner of command, control and operations he had experienced with Force H in the Mediterranean.

Many years later VAT omitted this liaison time on the *Chicago* from a precis of his active service. He wrote that after Fulmars there had been "some more Swordfishing" and then "some Walrusing". That Walrusing time was now to prove profoundly memorable.

Supermarine Walrus P5715 as flown by VAT from HMAS Canberra in 1942.

Supermarine Walrus (Seagull V)
Powerplant: 750 hp Bristol Pegasus VI 9-cylinder air-cooled radial
Speed: 117 knots
Range: 520 nautical miles
Max Weight: 8,050 pounds
Crew: 3/4
Armament: 2 x 0.303-inch calibre Vickers K machine guns
Bomb Load: 6 x 100-pound bombs or 2 x 250-pound bombs or depth charges

Needing a replacement for their diminishing numbers of naval cooperation Seagull IIIs the RAAF submitted specifications to Supermarine for a robust catapult-launched amphibian to undertake fleet-spotter duties. The Seagull V prototype, designed by RJ Mitchell who went on to design the Spitfire, was completed in 1933. The first aircraft to combine a metal fuselage, completely enclosed crew compartment and fully retractable undercarriage, the single-engine biplane went on to arguably fly a greater variety of military tasks in WWII than any other type.

With Australia recovering from the depression, extra money was available from the Treasury and the RAAF ordered 24 Seagull Vs, the first entering service in 1935. With some minor design changes the RN subsequently ordered an initial twelve. In October of that year Admiral Sir Roger Backhouse, keen for a modern "Admiral's Barge", was a passenger in the third prototype K4797 which overturned and sank whilst landing alongside his home fleet flagship *Nelson*. It was later recounted that never had so many senior officers vied to man the oars of a rescue boat, although it was a midshipman who dived overboard and reached the sinking aircraft first.

Instead of calling their airframes Seagull Vs the British adopted the name Walrus, which passed into general use in Australian service when not using the more common shipboard designators of Shagbat, Pusser's Duck or Steam Pigeon. During the war the RAAF received a number of Walruses with British serial numbers to supplement the surviving fleet of Seagull Vs.

Wartime expansion saw the type eventually equip 24 FAA squadrons and 18 RAF squadrons. Initially used mainly in the spotter reconnaissance role, the ability to land in swells of up to four metres saw it save many lives flying air-sea rescue missions. Capable of being catapulted with a full military load carrying bombs and depth charges the Walrus saw service in the anti-submarine role and even, on occasion, bombed shore targets. Given its low stalling speed, landing on a carrier's deck without an arrestor hook or flaps was routine.

During the war 270 Walrus Mk IIs were produced with a wooden hull to conserve scarce light alloys. After 740 airframes had been built for nine countries, production finished in July 1943, the year most catapults and ships flights were being removed as escort carriers became more widely available.

HMAS *Canberra* 11 May 1942 – 9 August 1942

Since February 1942 *Canberra* had been undergoing a refit period in Sydney where Flying Officer Duncan Murchison had disembarked the Walrus flight to Rose Bay as a duty aircraft. Her major year-long modernisation to improve fighting efficiency and reliability, which *Australia* had completed in 1939, had been deferred because of the shortage of cruisers. Minor refit complete she needed an observer and Sub-Lieutenant (A) George Jackson had been designated. Jackson, however, injured in the crash when landing alongside *Australia* on 19 February, was not yet fully recovered.

This led to VAT being given a "pierhead jump" when *Chicago* arrived in Sydney.[13] On 11 May 1942, a 29-year-old VAT reported for observer duties onboard the cruiser he had first joined aged seventeen in 1931, and then again in 1935. This latest posting was to be the shortest of the three.

Joining VAT as pilot was Duncan Murchison. A clerk in civilian life, he had served as a corporal in the part-time militia for

An RAAF Seagull V seaplane mounted on a catapult on an RAN cruiser. The aircraft were delivered in the late 1930s in natural metal finish but by the time of the Pacific War had been camouflaged.

three years before joining the RAAF for pilot training in March 1940. Although having fewer than 500 hours of total flying, he was well reported. In almost exact correlation with VAT's confidential reports, he was particularly noted for his zeal, leadership and reliability. Duncan obviously had the tact, and perhaps sense of humour, necessary for a junior RAAF officer aboard an RAN cruiser. He was also an officer who kept himself fit so he and VAT would have meshed well as a crew. Indeed, the navy considered Duncan their best air force officer and naval co-operation pilot.

The newly promoted Flight Lieutenant Murchison embarked Walrus W.2768 aboard *Canberra* and VAT catapulted with him for the first time on 15 May. Strapped in on Murchison's right, they both braced and leaned back against their headrests as, with full throttle and boost on the Pegasus engine, the cordite charge accelerated them to 55 knots in as many feet with a force

---

13   A "pierhead jump" or "crash draft" is when an officer or rating is appointed from one posting immediately to another at very short notice.

A Walrus launches from Canberra in 1942, very likely crewed by VAT and Duncan Murchison.

of up to 4g. Airborne they flew to Mascot for the obligatory compass swing.

Several weeks of work-up for the ship and ship's flight followed which included early radar trials, photographing torpedo runs and spotting for the 8-inch main guns. Five more times Murchison and VAT were catapulted into the air when not being hoisted out for take-off.

In Port Phillip, after practising bombing, the Walrus was recovered by the underway boom method for the first time. Used in rougher swells, this involved VAT getting very wet standing in the fore hatchway to attach a towing line while the TAG clambered onto the upper wing with the propellor turning to secure the sling hook for the aircraft to be hoisted inboard.

Recovery with the ship underway was always hazardous for the Walrus crew. A rapid evolution minimised the ship's vulnerability so recovery with the ship steaming at up to 15 knots was often required. Landing was in the "slick" created by the officer of the watch. Assessing the wind direction for recovery he would put the ship's head some 60 degrees off then order full helm for half a turn before steadying on the recovery course. This created a smooth patch of water on *Canberra*'s lee quarter. The pilot would judge his approach to touch down inside the slick then taxi to the ship's side, matching course and speed. From landing to hoist clear could approach

A normal recovery of Canberra's Walrus in calm seas. While Duncan manoeuvres them alongside, VAT can be seen in the right-hand seat watching the TAG attach the hook in front of the spinning propellor.

90 seconds but there were many points of hazard in the process. It was during one such evolution that VAT was hit by the swinging block while hooking on and suffered the facial injury that left him with a permanent scar on his lower left cheek. Scores of junior officers in the years to come learnt to beware when this "war injury" turned from a healthy pink to a startling white.

Canberra returned from work-up and secured to No. 1 Buoy, Farm Cove, on 29 May just

An E9W1 Slim floatplane from the submarine I-21 flies over Sydney Harbour in the early hours of 29 May 1942. (courtesy Michael Claringbould)

as five large Japanese I-class submarines gathered off Sydney Heads. In the pre-dawn hours, the *I-21* launched her E9W1 Slim floatplane for a reconnaissance mission.[14] It flew as low as masthead height plotting the positions of the twelve major Allied warships in Sydney Harbour. When ground lookouts finally realised that the floatplane overhead was not *Chicago*'s, Airacobra fighters from Bankstown were scrambled, but failed to sight the intruder. Inexplicably, only two weeks after the merchantman *Wellen* had been shelled by a submarine off Newcastle, the naval hierarchy failed to appreciate the significance of this aircraft as a harbinger of looming danger.

In the early evening of 31 May, the *I-22*, *I-24* and *I-27* each released a two-man Type A *Ko-hyoteki* midget submarine they had piggy-backed down from the Fourth Fleet's main base at Truk in Micronesia. All three young commanders of the *Toku-tai* Special Attack Force were graduates of *Kaigun Heigakko*, the Imperial Japanese Naval Academy at Etajima, and had been instructed along Royal Navy lines.[15]

---

14   Incredibly in the four months prior to this daring flight the Slims of *I-25*, *I-29* and *I-21* had overflown Sydney (twice), Melbourne, Hobart, Wellington, Auckland (twice) and Suva (twice).

15   On initial founding 34 RN officers organised the academy, to which they bequeathed a lock of Horatio Nelson's hair and his fighting spirit. Marshal Admiral Marquis Heihachiro Togo (1848-1934), the academy's most famous alumnus as victor at the Battle of Tsushima against the Russians in 1905, was referred to as "the Nelson of the East" and himself believed he was an oriental re-incarnation of Nelson.

A two-man Type A Ko-hyoteki midget submarine.

Despite warnings from New Zealand of enemy submarine activity off Sydney and reports of an unidentified aircraft over the harbour, a sense of naval complacency within the harbour existed. This was reinforced by feeling safe behind the numerous indicator loops, anti-submarine boom nets and harbour defence vessels. Rear-Admiral Gerard Muirhead-Gould DSC RN, Flag Officer-in-Charge Sydney, hosted the captain and officers of *Chicago* at his official residence *Tresco* that evening for a libatious dinner. Muirhead-Gould's heart condition precluded sea-service but not, evidently, drinking.[16] As a commander Muirhead-Gould had sat on the board of inquiry investigating the sinking of *Royal Oak* by *U-47* at Scapa Flow in October 1939, so he should have been more alert than most to the danger from submarines commanded with skill and daring.

At 2001 a small blip on the trace for Inner Loop 12, two minutes after the larger blip of a Manly ferry, went unnoticed. This was *I-27*'s midget, which soon became entangled in anti-submarine nets close to the western boom gate. Unable to get free the crew followed *samurai* tradition, and triggered the submarine's demolition charges at 2237. Meanwhile *I-24*'s midget had more success after they penetrated the harbour at 2148. Fired on by an alerted *Chicago* their two torpedoes missed the heavy cruiser, but one exploded under the ex-ferry *Kuttabul* at 0031, killing 21 sailors.

With the harbour a confusion of firing surface ships, searchlights and depth charges, *Canberra*'s Captain George Moore, with two-thirds of his crew ashore on leave, had sufficient steam raised for slow speed.[17] Ordering VAT to fully darken the ship, he calmly had the ship's head kept pointed to avoid silhouetting the ship against shore lights while minimising its target profile. VAT maintained that it was a very wise move in the confusion pertaining that night. When an enraged Captain Bode arrived back onboard *Chicago* he accused his officers of being drunk and refused to believe they had seen a submarine. Proceeding hurriedly out of the harbour just before 0300, Bode turned once again on his executive officer declaring "You wouldn't know what a submarine looks like". Lieutenant-Commander Jimmy Mecklenberg pointed at the

---

16   Rear-Admiral Gerard Muirhead-Gould DSC (1889-1945), who had surreptitiously kept Churchill informed of German rearmament while posted to the British Embassy in 1930s Berlin, was appointed Flag Officer, Western Germany, where he died of a heart attack aged 56 on 26 June 1945.

17   Later Rear-Admiral George Moore CBE RAN (1893-1979). As Acting First Naval Member on 15 August 1945, he sent the signal "Japan has surrendered. Cease offensive action. Take all wartime precautions for self-defence". A Queenslander, Moore had trained as a merchant navy officer before WWI and joined the RNR. Transferring to the RAN he had been executive officer of *Albatross* and during the war became the first Australian to command *Australia* in August 1941. Postwar Moore turned diplomat and was Australia's first ambassador to the Philippines in 1950.

midget submarine then passing down *Chicago*'s side, too low for the ship's guns to bear, and replied "They look like that, Captain!"

This was *I-22*'s midget, which had patiently waited four hours off Sydney heads before entering. At 0350 the armed merchant cruiser *Kanimbla* opened fire on a suspected submarine sighting and at 0440 a lookout on *Canberra* reported a suspected torpedo track. This may have been the long stream of compressed air bubbles as the crew attempted to fire, not knowing their torpedo bow caps had been damaged and were jammed. At 0500 in Taylors Bay, on the northern side of the harbour, the submarine was spotted once more and successfully depth charged. When the wreck was raised it was discovered that this crew had also followed the *samurai* code.

Muirhead-Gould ordered, in the face of some criticism, that the funeral of the four Japanese servicemen be conducted with full naval honours, as were those of the 21 sailors from *Kuttabul*. Despite an almost wilful disregard of intelligence warnings and overflights, followed by inactivity and indecision on the night, little blame was ever apportioned for the command failures during the battle of Sydney Harbour.

Recovered sections of submarine wreckage were transported around Australia to raise funds for the Naval Relief Fund, of which VAT would become chairman twenty years later. The wreck of *I-24*'s midget, apparently making their way to the northern rendezvous position, was not discovered until 2006 off Sydney's northern beaches. It remains undisturbed as a war grave.

The next day, 1 June, *Canberra* left a disturbed Sydney, where fortunately no civilian casualties had been caused by hastily fired shells landing in the suburbs. Joining *Chicago*, they sailed to Brisbane for Task Force 44 to conduct working-up exercises under Crace in *Australia* and shortly afterwards his replacement, the impressive Rear-Admiral Victor Crutchley VC DSC.[18]

Captain Frank Getting who assumed command of the Canberra in June 1942.

During the work up off Brisbane, amongst the height finding exercises, anti-submarine patrols and the odd mail run, Murchison and VAT flew ashore to swap Walrus W2768 for Walrus P5715 which had been flown up to RAAF Amberley. This was an ex-RN airframe, crated for shipment from the UK and newly erected by the Qantas facility at Rose Bay. *Canberra* also saw a change of command when Captain Frank Getting arrived on 17 June. It was Lieutenant Getting who had taken VAT and his classmates to sea in

18   Later Admiral Sir Victor Crutchley VC KCB DSC (1893-1986). A godson of Queen Victoria he joined the RN in 1906 and was awarded the Victoria Cross for actions in the Ostend raid of May 1918. A fighting captain in the tradition of Nelson, he took his battleship *Warspite* into the restricted waters of Ofotfjord during the second battle of Narvik in 1940, where she helped sink eight sheltering Kriegsmarine destroyers. *Warspite*'s embarked Swordfish floatplane, airborne to spot for the guns, sank *U-64* with 250-pound bombs. Crutchley is mentioned in Chapter 3 when commanding the New Zealand based cruiser *Diomede* which exercised with *Canberra* (with Midshipman VAT Smith aboard) in 1932.

a submarine in 1929 and Commander Getting had been on the admiral's staff when VAT had been the flagship's junior watchkeeper in 1935.[19]

The USN had demonstrated that there was to be no quiescent period of defensive operations in the Pacific despite bearing heavy losses. Having already struck at Tokyo itself with carrier launched army B-25's in April, turned back the Port Moresby invasion fleet in May and won a decisive victory at Midway in June, Admiral King was determined on quickly mounting the first Allied offensive amphibious operation of WWII. Operation *Watchtower* was ordered on 2 July for the occupation of Guadalcanal in the Solomon Islands, where the Japanese had just commenced airfield construction.

VAT always remained succinct in his reminiscences of the following weeks:

> Shortly afterwards *Canberra* sailed … to form part of the covering force for the US Marines landing at Guadalcanal, and subsequently she became a casualty in the Battle of Savo Island on 9 August 1942. I have nothing to add to the many accounts which have been written.

On 14 July TF 44, now strengthened by the USN's 4th Destroyer Squadron, sailed from Brisbane to rendezvous in Wellington, New Zealand, where the invasion's spearhead, the South Pacific Amphibious Force ships of TF 62 waited. These ships would carry the 16,000 men, mainly the 1st Marine Division, who had been hurriedly gathered for the operation. In Wellington the dock workers, despite the Pacific crisis, were on strike, so the marines took on the logistical challenge of loading. Not able to properly combat-load the 23 transport and store ships, their 155mm howitzers were left behind, but of graver consequence no mosquito nets or insect repellent were loaded.[20]

The amphibious force sortied from Wellington on 22 July and the Walruses from *Canberra* and *Australia* flew anti-submarine patrols. The force then made rendezvous south of Fiji with the three carrier groups of *Saratoga*, *Wasp* and *Enterprise*. Merged together these became Task Force 61 which would conduct America's first amphibious operation since 1898. The 70 ships conducted three days of landing rehearsals on Koro Island. Unsurprisingly, given the lack of training and staff work accompanying this hurried assault - soon nicknamed Operation *Shoestring* by the marines - the rehearsals were a shambles with few landing craft getting past the coral reefs. One marine officer recalled *Canberra's* aircraft spotting for *Australia*, *Canberra* and *Hobart* during the practice firing runs as:

> … an ancient Walrus biplane, a relic … the old string-bag strutted proudly along at its top speed of about eighty knots.[21]

---

19   A member of the 1913 Pioneer class Frank Getting was the RAN's first submarine captain. That specialist branch suffered even more vicissitudes than aviation and Frank returned to general service in 1930 when the economies of the depression saw the RAN's two O-class submarines transferred to the RN. At the beginning of the war, he commanded the armed merchant cruiser *Kanimbla* before being appointed Deputy Chief of Naval Staff in Melbourne.
20   At Guadalcanal 650 marines were killed and 1,278 wounded. A staggering 8,580 contracted malaria.
21   Lieutenant Colonel Merrill Twining who later commanded the 1st Marine Division in Korea.

The command conference evinced antipathy between Marine General Alexander Vandergrift and the carrier commander Vice-Admiral Fletcher. Frank Fletcher, doubtful of the chances of success and fearful of losing a valuable carrier, arbitrarily declared he would only cover the invasion forces with his aircraft for two days rather than the five required to unload all the marines' stores and equipment. With some difficulty he was persuaded to commit to three days of air cover. VAT, along with all RN and RAN officers, would scarcely credit this attitude. They innately adhered to an inter-service staunchness, so ably demonstrated under Admiral Sir Alan "ABC" Cunningham during the recent Battle of Crete where the RN endured nine warships sunk and fifteen severely damaged whilst ensuring the navy did not let down the army.[22]

Steaming north-west between the New Hebrides and the Loyalty Islands, *Canberra* received a signal that Murchison's wife Marjorie had given birth to a girl on 3 August in a Sydney hospital. As they were in an operational area, celebrations within the close camaraderie of an embarked ship's flight were heartfelt but muted, and the popular pilot's first child Robyn was toasted with cold tea. The occasion would have been extra poignant for Leading Aircraftman Fred Rivers whose wife, Daphne was also expecting.

At 1000 on 6 August, approaching the Solomons undetected, the force went to action stations which they would exhaustingly maintain day and night until the evening of 8 August. In the early dawn of 7 August VAT and Murchison with their Telegraphist/Air Gunner Harold Davis catapulted on an anti-submarine and anti-torpedo boat patrol ahead of the amphibious forces entering the restricted littoral waters, while the carriers remained south of the archipelago. Passing Savo Island, midway between Florida Island and Guadalcanal, *Canberra* hoisted her battle ensign as she passed the troop transports and commenced the pre-assault bombardment of Tulagi as the dive-bombers went in. *Australia*'s aircraft was damaged while being recovered underway, so more patrol and reconnaissance work devolved onto *Canberra*'s flight. The next two days assumed a pattern of desperate Japanese bombing and torpedo air strikes by day, and guarding the three sea approaches to the vital transport ship anchorage at night as the marines established their perimeter ashore. The daylight had the advantage for Australian

HMAS Canberra with her Walrus embarked sails from Wellington on 22 July 1942.

22   "It has always been the duty of the Navy to take the Army overseas to battle and, if the Army fail, to bring them back again … it will take three years to build a new Fleet … it will take three hundred years to build a new tradition" - Admiral Sir ABC Cunningham, 26 May 1941, on board his battleship *Warspite*.

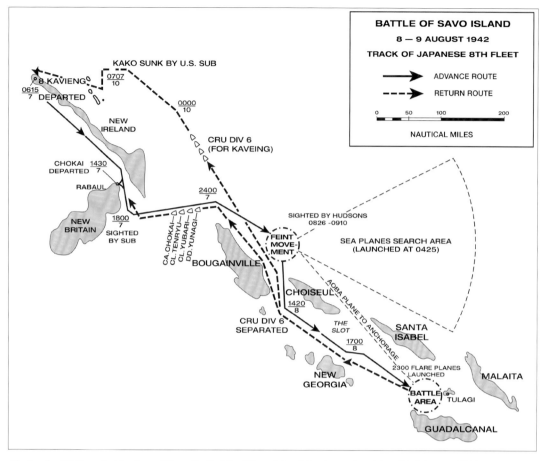

The track of Mikawa's ships to and from the Battle of Savo Island fought on the night of 8-9 August 1942.

coastwatchers such as Petty Officer Paul Mason RANVR (41) who, from his elevated jungle post in Bougainville, was able to give significant notice of inbound strikes leading to the memorable pipe aboard *Canberra*:

> The ship will be attacked at noon by 24 torpedo bombers. All hands will pipe to dinner at eleven o'clock.[23]

In Rabaul Vice-Admiral Mikawa Gun'ichi, commander of the Eighth Fleet, immediately gathered his naval forces for a bold night attack on the Allied forces 600 miles to the south-east, pursuing the IJN doctrine of the *Kantai Kessen* or "decisive battle". Tokyo Naval Headquarters initially rejected his proposal as dangerous and reckless, but then deferred to Mikawa as the local commander and gave permission. The admiral and his staff boarded the heavy cruiser

---

23   Later Lieutenant-Commander Paul Mason DSC RANVR (1901-1972). A plantation manager who remained behind when the Japanese invaded, Paul was overage, undersized, slightly deaf, short sighted, gauche and ill-kept. Recruited by Commander Eric Feldt (1913 Pioneer class) into the coastwatching organisation, he was given naval rank as a possible safeguard against being executed as a spy in the event of capture. Also awarded the US DSC for "extraordinary heroism in action", Admiral William Halsey stated that the coastwatchers "saved Guadalcanal" and "Guadalcanal saved the South Pacific".

Chokai and sailed with cruiser *sentai* (division) No.18 at 1430 on 7 August to rendezvous with cruiser *sentai* No.6 from Kavieng, making a force of seven cruisers and one destroyer heading for one of the great naval exploits of the Pacific War.[24]

Just before sunrise on 8 August the cruisers catapulted five Jake floatplanes for reconnaissance. *Aoba*'s Jake had the longest mission, flying 330 miles to Savo Sound and accurately reporting all ships and their dispositions between Tulagi and Guadalcanal. With this intelligence the admiral confirmed his attack intentions and at 1300 set course at 24 knots to pass through the Bougainville Strait and then down the New Georgia Sound. Although sighted by an Allied submarine and aircraft this course was, crucially, out of sight of any coastwatcher who would have broadcast the sighting immediately in plain language, just as they were doing for the Japanese air strikes passing overhead.

Having manned their action stations continuously for 60 hours in the enervating tropical conditions, a modified second degree of readiness was assumed as *Canberra* took up her night screening position astern of *Australia* on the evening of 8 August. Damage control parties and two turret crews were fully closed up as was one 4-inch gun each side and one set of top torpedo tubes. The other two turrets were manned by a communications number and the men off watch were resting near their stations. VAT had seen the Walrus de-fuelled at dusk, keeping it armed with four 100-pound bombs. The ship's guns were not loaded but half the cruiser's armament was ready immediately, the remaining half would be ready within 20 seconds. It was estimated to take 45 seconds from first sighting a target to train the guns and fire, but this proved to be 45 seconds they did not have.

Vice-Admiral Fletcher (Expeditionary Force Commander, *Saratoga*) signalled Vice-Admiral Ghormley (Commander South Pacific, Noumea) at 1807 that evening recommending withdrawal of the carriers. Without waiting for a reply, he immediately turned the Air Support Force south. Intercepting this signal, Rear-Admiral Richmond Turner (Amphibious Force Commander, *McCawley*) summoned Rear-Admiral Crutchley (Screening Group Commander, *Australia*) at 2045 for an urgent conference with General Vandergrift (Marine Commander) aboard his flagship, twenty miles away in the transport area. Lacking the promised air cover Turner felt he had no choice but to withdraw his transports the next day, leaving the marines unsupported with less than half their stores landed. By precipitately leading his carriers out of harm's way, later unsparingly called desertion by Turner, Fletcher sailed away from his responsibilities as Expeditionary Force Commander. He had earned the lasting disdain of the Marine Corps and put at grave risk the Tulagi-Guadalcanal operation.[25]

---

24   A 1910 graduate of the Naval Academy, and later the Naval War College, Mikawa (1888-1981) had been a naval attaché in Paris between ship commands. As a vice-admiral he was second-in-command of the Pearl Harbor Striking Force leading a battleship division. Taking responsibility for the eventual loss of the Solomon Islands he was reassigned to minor commands.

25   The then Rear-Admiral Philip Vian DSO*, commanding the carriers of Force V supporting the landings at Salerno in September 1943, was asked by the commander of the American Fifth Army if he could stay longer despite fuel shortages? Vian replied "My carriers will stay here if we have to row back."

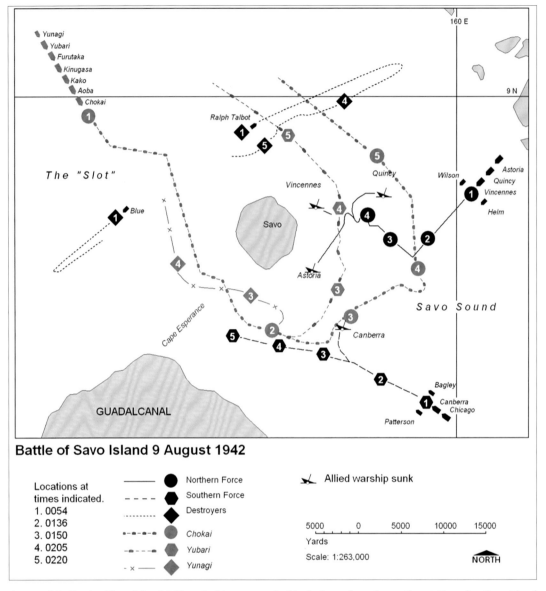

A map of the Battle of Savo Island. Mikawa's ships approached in darkness from the northwest. Rounding Savo Island off the coast of Guadalcanal, they surprised and scored a decisive victory against two groups of Allied cruisers.

Although Captain Bode USN was senior, *Chicago* remained astern of *Canberra*, flanked by the destroyers *Patterson* and *Bailey*, as they continued their screening patrol at 12 knots between Lunga Point and Savo Island. At 2300 *Chokai*, *Aoba* and *Kako* catapulted three Jakes for a final reconnaissance - which reported cruisers south of Savo Island - and to loiter in the area as flare droppers before diverting north to Shortland Island. Supremely proficient at visual night manoeuvres in close company and restricted waters, the IJN had further exercised their cruisers and embarked flights in the tactic of aircraft illuminating targets. At midnight the ships went to action stations, speed was increased to 26 knots, and a battle column astern of *Chokai* was formed.

Several hours after midnight in a Sydney hospital Marjorie Murchison, recovering from the birth of her daughter, was startled by the dressing table picture of her husband Duncan suddenly falling over. Distressed, she called out to a disbelieving nurse "Sister, my husband's been killed!"

When the action alarm sounded at 0143, VAT, having flown several times during the day, was sleeping aft in his cabin. Ten seconds after the alarm started ringing the first hit shook *Canberra*. Dashing to the upper deck and forward to his aircraft he felt the shock waves from explosions as the cruiser was repeatedly struck, hit 24 times in two minutes. To VAT "everything in the world seemed to hit the ship". Reaching the mass of flames enveloping the Walrus and catapult structure he found his entire RAAF flight had already been killed or wounded, only VAT and the naval TAG Harold Davis escaping death or injury.[26]

The northern and southern screening groups had been aware of aircraft overhead after midnight but, dangerously dismissive of IJN night capabilities, assumed they were friendly. Ahead of the groups were two radar equipped picquet destroyers. *Chokai* sighted one of these, the *Blue*, just after 0040. The heavy cruiser slowed to 22 knots, reducing her bow wave, and passed within 500 metres undetected by *Blue*'s lookouts or radar. Once clear, speed was increased to 30 knots and the attack order was given, the airborne observers having reported the position of Allied cruisers. *Canberra*'s newly fitted Type 271 radar, hampered by land returns, also failed to detect the approaching Japanese, whose 34 x 8-inch guns and 60 torpedo tubes were loaded and trained to starboard.

Suddenly *Canberra* and *Chicago* were illuminated by parachute flares from the Jakes overhead. As action stations sounded throughout both ships the Type 93 Long Lance torpedoes and then the guns from the Japanese column were fired at the closest cruiser some 4,500 metres away. With outstanding seamanship, and a large measure of luck, the Japanese had achieved a surprise Nelsonian "crossing the T". Unfortunately, fate had decreed *Canberra* to be lead ship of her column at the point of that T and facing the concentrated fire of six cruisers.

Before *Canberra*'s guns could be brought to bear as the ship turned violently port and then hard to starboard to avoid torpedoes, the first salvo struck, hitting the Walrus, catapult, plotting office, port torpedo space and the 4-inch gun deck. The second salvo hit the compass platform killing several and mortally wounding Captain Getting. This salvo also killed all the watch keepers in A and B boiler rooms and a shell went through the RAAF mess under the catapult mounting. Everyone in the damage control headquarters was killed or wounded as was the USN Liaison Officer, Lieutenant (jg) Joseph Vance Jnr, who had been in the cypher office.[27] *Canberra*'s enemy sighting report, to alert the northern group of four USN cruisers

---

26   Killed in action: Flight Lieutenant Duncan Murchison (26), Corporal Joseph Croft (26), Leading Aircraftmen Geoffrey Chapman (19) and Victor Eggington (30). Died of Wounds: Corporal James McCormack (21). Seriously Wounded: Leading Aircraftman Fred Rivers (35). Slightly Wounded: Leading Aircraftman Donald Poole (29).

27   Ensign Joseph Vance USN (23), torpedo officer of the destroyer *Parrott* at the Battle of Makassar Strait and the Battle of Badoeng Strait, was decorated with the Bronze Star and promoted before reporting aboard *Canberra*. His mother launched the destroyer escort USS *Vance* on 16 July 1943.

and the eastern group which included *Hobart*, was cut off when the power failed. *Chicago* failed to broadcast her own enemy sighting report.

By 0146, the Japanese were hauling away to the north where they sank the cruisers *Astoria*, *Quincy* and *Vincennes* along with their nine Curtiss Seagull floatplanes, leaving *Canberra* a drifting hulk without steam or electrical power. Lacking back-up generators, she had lost all water mains pressure, lighting and communications. There were blazing fires amidships and below decks being fed by exploding ammunition with the deck already listing eight degrees as water flooded into ruptured compartments. Survivors reported that the Walrus burned particularly fiercely with a distinctive crackling roar.

VAT was ever reticent about what he saw in these scant minutes and could never be drawn to describe the following hours in detail. County-class cruisers, sometimes described as "eggshells armed with hammers", were designed to mete out punishment but were not armoured to take this amount in return. The main magazines and 8-inch shell rooms were ordered flooded, which increased the list, but VAT's immediate concerns were in his part of the ship where the blazing aircraft illuminated the grim sight of huddled bodies and wounded on the 4-inch gun deck and the flat below as well as the torpedo space where spare wings and boat stores were burning in the overhead.

The executive officer Commander John Walsh (1919 class), burned and with shrapnel in his back, directed VAT and Lieutenant David Logan, a rugby teammate on that winning 1929 College XV, to the starboard waist to take charge of firefighting. Petrol tanks had been released and pushed over the side as were the 44-gallon drums of aviation fuel adjacent to the torpedo space. This was done by the engineering commander since the stoker detailed for that duty had been killed. Signal halyards were cut from the flag deck to allow buckets to be lowered into the sea as bucket parties were organised to fight the fires amidships. All ammunition that could be reached in the ready-use lockers was dumped overboard amidst constant worry that the aircraft bombs on the burning aircraft would explode. The 4-inch magazine was immediately below the blazing aircraft workshop so it was ordered flooded shortly after 0200.

The port pom-pom magazine, containing spare aircraft bombs, needed to be cleared and the bombs thrown overboard. VAT volunteered to enter the magazine with commissioned Gunner Harold Hardiman MBE and by torchlight, amidst the fumes and smoke, they manhandled the 100-pound bombs, shells and Oerlikon ammunition to be disposed of. In the darkness with occasional heavy rain, lightning added its thunder to the exploding ammunition and decks started to buckle underfoot from the intense heat of the fires.

Some wounded were put into the ship's cutters in case the cruiser capsized, and VAT had all boats and rafts in the water moved forward to comparative safety under the port bow. With the sick bay out of action, stretcher cases were taken to the forecastle. VAT described the ship's doctors as doing a marvellous job, probably thinking in particular of Surgeon Lieutenant Kenneth Morris who had done what he could for the wounded RAAF men under the burning

Walrus, glancing up occasionally to see the flames spreading along the wings to the attached bombs. He cleared the casualties, and himself, just as the wings fell off.[28] Fortunately, the bombs failed to explode. Three medical parties worked frantically on to save as many of the 193 casualties as they could.

Signalling *Patterson* by torchlight, she came alongside at 0325 after initially standing off when further ammunition started exploding. While transferring wounded, *Patterson* relayed the order from Rear-Admiral Turner that if *Canberra* could not be underway by 0630, she was to be abandoned and sunk. *Patterson* had to hurriedly cast off when it was thought an enemy warship was closing the scene. The ship that commenced firing at *Patterson* turned out to be *Chicago*.

All hands were piped to the quarterdeck and forecastle to prepare to abandon ship. While the men were mustering Commander (E) Otto "Mac" McMahon (1914 class), assisted by VAT, attempted to investigate conditions below decks. Soon driven back from the flat spaces because of fires, they realised that even if the ship could be kept afloat, she would be a burned-out hulk unable to raise steam or fight. *Patterson* reported that abandoning ship was delayed as none of *Canberra*'s crew would leave until all the wounded had been passed across. First light came at 0550 and by 0645 every survivor was aboard *Blue* and *Patterson*. The destroyer *Ellet* later sank the floating wreck with torpedoes.

A colourised photo of the Canberra at dawn, still burning and listing 35 degrees. A short time later the wreck was sunk with torpedoes.

All survivors were trans-shipped to the attack transports *Fuller* and *Barnett* which set course for Noumea. Ten of the wounded died on the passage.

Canberra was the eighth ship of the RAN to be lost; the three cruisers (all with embarked flights), three destroyers and two sloops, only being one short of the nine warships in commission in July 1939, just before hostilities commenced.[29] The RAN was now five times the size it had been then with manpower exceeding 24,000. In his official announcement of *Canberra*'s demise the Prime Minister said:

These losses in various theatres show the part being played by the Navy … in the world-wide

28   Only recently qualified, Surgeon Lieutenant Morris RANR (1917-2001) was Mentioned in Despatches for his skill, resolution and coolness aboard *Canberra*. Later qualifying as a surgeon, he performed Australia's first open-heart surgery in 1955.
29   *Waterhen*, 30 June 1941, Mediterranean. *Sydney*, 19 November 1941, Indian Ocean. *Parramatta*, 27 November 1941, Mediterranean. *Perth*, 28 February 1942, Sunda Strait. *Yarra* 4 March 1942, Indian Ocean. *Vampire*, 9 April 1942, Bay of Bengal. *Nestor*, 15 June 1942, Mediterranean. *Canberra*, 9 August 1942, Savo Island.

conflict in which we are engaged with the other parts of the Empire, and the United Nations against the common foe.

In the jungle ashore, the marines, short of ammunition and food, fought on unsupported until a naval convoy arrived on 18 September. Thirty marine fighters and bombers did reach the newly completed Henderson Field at Lunga Point on 20 August. They had launched from the USN's first "baby flattop", the escort carrier *Long Island*, which had approached from Fiji to a launch point 170 miles southeast. For six months the nautical equivalent of attrition trench warfare was fought through six further naval battles until the campaign's victory in February 1943. By that time dozens of ships had followed *Canberra* to the sea floor between Tulagi and Guadalcanal, Savo Sound truly earning the sobriquet "Iron Bottom Sound".

VAT hesitated to be critical post-war but felt that some of the costly lessons learned at Savo Island should have been learnt before the battle took place. A comprehensive analysis by the US Naval War College listed 26 points, ranging from correct location of the expeditionary force commander to functions of a carrier covering force. Many lives were lost for the Allied navies to learn, and in too many cases to re-learn, the lessons of the defeat that night.

Most of the survivors, often like VAT wearing US surplus uniforms, returned to Sydney on 20 August in the transport *President Grant*. They were welcomed by the Governor-General Lord Gowrie VC and Rear-Admiral Muirhead-Gould. Berthed alongside a RAN ship there were officers and men waiting to issue new kit and pay to those not immediately transported to hospital. Also attending were postal officials to accept one free telegram home before the men began survivors' leave. Chalked on a blackboard were samples for those traumatised and having difficulty in deciding what to say: "Expect me home, love" and "Safe and well, proceeding leave tonight, love".

A relieved VAT and Gunner Hardiman, wearing surplus US uniforms, arrive in Sydney on 20 August 1942.

Leading Aircraftman Donald Poole was taken to No. 3 Hospital at Bradfield Park where he slowly recovered. Released from hospital in January 1943, Poole worked as an RAAF stores hand for the rest of the war, to the no-doubt relief of his wife Eveline and children. On discharge in 1945 he was awarded a 20% disability pension. Daphne, wife of Leading Aircraftman Fred Rivers, had been informed her husband was seriously wounded but then nothing further. Writing to the authorities for news several weeks later as "an anxious expectant mother" it transpired that Rivers had gone from the destroyer *Blue* to the *Fuller*, and then to the hospital ship *Solace*. He had further surgery and bone grafts at the USN hospital in Auckland before returning to Sydney in a body cast. Fred was still in the Naval Wing of Randwick's Prince of Wales

Hospital when his daughter Wendy was born. When he returned home a year later one leg was four centimetres shorter than the other and he received a 100% war disability pension.

There is no record, but it is inconceivable that VAT would not have visited the bereaved widows, and those men of the flight recovering in hospital, during the months before he once more left Australian shores.[30]

The final casualty of the Battle of Savo Island occurred on 19 April 1943, when Captain Howard Bode USN, learning that he was to be formally censured for his conduct at Guadalcanal, took his own life.

The Pacific Star, awarded for operational service in the Pacific Theatre of Operations between 8 December 1941 and 2 September 1945.

---

30   Captain Getting's widow Hazel visited Marjorie Murchison with a present for her daughter. Hazel had been told of her husband's death before attending a tea party with other *Canberra* wives where she had to keep the news secret.

135

CHAPTER 8

AIR STAFF OFFICER AFLOAT 1942 – 1944

GUADALCANAL HAD SHOWN CRUISER EMBARKED AIRCRAFT still had value in Pacific fleet operations but, with *Canberra's* loss, VAT as an observer was once again surplus. *Perth* had become the fifth RAN cruiser fitted with a catapult in March 1940. In addition, *Manoora* and *Westralia*, whose conversion to armed merchant cruisers for convoy escort duties had included a seaplane platform and derrick, were allocated flights that same month. The navy's preferred wartime complement of two aircraft per ship the RAAF refused to countenance, since pre-war plans had not allowed for it, and they had neither enough airframes or pilots.

With insufficient observers for even one aircraft per flight in early 1940, the shortage had been made up when two RANR officers were given a rushed four-week local course and three RN observers were loaned, while eight RANR officers volunteered and began training in the UK. By mid-1941 RN policy held that unprotected cruiser aircraft in the Mediterranean were a liability, and *Hobart's* catapult accordingly was removed when she replaced *Perth* in that theatre. Coupled with the loss of three cruisers, this meant there were suddenly more observers than billets.

Australia conducted Coral Sea patrols with her single Walrus in the final months of 1942, fortunate to be in company with *Phoenix* which had three floatplanes embarked. After the loss of Walrus P5715 at Savo Island there were only twenty left in RAAF service, when thirty-two were needed for both air force and navy tasking. The Admiralty was approached and released seven additional Walrus airframes. VAT had been recommended for both a squadron command and for staff duties but, with no naval air squadron or air station organisation in Australia, VAT's employment mandated a return to executive branch service and the inevitable staff appointments.

In this he was following the path of almost all the pre-war observers. Only "Pally" Carr and Harrie Gerrett were still flying as observers aboard *Australia*.[1] Commander Henry Chesterman, the original observer, had left Darwin after a further 36 Japanese air raids and was a senior staff officer for the Naval Commander South West Pacific, while George Oldham was commanding the sloop *Swan*. Another was on an admiral's staff with the Eastern Fleet based in Colombo and one was a staff officer and naval liaison with the American Fifth Air Force. VAT was not yet, however, to experience the dedicated drudgery of desk work in a headquarters ashore. His appointments would take him from a storm-tossed Atlantic into the arctic waters of the Barents Sea and eventually to the battlefields of Normandy.

---

1   Lieutenant-Commander Palgrave Carr KM DFC (1908-1993) was the only RAN officer to be awarded a DFC in WWII. Leaving *Hermes* the day before she was sunk by Japanese aircraft, Carr was later seconded to the RAAF for a secret mining campaign by the famous Catalina "Black Cats". The sole survivor when shot down during a night torpedo attack in the Celebes, Carr was stoic under torture as a POW. Post-war he joined the Bureau of Meteorology.

VAT's initial staff appointment to HMAS *Assault* was a new and unusual one. Admiral Ernest King in mid-February had envisaged establishing a series of strong points "from which a step-by-step general advance could be made" against the Japanese homeland. This island-hopping strategy, in which both Australia's navy and army would take their part, was still being codified after the lessons of Operation *Watchtower*. Port Stephens north of Newcastle was identified by Commander Frederick "Freddie" Cook DSC (1919 class) as the ideal location to train for amphibious landings and it was there that General MacArthur ordered the establishment of the Joint Overseas Operational Training School.[2] The establishment commissioned as *Assault* on 1 September 1942 and VAT joined when his survivor's leave finished a fortnight later. He would have been welcomed by Cook, a Year Officer when the college moved to Flinders Naval Depot in 1929 and VAT was a trusted cadet captain.

Assault was to train army and navy personnel in the employment and handling of landing craft and the tactics of landing over beaches, getting vital stores ashore and the establishment of ship to shore communications. It was the very early days of such operations and with no proper landing craft available, civilian motor cruisers were requisitioned. In those first landing exercises six motor cruisers would tow foldable boats to simulate landing craft.

The HMAS Assault badge.

While buildings and workshops were being constructed, the 8,000-ton AMC *Westralia* was anchored as an accommodation ship for staff and trainees. Her Walrus was disembarked to RAAF Base Rathmines, the seaplane base at Lake Macquarie south of Newcastle, from where they would conduct anti-submarine patrols as the 3,100-ton tender *Ping Wo* went to Newcastle for food, stores and water. *Ping Wo* was a China Navigation Company river steamer requisitioned by the RN in 1941, becoming part of the RAN's "China Fleet" of similar vessels.[3] Another tender, *Allandale*, transported classes to and from Nelson Bay for the landing exercises.

Aboard *Westralia* VAT found in the ship's office a fellow Chatswood local, Leading Writer Jeffrey Britten, to help in his staff duties.[4] Britten had joined the Navy as a 17-year-old probationary writer on the eve of war. He had served in *Sydney* throughout her Mediterranean battles of 1940-41 and was fortunate to have been posted ashore just before that cruiser's loss with all hands. Their respective careers would intertwine regularly as senior and subordinate for the next three decades.

<hr>

2   Later Captain Frederick Cook DSC MiD (1905-1985), the only Australian survivor from *Royal Oak* in 1939 who also survived the sinking of *Curlew* off Narvik in 1940. Commanded the commando training establishment *Tormentor* and decorated for the Bruneval Raid on a German coastal radar station. Participated in amphibious operations in New Guinea, Borneo and the Philippines and was present in Tokyo Bay for the formal Japanese surrender.

3   After the fall of Singapore, with a mixed crew of RNR, RANR and Chinese seamen, *Ping Wo* ("Equitable Harmony") took the disabled destroyer *Vendetta* under tow at 3 knots from Batavia to Fremantle. At 62 days it became the longest tow in RAN history.

4   Later Commodore Jeffrey Britten OBE (1922-1990), the first Australian to rise through every rank from Ordinary Seaman, Second Class, to Commodore. His final posting was as Director General Manpower Division in 1973 before retiring in 1976.

VAT underwent a small but significant uniform change at this time. During WWI wings were awarded to observers of the RNAS and the RFC. Post-war no further "O" wings were awarded although RAF and RN pilots continued to be awarded pilot wings on their graduation. The Admiralty accorded observers specialist status but into the 1930s the perceived attitude was that observers wished to preserve their

The new observer wings insignia introduced in September 1942.

executive branch identity. There was a fear that wings insignia would be interpreted as a shift in allegiance to the very junior air branch, which might damage their career prospects.

By 1942 naval observers were the only unbadged aviators across the entire British air services. With 80% of observers now wartime voluntary aircrew the old peacetime executive branch attitudes were no longer predominant. Rear-Admiral (Naval Air Stations) Clement Moody in 1941 recognised the pent-up demand for observer wings and urged a suitable badge be introduced. On 17 September 1942 badges were approved for commissioned naval observers and rating observers/TAGs. VAT was finally able to wear on his left sleeve the wings he had qualified for almost five years before.

This rather idyllic spring existence at Port Stephens, ignoring an epidemic of mumps and measles onboard *Westralia* in October, did not last long. Churchill announced that to make up for the loss of *Canberra* the RN would transfer the County-class cruiser *Shropshire* to the RAN. *Shropshire* was recalled from the South Atlantic and entered refit at Chatham Dockyard. It had been intended to re-name her *Canberra* but when the USN, in rare tribute, decided to commission one of their impressive 13,600-ton Baltimore-class heavy cruisers as USS *Canberra*, the county name was retained.

Commander "Darbo" Harries, whose minesweeping *Seagull* had safely seen *Ark Royal* to and from her anchorage at Scapa Flow, was posted from naval attaché duties in Washington to temporary command of the refitting cruiser.[5] Suddenly an observer was needed again, and VAT was appointed after only ten weeks at *Assault*. On completion of pre-embarkation leave VAT took charge of an initial draft of men for *Shropshire*.

The first leg was sailing to New Zealand in the huge 81,000-ton *Queen Mary*, the Cunard liner converted to a troopship in Sydney and known as the Grey Ghost. It was capable of carrying over 10,000 troops unescorted, relying on her average 29 knots to avoid submarines. After several days in Auckland the journey continued aboard *Rimutaka* via the Panama Canal, celebrating Christmas and New Year on passage. Overall, it was a pleasant voyage to New York for VAT, especially since waiting for a UK bound convoy allowed several days of sightseeing and shopping. On disembarking in Avonmouth the draft travelled by train to Chatham.

It must have been an unpleasant surprise for VAT, and perhaps for Navy Office in Melbourne,

---

5   The Halcyon-class minesweeper *Seagull* was the first "rivet-less" ship in the RN, being all welded.

The HMAS Shropshire badge.

Decorated Shropshire officers: "Braces" Bracegirdle is third from left next to VAT whose facial injury, suffered while hooking up a Walrus for re-embarkation on the Canberra, is still prominent.

that although appointed to stand-by *Shropshire* as her observer he discovered on joining that her EIIH catapult had been removed by the dockyard weeks before.

Being freed of that topside weight enabled a myriad of close-range anti-aircraft weapons to be fitted, reflecting the combat needs experienced in all theatres where enemy aircraft ranged. The previous fit of 4 x 4-inch, 4 x 3-inch and 4 x 2-pounders was expanded to 8 x 4-inch, 18 x 20mm Oerlikons (in seven twin and four single mounts) and 2 x 8 barrelled pom-poms. In addition, torpedo tubes and depth charge racks along with the latest radar and sonar were installed.

Also standing by the refitting cruiser was the gunnery officer, Lieutenant-Commander Warwick "Braces" Bracegirdle DSC (1925 class).[6] What gunnery officer would not have been delighted with this increased secondary armament? A disappointed VAT, however, requested appointment to the RN Fleet Air Arm. Any impatience he may have felt waiting for his request to be approved was not reflected in his efficiency. The sole seaman lieutenant under two lieutenant-commanders he carried out all duties with his usual zeal and energy. VAT had seen Bracegirdle graduate from the college in 1928 and it was his father, then Captain Leighton Bracegirdle DSO MiD**, who had exposed Midshipman Smith's subterfuge in swapping King's Medalists at the 1932 award ceremony aboard *Canberra*.

Amid the dockyard dreariness it would have been some mollification when VAT was notified in February that compensation of £200 sterling had been agreed for the loss of his uniforms and other belongings that went down with *Ark Royal*. Two months later he received £125 Australian for the loss of his effects in *Canberra*.

---

6   Later Commander Warwick "Braces" Bracegirdle DSC**MiD*. The gunnery officer when *Shropshire* and others sank the battleship *Yamashira*, Bracegirdle commanded *Bataan* during the Korean War. His father Rear-Admiral Sir Leighton Bracegirdle was known as "Brace" and his daughter Phillada was known as "Bracelet".

The RN's eleventh escort carrier, HMS *Tracker*, had commissioned on 31 January 1943, in Portland, Oregon. Another twenty "Woolworth carriers" were due to commission that year alone and, from April 1943 the first of nineteen Merchant Aircraft Carriers started coming into service.[7] With this expansion of the FAA there was an extreme shortage of qualified observers, most especially general list officers with the level of operational experience VAT held. *Tracker*'s delivery voyage across the Atlantic had ferried aircraft to Casablanca. It then took ten weeks at Harland and Wolff's dockyard in Belfast to modify the carrier to RN standards. Losing the ice cream maker, she gained a Type 272 surface search radar and extra safety measures for aviation fuel stowage recommended after the loss of *Dasher*. The hangar was modified, and British guns replaced the American.

Captain John Collins CB took command of HMS *Shropshire* on 7 April with Harries as his executive officer, the main draft of ten officers and 426 men arriving two weeks later. Many of this draft were survivors of Savo Island. Commissioned HMAS on 20 April, the long refit was not finished until June, and she sailed for Scapa Flow at the start of July. There the cruiser was inspected by King George VI before sailing for Australia in August. But VAT was not onboard to salute his King having travelled south from the Orkneys on the "Jellicoe Express". His transfer request had been approved and he had been appointed to *Tracker* as her air staff officer.

VAT left *Shropshire* with an impressive personal endorsement from Collins, perhaps the premier RAN officer of the war who assessed VAT's leadership and personal qualities as outstanding. Having watched him as a duty commanding officer, he commented that VAT was:

> … an outstanding officer who despite his eagerness to continue his observer duties applied himself loyally and energetically to his ship's duties. It was with regret that I agreed to the loan of this able officer to the RN in view of shortage of observers.

There was additional welcome news when VAT heard that he now had two nephews, John and Peter, his sister Bess having been delivered of twins by Caesarean section on 3 July. Tragedy quickly struck the young family when she suffered severe puerperal sepsis after returning home with her new-borns to Chatswood. Bess was re-admitted to Prince Henry Hospital, but died on 6 August of total kidney failure, aged only 23.[8]

Reporting to *Condor*/Naval Air Station Arbroath, VAT was given a week's training in his new duties before joining the 14,170-ton *Tracker* on 21 July in Belfast. Wearing the two and a half stripes of an acting lieutenant-commander, in accord with his new role, VAT walked the smallest flight deck he had yet experienced at only 442 x 80 feet. It was not armoured as the *Ark*'s had been but was Oregon pine (naturally) laid over mild steel plate. There were nine arrester wires, three barriers, two lifts and one hydraulic accelerator. Embarked capacity was twenty aircraft, crew numbered 646 and she was designed for a service life of only three years.

---

7   A working grain or oil bulk carrier with a flight deck added and three or four Swordfish embarked.
8   A distraught John Hall was unable to come to terms with the loss and abandoned the twins. John and Peter were lovingly raised by their uncle Donald Hall and ageing grandparents.

The new escort carrier HMS Tracker in 1944 with two Swordfish of No. 816 Squadron parked forward.

Approaching maximum speed of 18 knots, escort carriers would take on a hull resonance that their officers delicately described as a "honeymoon motion".

The small box island was only 14 feet wide with barely room on the bridge for captain and commander (air) to take a worried six paces fore and aft. Underneath the flight deck was a gallery deck and the sea cabins of all who must be on immediate call: captain, navigator and the air staff officer. Adjacent was VAT's new home - the Air Operations Room - with the meteorology office and signals office close by. Here he would gather and co-ordinate the intelligence to efficiently task and brief. In many respects the safety and fighting ability of *Tracker* rested on his shoulders.

Admiralty decrypts of U-boat transmissions and *Kriegsmarine* orders, western approaches situation reports, signals from other ships and aircraft; all would be incorporated by VAT into his plot, the big chart in the operations room. Showing the tactical situation at a glance, its coloured pin heads represented the carriers, escorts, convoys and U-boats in the North Atlantic.

The commander (air), Lieutenant-Commander Alexander Harding DSC, had commanded No. 823 (Swordfish) Squadron the previous year. He was responsible for flying on and immediately around the carrier while VAT as air staff officer was responsible, in consultation with the captain, for the tasking of those aircraft and their effective use in action. Together they ensured the ship became a warship with aircraft able to patrol and strike out to a range of several hundred miles. From the operations room VAT, having tasked the squadron, would brief the aircrew on the tactical situation in the immediate area of operations and give them their orders. This would include known enemy dispositions and hostile aircraft, expected friendly aircraft on patrol and Allied vessels, plus the all-important weather and wind conditions.

"Hands to flying stations" was first piped on 9 August for deck landing trials with a Swordfish. Several days later No. 816 Squadron embarked nine Swordfish IIs and six Seafire fighters from *Shrike*/Naval Air Station Maydown. VAT knew this squadron as it had been with the *Ark* for several months before she went down. After reforming, No. 816 Squadron had been aboard the escort carrier *Dasher* when she blew up in March 1943 with only 149 survivors. Reformed again, the unit was suffering from low morale after so many losses and the new commanding officer, Lieutenant-Commander (P) Fred "Freddie" Nottingham DSC RNVR, would rally them in his South African accent saying: "Fly with me, lads, and you'll live to see your grandchildren." Freddie himself had been fortunate to be disembarked ashore with his previous squadron when *Hermes* had been sunk in the Indian Ocean.[9]

Working up the ship's air department and squadron in the Firth of Clyde there were two major accidents. A Swordfish went over the side during night deck landings killing two of the crew and Captain Godfrey Dickins, an FAA pilot since 1925, was seriously injured while inspecting the accelerator (catapult) machinery. He was replaced by Captain Donal McGrath MiD*, a black van Dyke bearded WWI torpedo-boat skipper who had commanded nine destroyers between the wars. Entering harbour at full speed he was soon known as "Dangerous Dan" for his habit of handling the carrier as if one of his destroyers. In early September *Tracker* was temporarily used by No. 767 Squadron, the deck landing training squadron, with its inevitable heavy landings and an embarrassing barrier entry by the squadron's commanding officer.

Carriers were a prime target and had suffered heavy losses proportionate to their numbers: *Courageous*, *Glorious*, *Ark Royal*, *Hermes* and *Eagle* all being sunk by August 1942. Escort carriers were desperately needed in the ongoing Battle of the Atlantic, most especially in the mid-Atlantic where a deadly "air gap" existed between 30 and 40 degrees west out of range of coastal command aircraft from Ireland, Iceland or Newfoundland. Half the length and one third the displacement of a fleet carrier and taking a fraction of the time to construct, the first of 45 escort carriers was commissioned in June 1941. Constructed in both US and UK yards, often from mercantile hulls purchased on stocks, their main machinery, whether diesel or steam turbine on a single shaft, could rarely exceed 17 knots. Not expected to keep up with the faster fleet carriers, their usefulness was, however, immediately valued. Unarmoured, intensely susceptible to torpedo and fire, the first few were rushed into service with lower standards of safety and by mid-1943 three had been lost. This vulnerability was accepted given the desperate lack of alternatives.

Once sufficient were available for the convoy escort role more specific tasking was given as ever more hulls commissioned. Relieving the bigger carriers from deck landing training duties, they also found wide use as ferry carriers. The Admiralty had recognised since early

---

9   Embarking with No. 854 (Avenger) Squadron on *Illustrious* in early 1945 Freddie's port wing was shot off attacking targets in the Sakishima Gunto Islands and he parachuted into the Pacific. His crew were killed but Freddie was picked up by the submarine *Kingfisher* where he remained for six weeks until her patrol ended. After the war he returned to South Africa where he died in 2005.

in 1943 that two carriers per convoy would be optimal. When not needed as close escort they would be assigned to detached hunter/killer groups, or converted to assault carriers, providing fighter air-cover over invasion beaches until airfields were captured ashore. This was done by *Avenger* during the November 1942 landings in North Africa before she was torpedoed off Gibraltar with only twelve survivors. By September 1943's invasion of Sicily, two fleet carriers and four escort carriers were able to be among the RN forces assembled.

On completion of work-up *Tracker* was allocated to Western Approaches Command for trade protection duties. She sailed from the Clyde on 23 September 1943 for anti-submarine operations as an Air Support Group working in conjunction with surface groups. The Battle of the Atlantic was still on the cusp. In November 1940 Captain Fogarty Fegen VC in *Jervis Bay* had been the only escort for convoy HX.84. The next month VAT and his pilot had been the sole air asset among a convoy's seven escorting destroyers and sloops, available for a one-shot sortie from *Pegasus*. CAM ships had then held the line against the Focke-Wulf Condors but not the U-boats. This was remedied when the first escort carrier *Audacity* embarked Swordfish and sailed with Convoy OG.74 in September 1941. August 1942 marked the first month that more U-boats were sunk than were coming into service, but the battle remained fierce.

From September 1942 to June 1943 a further 700 ships, totalling four million tons, were sunk by U-boats. Thrown into the battle were increasing air assets, both shore-based and at sea, improved sonar, radar and HF/DF (huff-duff) direction-finding equipment. Torpex gave 50% more depth charge explosive power than TNT and the new surface group tactics were using it to deadly effect. U-boats introduced radar detection, increased their anti-aircraft gun armament and each boat loaded some Gnat acoustic torpedoes specifically to target manoeuvring escorts. Although Karl Dönitz had been promoted to grand admiral and was now *Oberbefehlshaber der Kriegsmarine*, Commander-in-Chief of the Navy, he retained personal control of the U-boat force. After committing that force to a mid-summer blitz, there had followed a brief lull, but now the autumn offensive was in the offing, Dönitz being well aware of the need to curtail the Allied build up for the forecast invasion of Europe.

VAT briefing aircrew in Tracker's Air Operations Room.

VAT encouraged the pilots and observers to drop in at any time and study his plot, holding that the more they knew about any forthcoming operation the better. When decrypts showed that U-boats were being directed to intercept a convoy, *Tracker* raced to support, and VAT said it was "interesting". When his plot showed a concentration of 30 U-boats in their path VAT described the tactical situation as "interesting". After the war when questioned about his wartime experiences he would reply that they had been "interesting"! VAT told his eager aircrew that:

A No. 816 Squadron Swordfish aboard Tracker in October 1943 having its wings unfolded ready for flight.

> … it'll be two or three days before we can expect any fun. But for the next three days we shan't need to do any flying; Coastal Command is giving us air cover, so we'll save our aircraft for the real fight.

When they joined the first convoy, VAT put up a separate plot showing the positions, names and numbers of all 57 ships; as he would for the next twelve convoys *Tracker* helped protect.

For six months *Tracker* with No. 816 Squadron operated to a roving brief in conjunction with surface forces; sometimes working as close escort to a particular convoy expected to be under attack, or as a separate striking force to find and break up U-boat packs before attacks could develop. First covering convoy ON.203 from Liverpool to New York with the Canadian 4th Escort Group, they switched mid-ocean to Johnnie Walker's famous 2nd Support Group. A typical Western Approaches tasking signal to them read:

> If no indication of U-boats in vicinity leave convoy at 1800 and sweep on course 170° as far as 49° North.

Captain Frederick "Johnnie" Walker CB DSO* in *Starling* would have a long association with *Tracker*. Passed over for promotion pre-war, he was now the RN's foremost U-boat hunter. The prime instigator of aggressive group tactics to seek out and destroy, he created creeping and barrage attacks while holding down a contact until it was sunk or had to surface short of oxygen, where it would be destroyed by gunfire or ramming. Not a believer in huddling around a convoy waiting for an attack, his group would form a patrol line and hunt down a huff-duff bearing from a U-boat transmission or aircraft sighting. Once it was acquired by sonar, Walker had a sixth sense for anticipating the U-boats' evasive tactics. Joining *Tracker*, becoming one of an eventual five hunter-killer groups each with an escort carrier, he already had a score of twelve and played *A-Hunting We Will Go* over his ship's loud hailer when leaving harbour.[10] Amongst his decorations a grateful Admiralty later backdated his seniority two years to make up for his stalled peace-time career.

---

10 The five escort carriers were *Tracker, Archer, Avenger, Biter* and the USS *Bogue*.

One early example among many during these months was when wolf pack *Siegfried*, eighteen strong, was formed in late October. Using enigma decrypts the Allies diverted most convoys south and designated the empty ships of convoy ON.207 to be a "bait convoy" sent directly towards the pack. The *Biter* escort carrier group were in close escort, while Walker's group with *Tracker* patrolled nearby as did another support group under Commander Peter Gretton DSO* DSC and the coastal command B-24s which were in range. *U-274* was attacked with rockets by a B-24 and then Gretton in *Duncan* with *Vidette* in company destroyed her with depth charges.

Fair weather in the gap would herald an intense flying effort well above the normal routine of dawn and dusk patrols. In one two-day period there were always two Swordfish airborne on patrol. In a single 24-hour period 21 sorties, each of more than two hours, were flown and VAT would have briefed every sortie. Even when no U-boats were sighted the presence of the aircraft would keep them submerged, unable to track the convoy or get in attack position, and even deterring them away completely.

Foul weather would often severely curtail flying. With the sea state barely marginal on 29 October, Walker from *Starling* watched anxiously as returning Swordfish attempted to land:

> … in half a gale in the middle of the Atlantic on a pint-sized flight deck like *Tracker*'s.

The first found the flight deck plunging down just as he cut power, overshooting the arrester wires to meet the now rapidly rising deck to be bounced over the side and rescued by the hovering *Wren*. The next landed safely and a third broke its undercarriage and wings, essentially crashing on deck. Captain McGrath signalled Walker:

> Many thanks for your help and moral support. My pilots have resumed their poker … and seem to wonder what all the fuss was about.

Walker chuckled as he turned to his XO commenting:

> Those chaps have got guts!

The third Swordfish which landed on Tracker in heavy seas on 29 October 1943, smashing its undercarriage and wings.

During a southeast gale in early November while covering convoy HX.264, a roll of 52 degrees was recorded by *Tracker*. This caused aircraft and stores to break free in the hangar, as flooding from a broken water line threatened to capsize the ship from the dangerous free-surface effect.[11] By the time all was secured again only three aircraft remained undamaged.

---

11   The weight of only a few inches of water on the hangar deck shifting with the ship's movement will change the centre of gravity and markedly increase the danger of capsizing. Try carrying a large tray with water in it.

Moving south to seek calmer weather, the escorts ran down a radar contact to sink *U-226* which had been lining up to attack *Tracker*. Several hours later a huff-duff bearing from *U-842* was plotted. While *Tracker's* Swordfish kept the U-boat down Walker in *Starling* attacked and then directed *Wild Goose* in a creeping attack. Walker was theatrically stomping on his cap thinking the second attack a failure when an underwater explosion brought wreckage and human remains to the surface.

Walker had seen *Audacity*, disregarding his "suggestions" to her more senior captain, torpedoed in December 1941 while escorting convoy HG.76. Although no blame was attached to him - indeed his group had just sunk four U-boats and he was awarded the DSO - he still felt partially responsible. Walker begrudged allocating ships from his group to screen a valuable carrier when he thought they would be better used hunting down U-boats with him. This attitude was especially prominent when the weather was foul and the carrier a target only, unable to launch aircraft to patrol and fight. *Audacity* though, in her fourteen weeks' service had proved the concept of escort carriers. Admiral Sir Max Horton, whose aggressive drive VAT had served under when *Australia* was part of Horton's First Cruiser Squadron in 1935 during the Abyssinian crisis, was now Commander-in-Chief Western Approaches and insisted Walker had a carrier when available.

On 8 November, in yet another Atlantic gale, *U-648* of the *Siegfried* pack, got within 2,000 metres of *Tracker* and fired three torpedoes at her. Aboard Tracker VAT had been more concerned that the aircraft did not again break their lashings than he was about the possibility of being torpedoed in such foul weather. All three missed as did the homing torpedo fired at

A Swordfish comes into land on Tracker after another anti-submarine patrol over the Atlantic. Note the rockets under the wings, for use against surfaced submarines.

Starling. As the ships, short of fuel, escaped behind rain squalls, VAT reflected on the irony that *Tracker's* aircraft had not had a submarine kill, rather the nearest they got was the other way around. One squadron line book entry for this period noted:

Very bad weather, and the biggest sea yet. No flying, much poker!

Tracker's squadron ready room, originally designed for briefing and fitted with the most comfortable chairs in the ship was the aircrew's usual gathering place. Wearing an odd assortment of sea-going clothes, usually old grey flannel trousers and a knitted sweater topped with a naval jacket, the aircrew would squat on the deck for hours playing poker. With several always trying to grow straggly beards to belie their youth, VAT fondly described the assemblage as:

Like a lot of thugs out of *Rake's Progress* gambling in a graveyard.

The almost continuous gales had damaged all the ships in the group. After disembarking her squadron to US Naval Air Station Argentia, Newfoundland, *Tracker* underwent dockyard repairs in Norfolk, Virginia. The repaired and repainted *Tracker* covering convoy HX.279 with the 2nd Support Group encountered yet more severe weather. They were back in the Clyde by 25 December where VAT joined the other officers in the naval tradition of serving Christmas dinner to the ship's company, followed by a concert in the hangar.

No. 816 Squadron disembarked with her Swordfish and Seafires to *Merlin*/Naval Air Station Donibristle. On 4 January 1944, No. 846 Squadron, the first composite Wildcat/Avenger squadron, embarked with twelve Avengers and four Wildcat fighters. Captain McGrath was replaced by Captain John Huntley and told him that VAT was a very zealous, conscientious and capable air staff officer who was a strong influence on the young FAA officers. McGrath also reported that VAT's staff work was sound and precise, and his ideas were always good. Noted now as having an excellent sense of humour, VAT was loyal, intrepid and a pleasant shipmate. Captain Huntly in turn would later record his own admiration for VAT as a real worker who knew his job thoroughly and was an asset to the carrier.

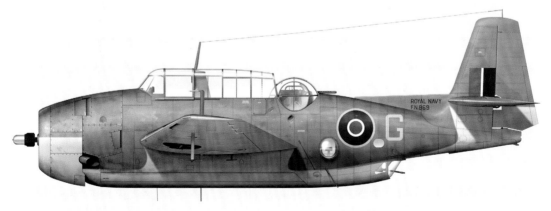

A Grumman Avenger of No. 846 Squadron, in which type VAT would get airborne when the opportunity arose from the carrier Tracker in early 1944.

Working up the new squadron saw four accidents (two Avengers and two Wildcats) and four fatalities before they joined *Biter* with her No. 811 (Swordfish/Wildcat) Squadron, becoming Air Group Two. The continual commissioning of new escort carriers now allowed two carriers to operate together for convoy escort, enabling one to focus on an anti-submarine duty and one to be a fighter carrier. In February 1944 *Tracker* and *Biter* were deployed to cover Gibraltar convoys. VAT had not been impressed with the Seafires' usefulness on a small flight deck and found the Avenger/Wildcat combination far more suitable.[12] When able VAT would get airborne in the large three-crew Grumman Avenger to familiarise himself with the capabilities of this latest American built type.

Gibraltar convoys enjoyed calmer weather, indeed sometimes too calm. In the Bay of Biscay *Tracker*, even at full speed, was unable to get sufficient wind over the deck to launch her Avengers for several days, losing one, with the crew picked up by *Clover*. The Wildcats could still be catapulted aloft. When he was able to send out Avengers, VAT could have patrols up to 200 miles from *Tracker* at a speed several times that of a Swordfish. A week alongside in Gibraltar at the end of February, with No. 846 Squadron disembarked to North Front, would have brought back memories of more desperate days with Force H for him. While covering the combined convoy SL.150/MKS.41 on 10 March *U-575* sank the corvette *Asphodel* at 0154. When an acoustic torpedo hit the stern of a small corvette it would often set off the readied depth charges, as this one did, leaving only five survivors. VAT sent out four Avengers hunting the U-boat, but they failed to find any trace of it.

Tracker gave a welcome week's leave to most when she reached Liverpool. VAT was not in the habit of taking all his leave, indeed Australia House compensated him several hundred pounds that January in lieu of many months of accumulated annual leave he had not taken since the start of the war. Perhaps he considered that two lots of survivor's leave along with foreign service leave had been sufficient time away from his duties? On 25 March *Tracker* sailed for Scapa Flow to join the Home Fleet where her aircraft were needed for the next convoy to Russia.

Described as "the worst journey in the world", the Arctic convoys were the lifeblood of the Russian front - but undertaken at a dreadful price. The disastrous losses of convoy PQ.17 in June 1942, when 22 of the 36 strong convoy were sunk, showed that protective air cover was just as desperately needed in the Arctic air gap as it was in mid-Atlantic or Mediterranean. A Russian convoy's passage, where no Allied land-based air cover was possible for perilous days, skirted the ice pack as far as possible from the long Norwegian coastline with its numerous Luftwaffe airfields and those remote northern fjords hiding *Luftwaffe* catapult ships and *Kriegsmarine* capital ships.

After a pause to consider losses and tactics, the following convoy PQ.18 in September 1942, had been escorted by a large force which included *Avenger*. Losing "only" 13 out of 39 vessels

---

12   During the July 1943 invasion of Sicily D-day began with 106 Seafires. Three days later only 39 remained available, the majority lost or damaged due to landing accidents in the low wind conditions.

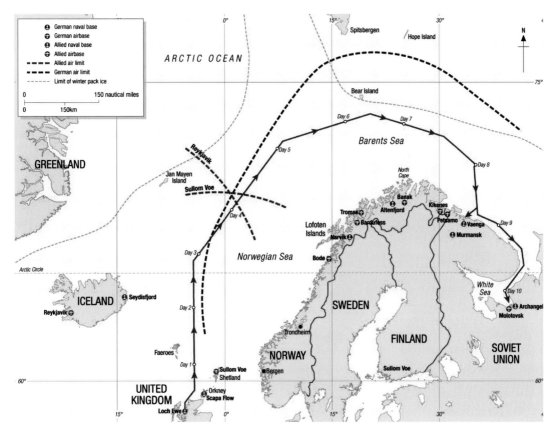

A map showing the ten-day voyage of the UK-Russia convoys. After day four these convoys went beyond the range of Allied land-based air cover and faced attack from German aircraft based in Norway.

the escort carrier's embarked Sea Hurricanes and Swordfish had helped close that Arctic air gap, but no further carriers could be spared until *Chaser* escorted convoy JW.57 in February 1944. Two carriers per convoy was only finally achieved with JW.58 in March 1944 when *Tracker* arrived at Scapa to join *Activity*.

Enigma decrypts reported the battleship *Tirpitz* repaired and in northern Norway's Altenfjord. Convoy JW.58 was to be formed around the US cruiser *Milwaukee*, a gift from the US to Russia now under RN protection. Walker was told that no matter what, *Milwaukee* was to arrive safely, avoiding Churchill the embarrassment of explaining to Roosevelt and Stalin its sinking. To deal with a possible sortie against the convoy by *Tirpitz* was *Tungsten*, a distant cover force, comprising two battleships, two fleet carriers, four escort carriers and eighteen cruisers and destroyers. Admiral Dönitz in Berlin had decreed that JW.58 "must not be allowed to get through unscathed".

When the convoy of 49 merchantmen, the largest convoy to Russia ever assembled, sailed from Loch Ewe on 27 March, 33 warships had been gathered for local and close escort under Rear-Admiral Frederick Dalrymple-Hamilton flying his flag in the new anti-aircraft cruiser *Diadem*. *Tracker* had twelve Avengers and seven Wildcats embarked while *Activity*'s No. 819 Squadron

The 1 April 1944 fire after Avenger "L" (FN877) struck Tracker's round down and crashed.

had three Swordfish and seven Wildcats. Rendezvousing on 29 March, *Milwaukee* was positioned in the centre of the convoy lines protected by the bulk of the merchantmen. The carriers operated to the rear of the convoy where they were free to manoeuvre while launching and recovering aircraft. Twenty destroyers and four corvettes in addition to Johnnie Walker's sloops of the 2nd Support Group surrounded them all.

Walker promptly destroyed *U-961*. The submarine was on passage to the Atlantic when it was literally stumbled upon by *Starling*. It is doubtful that the crew of 48 were even aware they were under attack. Two Wildcats from *Activity* shot down a reconnaissance Ju 88D-1 on 30 March, but the aircraft's sighting report saw twelve U-boats form attack groups *Blitz*, *Hammer* and *Thor* of four boats each. These groups patrolled a line southwest of Bear Island, while another five boats were hurried towards the fray. From 31 March the convoy was almost continually shadowed, but at a cost to the *Luftwaffe*. VAT plotted a long range Fw 200 Condor and had Wildcats launched to intercept (vectored by a Fighter Direction Officer), becoming No. 846 and *Tracker*'s first kill. Meanwhile Wildcats from *Activity* accounted for two more. All twenty crew members of the three Condors were lost. One Wildcat was written off in *Tracker*'s crash barrier. From the early morning of 1 April, the seventeen converging U-boats began their attacks - eighteen over the next 48 hours - and VAT's plot needed continual updating.

The first day of April started poorly for *Tracker*, when patrolling Avenger "L" spotted a U-boat at 0952 but could not release its depth charges while evading fire. VAT recalled the aircraft as the U-boat submerged. On final approach the Avenger flew into the round down despite signals from the deck landing control officer to go-around. The serious fire on the aft end of the flight deck and on the quarterdeck below, with both aircraft and ship's ammunition exploding inside it, took fifteen minutes to get under control. The pilot, a mass of flames, had stumbled into the hangar before dying. His observer was seriously burned, the TAG was severely shocked and one gunner from a Bofors mounting was slightly burned.

Later that morning Avenger "H" damaged *U-355* with rockets, allowing her to be finished off by *Beagle*. A Wildcat shared with one of *Activity*'s fighters in the destruction of a BV 138C-1 seaplane and her five crew in the afternoon. During the evening Sub-Lieutenant (A) Allen

Ballentyne RNVR (22) was buried at sea, with all ships in the convoy lowering their ensigns to half-mast during the service.

Two more aircraft were lost the next day, one in a barrier crash and the other during a strafing attack on a U-boat, going so low that he hit the conning tower and had to ditch. After monotonous months of patrols, it was a known problem that many aircrew, when finally in action against a U-boat, allowed their excited aggression to outweigh sound airmanship. Sub-Lieutenant (A) Tom Lucey RNVR managed to rapidly get out of the freezing water into his dinghy and incredibly was still alive when recovered by *Beagle* almost two hours later. *Keppel*, screening 25 miles from the convoy that evening conducted a successful forward hedgehog attack on *U-360*.

At dawn on 3 April *Tracker*'s loudspeakers suddenly piped:

> Flight and aircraft handling parties fall in at the forward end of the hangar at the hurry ... squadron commander and duty aircrew report to the air staff officer in the Air Operations Room at the hurry. Range a strike of one Wildcat and one Avenger immediately. Hands to flying stations.

U-288 had been sighted on the surface to the convoy's starboard quarter by *Activity*'s patrolling Swordfish "C" at 0518. *Oberleutnant zur See* Willi Meyer's gunners took the slow Swordfish under heavy anti-aircraft fire and the observer called for assistance. VAT immediately tasked an Avenger and a Wildcat on standby to strike, briefing the crews while *Tracker* turned out of the convoy lines into the wind as *Starling* and *Magpie* of the 2nd Support Group raced to the scene. Less than fifteen minutes after the order to ready aircraft was given, both aircraft launched.

Avenger "G" and Wildcat "Y" were on the scene at 0543 and positioned themselves for combined strikes. Meyer was determined to fight it out on the surface, trying to always keep his stern towards the aircraft, presenting a smaller target and allowing most of his flak

U-288 under attack by aircraft from Activity and Tracker on 3 April 1944. The picture was taken from the attacking Avenger.

armament to bear. The Wildcat used up 1,300 rounds attempting to silence those flak guns while the Avenger on her first run was unable to release its depth charges. *Activity*'s Swordfish then attacked with rockets, scoring multiple hits and *U-288* started to founder. The Avenger attacked again, managing to release its depth charges this time and straddling the U-boat with explosions close to the conning tower. Shortly afterwards the submarine itself

A No. 846 Squadron Wildcat fighter "at readiness" on the deck of Tracker. While escorting convoy JW.58 to Russia VAT faced the constant problem of keeping the flight deck relatively free of ice so the aircraft could operate.

sank and exploded with no survivors from the 49 crew.

When *Starling* and *Magpie* arrived they found Meyer's cap, with its distinctive U-boat commander's white cover, floating among the grim and oily detritus of the kill.

Closely following the staunch early defence of the convoy Vice-Admiral Sir Bruce Fraser aboard *Duke of York* decided that his *Tungsten* force no longer needed to be held in readiness as distant cover. By 3 April, as *Tracker's* aircraft were attacking *U-288*, Fraser was in position off Norway to launch 82 aircraft from his carriers against *Tirpitz*. Launching off *Victorious* in his Albacore Sub-Lieutenant Jeffrey "Jeff" Gledhill RNZNVR struck the battleship with his armour piercing bomb, one of several hits that put *Tirpitz* out of action yet again.

When Convoy JW.58 met the Russian local escorts and entered Kola Inlet for Murmansk on 4 April, they had not lost a single merchantman. VAT had played a small part in the most successful Arctic convoy of the war, where there could be no greater demonstration of the vital role naval air power now played to ensure effective sea power. Not a single attack had got through to the convoy lines, four U-boats had been destroyed and six shadowing aircraft shot down. German high command imaginatively claimed nine destroyers sunk, but the only Allied losses were seven aircraft including those damaged beyond repair.

The return convoy RA.58, which sailed on 7 April, benefited when the *Luftwaffe* refused to fly further daylight reconnaissance missions, restricting themselves to short night flights with radar searches. Accordingly, they did not locate the convoy until 9 April. The ten U-boats of packs *Donner* and *Kiel* failed to make any successful attacks and all 38 empty merchantmen arrived safely in the UK.[13] *Tracker* returned to Belfast and entered dock on 16 April to repair the damage from the Avenger crash and fire. VAT was lucky not to endure more trying weeks in dockyard, as he was appointed six days later to secret staff duties in London.

The Arctic Star was approved by Queen Elizabeth II in 2012 for retrospective award to those who served north of the Arctic Circle. The award, primarily intended to commemorate service in the Arctic convoys to north Russia, was issued to Mark Smith who applied on behalf of his late father.

The Arctic Star.

---

13 The Arctic convoy route was twice that of a Mediterranean convoy and both routes were constrained in the ability to manoeuvre compared with Atlantic convoys. Of the ships which sailed in the 78 Russian convoys 5.7% were lost compared with an overall convoy loss rate during the war of 0.33%. One escort carrier was severely damaged and two cruisers, six destroyers and eight corvettes sunk as were 30 U-boats.

D-Day, Normandy, 6 June 1944

At 0502 on 6 June Lieutenant Kenneth Hudspeth DSC* RANVR, a trainee schoolteacher from Tasmania, surfaced his midget submarine *X-20* off the invasion beach *Juno*.[14] The 30-ton craft had been slipped from her tow at 0430 on 3 June and slowly made her submerged way towards the Normandy beaches. On the night of 3-4 June Hudspeth crossed the German minefield on the surface before submerging again, reaching his marking position off the beach at 0400. The five crew, in a compartment measuring just 5 feet 8 inches by 5 feet, had then lain submerged and short of oxygen close inshore for two days. On surfacing, they immediately raised a telescopic mast and the periscope to which were attached lights, a radar beacon and a naval ensign to act as navigation markers for the approaching invasion forces. Preceded by the naval bombardment the first of 187 ships making up the *Juno* assault force reached their lowering position at 0550.

Lieutenant Kenneth Hudspeth who captained midget submarine X-20 on 6 June 1944.

Among the 7,000 vessels, including 1,213 warships and 2,490 assault craft, involved in the largest amphibious operation ever attempted, there were several thousand Australians not far behind Hudspeth, serving in the landing craft, motor torpedo boats, minesweepers and destroyers at the British/Canadian landing beaches of *Gold*, *Juno* and *Sword* and the US beaches *Omaha* and *Utah*. One of the 10,000 allied casualties on D-Day was Sub-Lieutenant Richard Pirrie RANVR, killed when a shell hit his landing craft approaching *Juno* beach on this his 24th birthday.

VAT was aboard the 11,500-ton *Southern Prince*, a temporary headquarters ship in the 600 vessel 100 mile long queue going back to the Solent off Portsmouth. Also in the Solent was Australia's first naval aviator, the recently retired Air Chief Marshal Sir Arthur Longmore. Unwilling to miss out on this great enterprise Sir Arthur, who had left his torpedo-boat command in 1911 to fly with the first RN aviator's course, had joined the yachtsmens' emergency service and was skipper of motor fishing vessel *MFV 124* working as a tender to the invasion fleet.

Leaving *Tracker* in April, no longer an acting lieutenant-commander as he had been promoted in March, VAT was among the influx of new junior staff officers joining the senior invasion planners who had been working from mid-1943, an indication the long-awaited D-Day was imminent. Reporting on 24 April to Norfolk House on St James Square, ten minutes' walk from the Admiralty, VAT commenced his top-secret staff air planning duties for Operation *Neptune*, the naval component of Operation *Overlord* to invade France.

Initially his task was to read the thousands of pages required to know the *Neptune* plan thoroughly.

---

14   Later Lieutenant-Commander Kenneth Hudspeth DSC** RANVR, who had taken his midget submarine *X-10* into Altenfjord in September 1943 attempting to attack *Scharnhorst*, VAT's target of June 1940. In January 1944 Kenneth in *X-20* had landed commando survey parties at night on Normandy beaches. Awarded three DSCs he returned to teaching in Tasmania after the war.

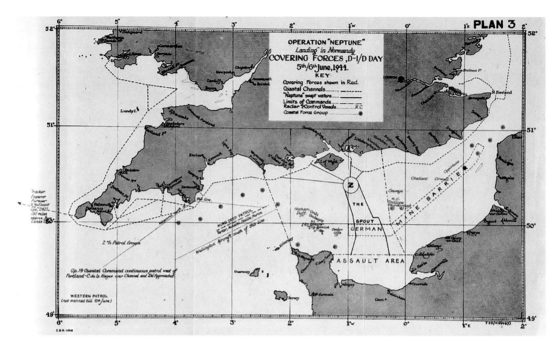

One of the planning maps used for Operation Neptune, the naval component of Operation Overlord. VAT was one of hundreds of staff officers from all services involved in months of detailed planning for the enormous undertaking.

As a staff officer (air) he needed to be especially familiar with those parts of the air force plan which would concern the navy. There were dozens of meetings, both single and inter-service to attend, but amidst his professional duties he took on the more pleasant task of courting. VAT had until now adhered without waver to the naval conventions that discouraged marriage until one's early 30s, leaving the bachelor to concentrate on his professional duties. A junior officer needed his commanding officer's permission to marry and the old adage that "a sub-lieutenant may not marry, lieutenants might marry and lieutenant-commanders should marry" was followed.

In *Shropshire* the previous year VAT had been friendly with Lieutenant James "Jim" Baker RANVR. On leave in London Jim introduced VAT to his friend Sidney Cotton who in 1917 had invented the Sidcot suit that was still keeping thousands of RAF aircrew warm. Cotton was a wealthy Australian entrepreneur who lived in a luxurious apartment on Curzon Street, overlooking Park Lane. He was one of the many who travelled to the UK in 1915 with the Australian Naval Board's blessing to become RNAS aviators. From 1938 the unconventional Cotton had taken spy photographs of German industrial areas and airports for MI6 while flying his personal Lockheed 12A on business trips. Modified with hidden aerial cameras operated by a switch under his seat Cotton's Lockheed was the last civilian aircraft out of Germany at the start of the war.

Now temporarily based in London, VAT resumed the friendship, and it was at Cotton's apartment that he was introduced to a Miss Nanette Harrison. Subsequent meetings quickly evolved into a courtship. Nanette, ten years younger than VAT, had been in the Women's

Sporting freshly painted invasion stripes, No. 846 Squadron Wildcats and Avengers on the deck of Tracker in June 1944.

Auxiliary Air Force but had taken ill and been discharged. She worked for a London solicitor, was appealingly vivacious and quickly took to calling VAT "Al", short for Al Capone in reference to his still livid facial scar. They spent increasing time in each other's company before VAT moved to Portsmouth, and subsequently embarked in *Southern Prince* with the rest of the staff comprising Naval Party 1570 under Rear-Admiral James Rivett-Carnac DSC.[15] Both VAT and his admiral were aware of the potential dangers in the coming assault area from friend as well as foe since *Rodney*, under Rivett-Carnac's command, had shot down two Fulmars from VAT's No. 807 Squadron on one hectic Mediterranean day in 1941.

Rivett-Carnac was Chief Naval Administrative Officer to the Allied Naval Commander-in-Chief, Admiral Sir Bertram Ramsay. Having successfully got the British forces off the beaches of Dunkirk in 1940 Ramsay was now tasked to return them to France, along with the American and Canadian divisions. Rivett-Carnac was designated to assume the duties of Flag Officer, British Assault Area (FOBAA) on completion of the initial assault phase. More simply known as "Rear-Admiral Beaches" the task was to ensure that the flow of men and material over the beaches of *Sword*, *Juno* and *Gold* continued uninterrupted after the first waves were ashore. Once a secure initial lodgement was established the beachhead needed expanding to allow the build-up of the following forces until they could break out. While coordinating the protection of those men and supplies as their vessels entered the assault area, FOBAA's teams of beach masters and communicators would keep the men and stores continually moving off the beaches and inland.

---

15   Later Vice-Admiral James Rivett-Carnac CB CBE DSC (1891-1970) had entered the navy in 1905 and served in the dreadnought battleship *Orion* at the Battle of Jutland in 1916. Flew his broad pennant as Commodore Commanding New Zealand Squadron 1938-1940 while captain of HMS *Leander*.

Aboard *Tracker* on 5 June the twelve Avengers and six Wildcats of No. 846 Squadron were painted with black and white "bumble bee" recognition stripes. All Allied aircraft in the invasion area were so painted, and they became known as "invasion stripes". *Tracker* joined *Pursuer* and *Emperor* patrolling a line 150 miles west of Land's End to intercept the dozens of French-based U-boats that Dönitz ordered to enter the English Channel and attack the invasion traffic. General Dwight Eisenhower, Supreme Commander of *Overlord*, had asked for two weeks free of U-boats to ensure his army's firm foothold ashore. Johnnie Walkers's 2nd Support Group was deployed in the area along with seven other groups, and he practically lived on the bridge for those two weeks and more.[16]

Captain Donal "Dangerous Dan" McGrath who after leaving Tracker next commanded Albatross during Operation Neptune.

Before commanding *Tracker*, Captain Donal "Dangerous Dan" McGrath, due to retire in 1941, had been mentioned in despatches commanding the landing ship *Glengyle* during the August 1942 Dieppe Raid. McGrath was now commanding *Albatross*, heading for Normandy as a Landing Ship (Engineering) with her hangar converted into a large machinery workshop. As well as repair duties from 10 June onwards Dangerous Dan, true to his nickname and destroyer heritage, undertook naval gunfire support with *Albatross*'s ageing 4.7" guns and was hit in return by shore fire. *Albatross* also provided anti-aircraft defence of the anchorage against the few *Luftwaffe* attacks that got through the patrol lines, truly earning her battle honour "Normandy 1944".

Buster Hallett, whose life VAT had saved off Sicily, was commanding No. 3 Naval Fighter Wing of 48 Seafires tasked with protecting the beaches themselves. No. 816 Squadron was conducting patrols under Coastal Command's No. 19 Group from *Vulture*/Naval Air Station St Merryn in Cornwall against U-boat and E-boat incursions. No. 807 Squadron, now trained in amphibious support for combined operations and tactical reconnaissance, remained in the Mediterranean, selected to embark on *Hunter* for August's invasion of southern France.

The main headquarters ship for each landing beach, with a commodore or rear-admiral and the army divisional commander onboard, were supplemented by assault headquarters ships in touch with the troops ashore in each sector of a main landing beach. Non-assault headquarters ships were assigned stationary tasks off the beaches, and it was off *Juno* that *Southern Prince* anchored on 8 June. Several days later, the coast inland had been cleared sufficiently for the staff to move ashore to a requisitioned chateau at the eastern end of *Juno* in the coastal village of Courseulles.

The chateau had been previously used by the *Kriegsmarine* and was surrounded by a garden and orchard where most of the staff lived in tents, which VAT found to be relatively pleasant.

---

16 Captain Frederick "Johnnie" Walker CB DSO*** (48) died from a cerebral thrombosis brought on by overwork and exhaustion on 7 July 1944.

As shipping streamed across the Channel through the spout to the beaches, the offloaded men and materiel were moved inland without delay.[17] A signals section was set up in the orchard, all signals from ships and services being routed through FOBAA. With thousands of aircraft and ships bustling to and fro, with patrol lines in the air and on the sea to protect against the increasingly desperate thrusts of U-boats, E-boats, *Luftwaffe* warplanes and even manned torpedoes, there were 1,600 signals a day requiring eight coders working watch on, watch off. On 13 June *Boadicea*, which VAT had boarded as a midshipman in Malta and last seen as one of the close escorts with *Tracker* in the Arctic, was sunk in the Channel by a *Luftwaffe* torpedo attack.

As well as air planning, VAT took his turn as duty staff officer and he felt everything flowed relatively smoothly from the naval aspect. VAT maintained a close working arrangement with the RAF group captain in command of the nearby radar site and with the senior air staff officer of the 2nd Tactical Air Force. He found both officers extremely helpful if any aid was needed for the protection of shipping in the assault area. Rivett-Carnac commented that he had found in VAT a reliable and efficient staff officer who maintained the necessary good liaison between air force and navy. Clearly VAT did not let any ingrained certitudes about his senior service stand in the way of inter-service co-operation that was friendly as well as professional.

By 16 June the shipping backlog caused by recent storms had been cleared, Mulberry harbours were proving their worth and, despite the continued shelling of *Sword* beach, half a million men and 77,000 vehicles had been landed. The situation was stable enough for King George VI with Churchill to land on *Juno* beach and they took tea with Rivett-Carnac. With the initial assault phase over Rivett-Carnac formally took the title of FOBAA on 24 June. In the last week of June U-boats that Dönitz had transferred from Norway and Germany managed to penetrate the spout, the main convoy route from the Solent to Normandy, torpedoing eight ships over several days, but the escort groups sank four U-boats. On 1 July *Sword* beach, the exposed eastern flank of the assault and still subject to enemy fire, was closed. Two weeks later the situation at *Juno* was stable enough to celebrate Bastille Day with the villagers.

At the beginning of July, the naval task force commanders hauled down their flags, ending Operation *Neptune* but FOBAA would continue his task for some months. The army had been given the ambitious object of securing the city of Caen, some twelve miles inland, on D-Day. An essential transport hub astride the Orne River, stubborn German defence meant it took six weeks to subdue. On FOBAA's staff was an army officer who had a jeep allocated to him for his liaison duties. This happenstance led to VAT seeing what few naval officers ever would, a major tank battle. They drove fifteen miles from their headquarters to a position not far from the frontline, so VAT had an unobstructed view. Three armoured divisions pushed off on 18 July with 1,100 tanks to break through the German *Panzergruppe* West and the battle raged for two days.

---

17   The "spout" was the narrow cross channel convoy lanes. Near Portsmouth it was ten miles wide marked by buoy "Z". Convoys hugged the English coast until they reached this buoy then turned south to cross the channel in various lanes within the spout until reaching its 30-mile-wide southern end from where they dispersed into the assault area. Huge Allied air and sea resources guarded the vital spout.

Albatross was off *Juno* beach on 11 August, having salvaged 79 landing craft from total loss and returned to service 132 others. Long years had passed since most of VAT's cadet class had first experienced *mal-de-mer* aboard her during a March 1929 college sea-day. Struck by a torpedo near Courseulles she suffered over 100 casualties with 67 killed and *Albatross*'s war was over.[18] It is not clear if VAT, finishing his staff duties

The France and Germany clasp.

with FOBAA the day before, saw any of this tragedy unfolding having been hastily recalled to the Admiralty. Several weeks after VAT left there was a serious friendly-fire incident which underlined the importance of the staff work he had been doing.

The British 1st Minesweeping Flotilla had their tasking changed to sweep off Le Havre, enabling *Warspite* to get closer to a troublesome German shore battery. The signal concerning the changed area of sweeping omitted FOBAA in the addressees. When the ships were spotted by a ground radar unit FOBAA's duty staff officer that watch, Lieutenant-Commander Robert Franks DSO OBE, was contacted. Having been himself the object of RAF friendly fire in Borneo's Arakan the previous year, Franks confirmed from the "Daily State" that there were no friendly vessels in that area. Unable to contact captain (minesweeping) in his command ship *Ambitious*, Rivett-Carnac could not risk enemy warships attacking unloading transports and approved a deadly Typhoon strike by Nos. 263 and 266 Squadrons.[19]

After more pounding from *Warspite*'s guns the bypassed port of Le Havre capitulated on 12 September. Combined with the already working port of Dieppe, there was no need to continue landing supplies over the beach, and *Juno*, the only landing beach still operating, was closed. From 24 June to 12 September almost 1.5 million tons of stores, 152,000 vehicles and 350,000 men had been landed in the British Assault Area.

The clasp "France and Germany" was added to the medal ribbon of those who, like VAT, had already qualified for the Atlantic Star if they then participated in land, sea or air operations in France, Holland, Belgium or Germany between 6 June 1944 and 8 May 1945.

With the gradual winding down of the naval war against Germany, the Admiralty was planning the formation of a British Pacific Fleet. This fleet was to have a large aviation component requiring considerable shore facilities in Australia. VAT, an Australian with extensive operational flying and carrier experience, who was additionally skilled in planning and inter-service staff work, was a natural choice among those called on despite his still relatively junior rank.

By late 1943 the Naval Board in Melbourne had started to consider the possibility of a post-war carrier-based fleet air arm but recognised that relevant experience was lacking in the

---

18   The war was over for *Albatross* but not yet for Captain Donal McGrath. He had commanded seven torpedo boat destroyers during and immediately after WWI, followed by another eight destroyers and two sloops before 1934. In the normal course he would have been on the retired list but held five wartime ship commands and was commanding *Adventure* at war's end.
19   The Typhoon's strike leader, Wing Commander John "Johnny" Baldwin DSO DFC*, thought the vessels friendly and sought confirmation of the attack order four times. There were over 200 killed and wounded with *Britomart* and *Hussar* sunk.

seaman executive branch. Captain Harold Farncomb DSO MVO RAN (1913 Pioneer class), pencilled in for an RN battleship after his outstanding years as flag-captain of *Australia*, was instead sent to the UK to take command of the assault carrier *Attacker* in March 1944. With 30 Seafires embarked *Attacker* went on to win the battle honours "South France 1944" and "Aegean 1944" under his command.[20]

Meanwhile *Australia* had been operating with the US Seventh Fleet since February 1943 and had supported offensive amphibious operations by the graduates of *Assault* in New Georgia, New Britain and Cape Gloucester. In these landings were *Westralia* and *Manoora*, converted from armed merchant cruisers to infantry landing ships, but their Walrus flights had ceased with the new role. As the RAN now operated with bountiful air assets from shore bases and accompanying carrier groups - eight US escort carriers were at the Hollandia assault in April 1944 - there was little tactical benefit from embarking the venerable yet vulnerable Walrus, whose aviation fuel and stores had proved volatile with battle damage. As new radars and guns threatened *Australia*'s stability some 60 tons of top weight, including catapult and starboard crane, were removed and the Walrus disembarked permanently. VAT's old teammate and shipmate, Harrie Gerrett, was now redundant as the flagship's observer.

Harrie, seeing the inevitable, was approved to transfer to general duties aboard *Australia*. As Farncomb left for the UK and *Attacker*, he recognised Harrie's feelings, writing that he was "… disappointed at being unable to follow an observer's career …" but "he would be suitable as first lieutenant of a small cruiser in a few months' time." Time, however, was to be in short supply. During the Battle of Leyte Gulf on 21 October 1944, Harrie was air defence officer manning the director above the bridge when a Japanese aircraft crashed into the ship mortally wounding him.[21]

In London VAT had proposed to Nanette in September 1944 and they became engaged. When warned on Monday 23 October that in ten days' time he would be leaving for Australia, VAT mustered his staff skills, immediately phoning Nanette and asked if they could get married the following Saturday. In making these arrangements he would have found a ready ally in Petty Officer Jeffrey Britten, now on the staff of the London Depot at Australia House, who had himself married a local girl, Jean Slaney, the previous September.[22]

Apart from a natural desire to be married, VAT recognised that post-war the wife of a serviceman would have some priority getting a passage out to Australia. With only five days' notice, on Saturday 28 October the 31-year-old VAT married 21-year-old Nanette at

---

20   Later Rear-Admiral Harold Farncomb CB DSO MVO who spent an astonishing 68 months of WWII in command of warships. For comparison Collins did 38 before being wounded on *Australia*'s bridge.

21   The *Canberra Times* reported "Mortally wounded the Lieutenant-Commander lay outstretched on the deck refusing medical attention while he gave orders to the fire-fighting parties … between orders he asked a seaman 'Did we get the plane?'… he died aboard the ship two hours after receiving his wound." As the cruiser withdrew south the 30 dead, including Captain Emile Dechaineux DSC (1916 class), were buried at sea. Harrie's widow Virginia with their two young daughters received a pension of £10 per fortnight.

22   Jean Fountain nee Slaney (1920-2011), widow of Corporal Jack Fountain RAFVR (1917-1941).

St George's, in Mayfair, undisturbed by the V2 rockets of the latest London blitz. Sidney Cotton stood in for Nanette's deceased father and pictures of their wedding appeared in the local papers. After a weekend honeymoon in Suite 539 of the Dorchester Hotel, the couple attended an investiture at Buckingham Palace where VAT, in the wording of the invitation, received the insignia of the Distinguished Service Cross "from the King's hand"..

Ten days after their wedding VAT embarked on the troopship *Queen Elizabeth* heading across the Atlantic to the United States. The couple were not to see each other again for a year.

"Lieutenant-Commanders should marry!" VAT and Nanette on their wedding day in London on 28 October 1944.

CHAPTER 9

AIR STAFF OFFICER ASHORE 1944 – 1947

I**N THE SECOND WEEK OF FEBRUARY** 1945 the British Pacific Fleet arrived in Sydney Harbour to popular celebration. Its Task Force 63 under Rear-Admiral Sir Philip Vian KCB KBE DSO** included the four armoured-deck fleet carriers *Indomitable*, *Illustrious*, *Indefatigable* and *Victorious*. On their passage from Ceylon, they had conducted the largest FAA strikes of the war against Japanese-held oil refineries in Sumatra, *Illustrious* alone losing 10% of her aircrew and 24% of her aircraft. On arrival, the carriers disembarked squadrons for continuation training, replenishment and maintenance to three new naval air stations ashore; that they were able to do so was in large measure due to VAT. The carriers' air engineering and supply officers also made demands for 2,300 air stores items.

When the carriers re-embarked their squadrons to sail for Manus in the Admiralty Islands, only ten percent of those demands had been met. Becoming Task Force 57 of the US Fifth Fleet for the invasion of Okinawa, the lack of air stores was at risk of becoming a major impediment to the fighting efficiency of the Fleet Air Arm in the Pacific. VAT and the rest of the air staff officers had been working untold hours since November to properly support the carriers with

Nabberley/Royal Naval Air Station Bankstown. Along the perimeter road are lines of airframes waiting for their wings and engines from the packing crates to the left. These are dozens of reserve aircraft ready for issue to the frontline BPF squadrons.

facilities ashore and to have new stores buildings erected and adequately stocked with spare parts. At its August 1945 peak the BPF air arm comprised 750 aircraft and 21 carriers; six fleet carriers and four light carriers supported by two maintenance carriers and nine escort carriers. These escort carriers were working as ferry and replenishment carriers for the Fleet Train which included the two maintenance and repair carriers. Providing combat air patrols for the vulnerable replenishment vessels, they would launch replacement aircraft and crews to the forward fleet carriers as needed, some escorts even taking their place on occasion in the fleet's line-of-battle as strike carriers.

VAT had spent several weeks before his wedding attached to *Flycatcher*, the shore headquarters for the proposed Mobile Naval Air Bases to support disembarked squadrons in distant operational areas. A MONAB of between 500 and 1,000 men included all the capabilities of a permanent air station - every facility from radio technicians to air traffic controllers and medics. Vital to the planned operations of the BPF the first MONAB commissioned as *Nabbington* on the day of VAT's wedding. Expected to support fifty Avenger and Corsair aircraft the unit's personnel, stores, equipment and vehicles sailed for Australia on 20 November 1944.

When VAT left his new bride and travelled west across the Atlantic he was with three other FAA officers destined for the staff of Rear-Admiral Reginald Portal CB DSC, Flag Officer Naval Air Stations (Australia).[1] Commanding the BPF was Admiral Sir Bruce Fraser KCB KBE, who had finally sunk *Scharnhorst* at the battle of North Cape in December 1943.[2] The four staff officers took the train to San Francisco, then travel onward to Australia was by aircraft. From *Golden Hind*, the rapidly expanding RN tented establishment at Warwick Farm racecourse, VAT travelled to Melbourne on 13 November 1944 where Vice-Admiral Charles Daniel CBE DSO had raised his flag as Vice-Admiral (Q) BPF in *Beaconsfield*, the requisitioned Port Melbourne Seamen's Mission building.[3] When MONAB 1 arrived at Sydney on 20 December, VAT had arranged with the air force for them to proceed to RAAF Base Nowra. On 2 January 1945, *Nabbington*/Royal Naval Air Station Nowra commissioned. It was to Nowra that *Illustrious* was able to disembark Nos. 1830 and 1833 (Corsair) Squadrons on 9 February followed by aircraft from another eight squadrons in the next few days. At one time the MONAB accommodated 130 aircraft.

The size of the logistics challenge was considerable. It had been estimated in mid-1944 that the BPF based in Australia, expected to number 675,000 by the end of 1945, would need one million square feet of naval and armament stores with an extra 300,000 square feet for air stores. These stores would require 1,200 personnel to man, in addition to the 100,000 that would be required in base support at Australian airfields, dockyards and ports. It was hoped by the British that at least 17,000 of these personnel would be Australian. Where the USN had

---

1   Later Admiral Sir Reginald Portal KCB DSC (1894-1983), a WWI observer who had been wounded over Gallipoli operating from the seaplane carrier *Ark Royal* in 1915. His older brother was a marshal of the RAF.

2   Later Admiral of the Fleet Bruce Fraser, 1st Baron Fraser of North Cape GCB KBE (1888-1981), who signed on behalf of Britain the Japanese Instrument of Surrender.

3   The Q had been borrowed from army terminology to encompass all naval logistics for the BPF.

taken two years to build up its supply organisation to maintain their remote task forces, the British only had months before Pacific operations commenced in early 1945.

That the inevitable deficiencies did not more adversely impact operations was directly due to the work of the inadequate numbers of staff officers working alongside VAT. When Fraser established his BPF headquarters in Sydney, Daniel remained in Melbourne with his Q staff. While the physical separation was not ideal, it still proved workable, helped by Fraser's chief staff officer Commodore Edward Evans-Lombe who had been VAT's executive officer in *Glorious*.

By agreement the RAAF loaned various airfields to the RN. Bankstown and Schofields in Sydney became Naval Air Stations *Nabberley* (MONAB II) and *Nabthorpe* (MONAB III) respectively, while the airstrip at Jervis Bay became *Nabswick* (MONAB V). MONAB IV was established as a forward station at Ponam in the Admiralty Islands and two other stations were formed at Maryborough and Brisbane. VAT pleasingly found both the RAN and the Commonwealth Department of Works to be of the greatest help. So often it seemed to him that when running out of time to produce some much-needed requirement, valuable and timely help was received from Navy Office and the Department of Works, which assisted his work enormously.

By July 1945, after eight months of exhausting work as an Air Staff Officer, VAT was being held by his commodore and admiral as:

> … responsible for a considerable part of the planning necessary for the establishment of naval air stations in Australia.

In a glowing report his personality and sense of humour were praised, noting that he was popular with both British and Australians. Presciently Daniel recommended VAT for accelerated promotion and affirmed that he would be:

> … invaluable to the RAN if and when they decide to start a Fleet Air Arm.

Not just aircraft spares were in short supply, so were new aircrew to make up "wastage". Some squadrons arriving on later escort carriers were disbanded as they disembarked ashore, their aircrew rushed north as replacements to the fleet carriers. The RAAF agreed once again to assist and 24 experienced RAAF pilots, bored with their training squadron duties, volunteered to transfer to the RANVR for carrier training and service with the BPF. Converting to Seafires with No. 899 Squadron at *Nabthorpe* they qualified in deck landings on *Arbiter* and the recently repaired *Indomitable*.[4] Their move to the forward areas coincided with the 6 August dropping of the first atomic bomb on Hiroshima, followed three days later by the second weapon on Nagasaki, and they did not see action.

VAT as an air staff officer ashore circa 1945, when an enormous amount of planning was undertaken to support the BPF in Australia.

---

4   *Indomitable* had been hit by three kamikazes in operations against the Sakishima Gunto islands.

With victory over Japan in the offing, VAT was called from *Beaconsfield* to visit Navy Office where he was briefed by Commander Galfrey "Gat" Gatacre DSC* MiD (1921 class), assistant to the Director of Plans Commander Claude Brooks MiD (KM) (1917 class). Brooks, a pre-war observer from 1927 had been with *Albatross* for her entire first commission from 1929 to 1933. Before his recent command of *Nizam* he was staff officer (operations) aboard *Warspite*, then flagship of the Eastern Fleet, when they lost a carrier, 45 aircraft and ten other vessels to strikes by Admiral Nagumo's five carriers in April 1942. Brooks knew exactly what air power at sea could now achieve.

Gatacre briefed VAT that they had been considering post-war plans for the RAN to include two carriers, two carrier air groups plus the shore organisation and facilities required to support such a proposed force.[5] VAT was asked to produce a draft plan. He knew this could only be a skeleton first draft, as so many details were not available and, in any event, it was well beyond the ability of one relatively junior planner. Despite these reservations the plan was drawn up and passed to the Plans Division of Navy Office. VAT afterwards considered this the first step towards the creation of the RAN carrier-based Fleet Air Arm two years later in 1947.

Certainly, it was the first step at his level, but these relatively junior officers were responding to nineteen months of high-level policy machinations. In January 1944 the prime minister had directed the Defence Committee, consisting of the chiefs of staff for each service and the powerful Secretary of the Defence Department, Sir Frederick Sheddon, to begin planning for the size and constitution of the armed forces post-war. The First Naval Member, Admiral Sir Guy Royle KCB CMG, who had entered *Britannia* as a cadet with Arthur Longmore in 1900, unofficially investigated the possibility of transfer "on loan" of a light fleet carrier and two cruisers. Umbrage was taken when he announced this proposal at a meeting of the Advisory War Council in March without prior consultation with Sheddon or the air force. Sheddon himself favoured further development of the RAAF after the war for "local defence". Recruitment per month at this time was 3,375 for the air force, 1,475 into the army and only 150 for the navy. Any proposals for new major fleet units, with its need for an extra 4,000 men, would require significant expansion of that naval figure.

When Prime Minister Curtin visited Britain in April 1944, the First Sea Lord offered *Venerable,* due to commission at the end of the year, plus two new cruisers. Curtin, who reasonably expected policy to be government led, also took umbrage with Royle when he found that the Admiralty knew of the Australian War Cabinet's most recent meetings over the question of a carrier. Churchill wrote personally to Curtin on 27 May with the carrier offer but, while the Defence Committee accepted that two carriers were desirable for a peacetime navy, manpower worries negated any concrete moves towards an Australian manned carrier in the present war.

The matter rested uneasily for months until the welcome arrival of Vian's impressive 1ˢᵗ Aircraft

---

5   Gatacre had been navigator of *Rodney* during the hunt for the *Bismarck* in May 1941 and was staff officer (operations) in *Australia* at the Battle of Savo Island.

Carrier Squadron in Sydney. It had been Vian who had commanded the eastern task force at Normandy. Catalyst or not, several days later on 14 February 1945 Curtin cabled Churchill asking for the transfer of a carrier. Since he requested the ship as a gift, further negotiations, now involving the British Exchequer and Australian Treasury Department, promptly stalled. The British thought asking for "freebies" while charging £26 million for the BPF facilities in Australia and £14 million for new works was tactless. With Curtin terminally ill, the final word was from the acting prime minister that manpower dictated a carrier decision would have to wait until peacetime.

The day before Hiroshima the Admiralty showed their undimmed desire to encourage a RAN carrier force when they cabled:

> No doubt the Defence Committee in considering the nature, strength and organisation of post war defence forces will take into consideration the prominent part which aircraft carriers play in the modern balanced fleet, especially in the waters of the Pacific Ocean.

The BPF carriers were at that moment striking at the Japanese mainland with the US Third Fleet under Admiral William "Bull' Halsey.

Emperor Hirohito broadcast the Imperial Rescript of Surrender on 15 August 1945. Into that uneasy void of intermittent clashes during the ceasefire period, Halsey signalled that if there was any doubt, the Japanese were to be "shot down in a friendly manner".[6] When the Japanese Instrument of Surrender was signed in Tokyo Bay on 2 September Australia had almost 600,000 men and women in army uniform and the air force, which had peaked at 6,200 aircraft in 61 squadrons with 182,000 personnel, was the fourth largest in the world. The navy had just under 40,000 in uniform but was predominantly a small ship navy. With only three cruisers in commission, it was, in many respects, less capable as an independent force than it had been in 1939 and, crucially, had no aviation assets.

Despite the central role naval air had assumed in British and American sea power, 1945 found only a handful of aviation specialists such as VAT in the RAN, with another handful of Australians who had served as RNVR aircrew.[7] By contrast Kiwi RNZNVR aviators had made up twenty percent of FAA aircrew in the Pacific, some 760 New Zealanders having qualified as naval aircrew during the war.

When Acting Admiral Sir Louis Hamilton KCB DSO* relieved Royle as First Naval Member he had been well briefed by the Admiralty and declared that he would revive the carrier debate, being convinced of the need for the RAN to have two. Recognising where policy power resided, he was immediately soothing in his dealings with Sheddon, stating that "If by so doing, we may get the requisite Naval Air Branch, all is well". When he received VAT's skeleton draft with its

---

6   Asked about the winning elements of the war in the Pacific Bull Halsey listed: submarines first, radar second, planes third, bulldozers fourth.

7   Such as West Australian Lieutenant Charles "Sprog" Lea DSC RNVR who, with his observer, released his torpedo at 600 yards from the battleship *Caio Duilio* at Taranto, putting an 11 x 7 metre hole in her.

outline for a naval air arm it joined the overly ambitious shopping list presented in November 1945 which included three light carriers, six cruisers, 32 destroyers and 50 escorts. While the debates continued at chiefs of staff level, VAT was sent to the UK. Hamilton also talked to the new Prime Minister Joseph "Ben" Chifley, arguing that a two-carrier force could act independently. He found the prime minister, a Labor defence minister in 1931 and historically wary of British self-interest at Australia's expense, receptive to the concept.

VAT had been working once again for Rivett-Carnac, now with a CBE for his success as Rear-Admiral Beaches, who had taken over the Q responsibilities from Daniel in March. When his appointment on the staff of Vice-Admiral (Q) finished towards the end of October 1945, VAT was sent by a Qantas Empire Airways Lancastrian mail service aircraft to London. His brother Bill telegraphed Nanette in London on 23 October that "Mick left this morning", VAT telegraphing that he expected to arrive late on 25 October and would go direct to the flat.

After his departure there was another laudatory personal report, again recommending accelerated promotion, written by Commodore Derrick Hall-Thompson, Chief Staff Officer. Derrick was the son of Rear-Admiral Percival Hall-Thomson who had argued so strongly for an RAN FAA in 1924 when on loan as First Naval Member. He said of VAT that:

> His general popularity both with British and Australians made him a most useful link, and he had a happy knack of persuading the RAAF and RAN to give help freely and willingly. He has now gone to London to carry out preliminary planning for an Australian Fleet Air Arm, a job for which he is particularly well fitted.

Hamilton had written personally to the First Sea Lord asking that Smith be afforded all necessary facilities.

An Avro Lancastrian airliner, the Lancaster bomber without armour or guns, was not comfortable but it was certainly quicker than any previous journey VAT had made between Australia and the UK. That speed VAT appreciated, as he had been away from Nanette for a year, and any discomfort of the journey was offset by joy in their anticipated reunion. Appointed to the staff of the Naval Liaison Officer, Captain (S) James Foley CBE at Australia House on the Strand, he was to fill in as many gaps as possible in his initial draft plan. An encouraging Admiralty provided him with a desk in the Directorate of Air Organisation and Training.

With the resumption of British control in Hong Kong and Malaya as British Commonwealth Occupation Forces started their duties in Japan, carriers of the 1st Aircraft Carrier Squadron frequented Australian waters for several years. In January 1946 *Glory*, *Implacable* and *Indefatigable* paid the largest naval visit to Melbourne since 1939. As they secured alongside Station Pier a funeral party mustered and went ashore, a Firefly pilot having died the previous day. He had ditched while recovering to *Glory* after the 72 aircraft fly past over the city led by

Implacable, Indefatigable and Glory visit Melbourne in 1946. The size difference between a 32,600-ton fleet carrier and an 18,000-ton light carrier is marked.

Lieutenant-Commander Buster Hallett DSC**.[8] Also in that fly past were several of the ex-RAAF/ex-RANVR pilots who had accepted RN commissions on the proviso that they could return to the RAN if subsequently required for flying duties.

In June 1946 exercises were conducted to demonstrate to the Naval Board and others the usefulness of carriers as RAN plans matured and VAT worked away in the UK. VIPs, including the ministers for navy and trade, embarked for the sea day. They enjoyed the live rocket firing exercise but saw a Firefly lose its wheels entering the first barrier until stopped by the second barrier and another hit the round-down. Both crews emerged from the wreckage unhurt and as the guests departed some were keen on an Australian carrier, others not so sure!

For most of 1946 VAT consulted - later recalling it as pestering - dozens of naval uniformed experts in admiralty departments and RN establishments where he found universal help and encouragement. He adopted a procedure of sending periodic information from Australia House to Navy Office where the Plans Division under Brooks now had Lieutenant-Commander (O) Gerry Haynes DSO working for him.[9] VAT had asked for Haynes to accompany him to London to help with the draft plan, but Gerry was committed to re-entering the shipping business he had run pre-war. If Brooks or Haynes found information lacking, or were unclear

---

8   Buster Hallett had finished the war leading No. 24 Fighter Wing as commanding officer of No. 887 (Seafire) Squadron off *Indefatigable* against the Japanese home islands. Hallett served in Australia instructing at the School of Land Air Warfare 1947-49 and married a local girl.

9   After surviving hazardous operations from Malta commanding No. 828 Squadron Gerry Haynes had operated with the Desert Air Force. Returning to Australia, he flew in RAAF Beauforts, was an air staff officer in *Golden Hind* and then instructed at the RN School of Naval Air Warfare.

on certain points, they would respond so that VAT could follow those aspects up. Foley reported that he had heard complimentary comments from many senior officers with whom VAT, a keen specialist officer, had tactfully dealt during his investigations where he had been particularly successful in what was a difficult assignment.

VAT had been free to plan with the Admiralty as long as no formal financial commitments were made, the same stricture the planning staff in Melbourne were subject to. At this time there were ten light fleet carriers in various stages of suspended construction. Knowing that they would not need, and could not afford, this number, the Admiralty informed Australia in September 1946 that the cost of a Majestic-class was £2.75 million. To further encourage the RAN in establishing a two-carrier FAA they offered the biggest "buy one get one free" deal in Australian history: two carriers for £2.75 million and two outfits of armaments and stores at £450,000 each for a total £3,650,000.

A lieutenant-commander, however competent, could only hold so much sway in the defence bureaucracy and, in any event, the scale of the plan was beyond even VAT's disciplined staff work ethic. It was apparent that the next major step towards an Australian FAA was to form a separate staff within the Plans and Operations Division of Navy Office. VAT flew to Australia by Lancastrian arriving in Melbourne on 25 October 1946. Nanette had left Southampton several weeks before in the RMS *Asturias*. Badly damaged by a torpedo in 1943 and converted to an emigrant ship in 1945, she was still painted RN grey and owned by the Ministry of Transport. Travelling via Cape Town and Fremantle, VAT was waiting to greet her on arrival in Melbourne.

The Naval Board sought Admiralty agreement for the loan of three senior RN officers to man an Aviation Planning Office in Navy Office. The experienced aviator Captain Edmund Anstice, air engineer Commander (E) Arthur "Attie" Turner DSC and a supply officer with knowledge of air stores Commander (S) Bernard Robinson, were sent out.[10] VAT was the fourth, and most junior member, of this planning staff. His tasks were dealing with organisation, personnel training and a host of other matters as they arose. A civilian officer of the Admiralty Director of Stores, who had considerable knowledge of air stores from the procurement and depot handling side, was also made available.

There were two principal objectives for this planning staff. One was to produce the final plan for the creation of a carrier FAA and the other, running concurrently, was to have open discussions with an RAAF team on the relative advantages and disadvantages of navy or air force manning that proposed air branch. The two teams were to produce a joint report for the Naval and Air Boards to be submitted to Cabinet. In essence, if the government should approve the RAN

---

10   Later Vice-Admiral Sir Edmund Anstice KCB (1899-1979), he had qualified on No.1 Naval Pilot's Course in 1924 and had commanded the escort carriers *Striker* and *Fencer*. Further service as Chief of Staff for Aircraft Carrier Training and commanding officer of *Daedalus*/Naval Air Station Lee-on-Solent (as well as being married to an Australian) made him the perfect choice. He served as Fifth Sea Lord before retirement.

Later Admiral Sir Arthur Turner KCB DSC (1912-1991), the first non-executive branch officer to reach that rank. Air engineer officer in *Indomitable* with the BPF, he pioneered the introduction of planned maintenance to improve the fleet's reliability in the 1950s.

obtaining two aircraft carriers, which service should provide the air component and shore support? The leader of the RAAF team was Group Captain Valston "Val" Hancock DFC whose personal view was that he was unsure that Australia could afford aircraft carriers but if it could, then the air component should be provided by the navy.[11] The RAAF generally took the strong line of their Chief of Air Staff, Air Vice-Marshal George Jones CBE DFC, against the RAN having a naval-manned Fleet Air Arm, making Hancock's view unpopular within his service.[12]

Rarely is a junior staff officer allowed to be as consequential as VAT had been. After his skeleton draft of 1945, which had flesh added to it by Haynes and himself in 1946, the four-member Air Planning Staff of which he was the junior fourth

The comprehensive naval aviation plan produced in February 1947 envisaged a force of two carriers supported by shore bases at Schofields and Nowra.

used that draft to produce the definitive *Naval Aviation - The Naval Plan* in February 1947. Although classified secret, time was pressing so Anstice and VAT "smuggled" Nanette into Navy Office to help them type up the submission for cabinet. The naval plan's objective was:

> To operate, man and eventually train and maintain a RAN Carrier Force of two CVL's and three Carrier Air Groups with RN co-operation as necessary.

Over hundreds of pages, the complex tasks and costs of building a naval aviation branch was comprehensively laid out in a ten-year plan to build up to the 4,000 personnel required. Stating that air warfare at sea is and will continue to be an integral part of sea warfare, it was boldly

---

11 Later Air Marshal Sir Valston Hancock KBE CB DFC (1907-1998), a graduate of Duntroon, he had been transferred to the air force in 1929. As Director of Personnel Services, he was involved in reducing the air force to its smaller post-war structure.
12 Later Air Marshal Sir George Jones KBE CB DFC (1896-1992), a humble man who had started WWI as an infantry private at Gallipoli and finished as a fighter ace. He was Chief of Air Staff from 1942 to 1952.

held as axiomatic that an air branch should be naval manned with a single allegiance. While the RAAF would provide basic flying training, advanced training would be a naval task, as would the maintenance and repair of aircraft and the vital air stores. Nowra was to be the station for the first and second CAGs when disembarked and Schofields a maintenance station. Only proven types of British naval aircraft would be purchased, with Sea Fury and Firefly aircraft and spares being available. Two Majestic-class carriers could be bought within a reasonable time for a reasonable cost and perhaps, most importantly, the Admiralty was ready to provide whatever assistance it could. The naval air planning staff's task as such was completed.

Anstice had found in VAT a thorough, painstaking and completely reliable staff officer who was well liked by his contemporaries and correct in his attitude to his seniors. He commented that the initiative and interest which VAT must have displayed when attached to the Admiralty had been of the greatest value in planning for naval aviation in Australia. Looking to the future, Anstice felt that VAT's strong sense of duty and his experience as a specialist in air work would be of great value to the RAN. Anstice recognised that he would do well in the higher ranks of the service and, although only of three years' seniority as a lieutenant-commander, recommended he be promoted immediately.

By May 1947 Hamilton's nuanced campaign within defence had won over Sheddon. Prime Minister Chifley provisionally approved the acquisition of two carriers and decided that the new air branch would be an RAN manned and controlled Fleet Air Arm. This became a fundamental part of the new five-year Defence Plan which saw the navy win the largest budget of the three services. After being agreed at the Commonwealth Defence Council it was announced in Parliament by the Minister for Defence, the Honourable John Redman, on 4 June 1947.

Among the traditional five core courses for lieutenants were sandwiched post-war additions such as combined operations and damage control. There was also a new "Air Course". In addition to lectures, it included instructional flying hours and a subsequent assessment of suitability to specialise in naval aviation. If the weather was fair, and the student apt, there were enough hours allocated to gain the basic civilian flying qualification. The 1941 college class, who had commenced active service aged sixteen in late 1944, had returned from these UK courses in 1947, most then deploying to Japanese waters in warships of the British Commonwealth Occupation Forces. The announcement by the Minister for Defence coincided with the 1941 class submitting their preferences for specialisation, ten of the thirteen immediately volunteering for pilot training. One of these ten young sub-lieutenants was Peter Goldrick, who felt that a rewarding and expansive career in the mooted multi-carrier navy beckoned.

Keen to demonstrate the capability that the recent Australian carrier decision would lead to in several years' time, it was decided that when *Glory* and *Theseus* visited Melbourne they would put on a show for senior service personnel and other VIPs. Poor weather during the voyage down from Singapore meant only two flying days for the embarked squadrons, although they had recently managed fly pasts and demonstrations for Adelaide.

Thousands queued to see the British carriers during their 1946 and 1947 Melbourne visits.

On the first Tuesday of their nine-day visit, they left Station Pier with all three members of the Naval Board, along with senior officers from the other services as well as a state minister and the mayor. All admired the professional recovery of carrier aircraft from RAAF Point Cook and watched the displays of bombing, rocketry and cannon firing at towed targets. The *Theseus's* captain, who as a midshipman had landed Anzacs under fire at Gallipoli, had his private Tiger Moth named *Montague* onboard. After a sixteen aircraft "T" formation was flown and following a Seafire rocket assisted take-off even *Montague* got airborne.[13] The RAAF were visibly impressed with the intricate flight deck operations and another demonstration was planned for the following weekend.

Overall, the nine-day visit was summed up as "boozy, romantic and practically sleepless". It culminated with the official farewell party on Saturday evening which extended well into the morning hours of Sunday 20 July 1947, a day scheduled for a 1000 departure with a major shop window of carrier operations in front of visiting dignitaries. In retrospect, the scheduling of intensive flying immediately after intensive socialising was not the wisest decision. *Glory* flew off Seafires from her large range aft allowing more visitors onto the flight deck. As they watched *Theseus's* aircraft forming up at 1500 for a farewell fly past over the city, two Fireflies

---

13   *Montague* was flown by Commander Robert Everett MiD (1913-1992), son of Admiral Sir Allan Everett KCMG KCVO CB (1868-1938) who had been First Naval Member of the Commonwealth Naval Board in the early 1920s.

The British carriers Glory and Theseus in Australian waters, in company with the cruiser Australia.

of No. 812 Squadron collided, spiraling into the water. All four aircrew were killed, with only one body being recovered by a destroyer for burial at sea the next day. Undeterred, *Theseus's* air group commander then flew a spectacular aerobatic display for the visitors.

As the shaken squadrons landed back on *Theseus* 30 minutes later a Seafire caught the wire off centre and slewed, narrowly missing the batsman but killing an ordinary seaman on the flight deck walkway. When *Glory's* Seafires returned the squadron commander came in fast, bounced over the barrier and crashed into the forward aircraft park. Two air mechanics were injured, with the most serious quickly transferred ashore by destroyer, but was dead on arrival. To the eyes of the Second Naval Member, the secretary to the Department of the Navy and the various senior RAAF officers and assembled press, *Glory's* flight deck now resembled the aftermath of a *kamikaze* attack.

Attempting to popularise the concept of Australian naval aviation in front of senior service and civilian guests had cost *Theseus* two Fireflies, while *Glory* wrote off a Firefly and three Seafires with three Fireflies badly damaged. If the day had demonstrated the capability of a carrier the loss of six lives had shown the considerable costs that capability incurred.[14]

In year one of the air plan, 1947-1948, capital expenditure of £3.9 million covered the start of

---

14   Several weeks later in August, after leaving Sydney *Theseus* lost four Fireflies in four minutes, one even hitting the bridge before cartwheeling into the water. *Glory* also had one written off in the barrier and the admiral decreed no further flying until after an intensive training period ashore.

recruiting and training the several thousand personnel to man an air branch, plus ordering its aircraft and acquiring a carrier. This also funded the establishment of an air stores organisation and upgrade work at Nowra's paid-off MONAB. The timetable was to have the first carrier commissioned in twelve months and the second a further eighteen months later. To achieve this, hundreds of RN senior sailors, together with warrant and commissioned officers would be required for loan service to the RAN in the formative years while hundreds of Australians would need training in the UK.

Within Navy Office the Air Planning Staff were absorbed into the new administrative structure detailed in the air plan document. Anstice became the inaugural Fourth Naval Member as Commodore (Air) responsible for all air branch matters. Turner was appointed Director of Aircraft Maintenance and Repair, and Robinson became Director of Air Equipment. VAT was briefly made Director of Air Organisation and Training.

In November 1947 VAT was again appointed to the staff of the naval liaison officer in London, his duties at Navy Office being taken over by two RN loan officers, a commander (O) and a lieutenant-commander (P). Farewelling him, Anstice recognised that he had cheerfully carried out the work of two as he had helped organise the first stages of the naval aviation plan with unflagging energy, always maintaining his high standards of staff work. As he had done six months previously Anstice reported that he considered VAT would do very well in the higher ranks of the service and that his value to the RAN in a more senior capacity warranted immediate promotion. Hamilton, the First Naval Member, concurred. It was in London on New Year's Eve 1947 that VAT's uniform was laced with the three broad stripes of a commander, signifying his first step into the senior naval ranks.

Australia was fortunate in the timing of the creation of the RAN's FAA. From the considerable pool of demobilised wartime pilots, selected ex-RANVR, ex-RAAF, ex-RNVR and ex-RNZNVR aircrew started their six-month naval orientation at *Cerberus* from February 1948 before proceeding to the UK and operational conversions to the Sea Furies and Fireflies selected for the RAN. The next month No. 1 Naval Air Pilots Course of new entries and selected ratings arrived at RAAF Point Cook for their basic training before heading in turn to the UK.

Many ex-RN air maintenance ratings also transferred, seeing it as an opportunity to emigrate. Furthermore, a sizeable number of RAN sailors proved keen to transfer to air arm categories such as aircraft handlers and armourers. Large numbers were taken into the various UK training establishments to learn their new skills until appropriate training facilities were constructed in Australia. VAT would be the Australian Divisional Officer for these scores of men.

CHAPTER 10

BRASS HAT AND THE KOREAN WAR 1948 – 1953

Promotion to commander gained VAT more than the embroidered gold oak leaves adorning the peak of his new Gieves cap, the proverbial "brass hat", it showed he was on the path to the service's higher ranks after only three years and nine months as a lieutenant-commander. The newest executive branch commander on the list, his immediate senior promoted six months prior was "Braces" Bracegirdle, who had entered the college two years before him. From VAT's 1927 class only three others made the leap to a brass hat. Keith Ridley, who had joined the paymaster branch was promoted at the same time, becoming a supply branch commander.[1] Of his seaman classmates John Dowson was not promoted until June 1949 followed by George Knox in 1951.[2,3]

Commander and Mrs VAT Smith at Buckingham Palace in May 1949 when they chatted to Princess Elizabeth and Lieutenant Philip Mountbatten.

In late 1947 Rear-Admiral John Collins, completing his Imperial Defence College course in London, invited VAT for a "chat" over tea to catch up on the new air branch. It had been 30 years since he volunteered for wartime balloon service but his enthusiasm for aviation had not waned. Collins replaced Hamilton as First Naval Member and Chief of Naval Staff in early 1948, immediately declaring he was "putting the carrier and naval aviation first".[4] Costs and manpower were his major headaches as he sought even more loan personnel. Although the King approved the names *Sydney*, *Melbourne* and *Albatross* in April, Collins found that only *Sydney* and *Albatross* were on schedule to commission, the timetable for a second carrier going under contentious review. There was to be no extra money to pay for further modifications to that hull on the slips until after the end of the present five-year plan.

---

1   Commander (S) Keith Ridley resigned for medical reasons in 1949. The best man at his 1939 wedding had been the RAN's original observer Lieutenant-Commander (O) Chesterman. Ridley served at sea as wartime secretary to both Rear-Admiral Crace and Commodore Farncomb in their flagships.

2   Later Acting Commodore John Dowson CBE (1913-1980), who had been a cadet-captain alongside VAT. During the war he commanded *Bendigo* and then *Condamine*. In the mid-1960s he was captain of *Albatross* and afterwards Naval Officer in Charge Victoria before retiring in 1970.

3   Commander George Knox (1913-1972). Mentioned in despatches for his command of *Quiberon* in the Pacific, he resigned his commission in 1958.

4   Prime Minister Chifley had insisted on an Australian as Hamilton's replacement. Collins, was only 49 and relatively junior, but the loss of so many senior RAN captains in the war meant that he was appointed, serving seven years as First Naval Member rather than the usual three.

VAT was instrumental in establishing wartime naval air stations in Australia and his later air staff work on the naval air plan, from August 1945 until his promotion to commander in December 1947, explains in large part his future accolade as the father of the RAN's carrier-based Fleet Air Arm, with Sir Louis Hamilton its slightly forgotten grandfather. His two years as the Staff Officer (Air) to the Naval Liaison Officer at Australia House in 1948 and 1949 reinforced that title when he became the Australian Divisional Officer for those gathering in the UK to man the first squadrons and aircraft carrier. A naval divisional officer is responsible for the training and welfare of his men - for the youngest ratings he is almost *in loco parentis* - and VAT's "division" numbered hundreds. Having done the staff work since 1945, he was now directly involved with overseeing that first tranche of men forming the core of the new air branch. After a four-year hiatus from the 1944 end of the second cycle of Australian naval aviation - catapult mounted amphibians - the third cycle comprising a fixed-wing carrier force was evolving with VAT central to its development.

After only six months at Australia House, Captain Foley declared that VAT was a tower of strength in dealing with the innumerable problems concerning the new air branch - problems which had been arising almost daily. He was proved yet again an excellent liaison officer as he assembled the new RAN aircrew, mixed with experienced RN aviators on loan, into the 20th Carrier Air Group (CAG). No. 805 Squadron, with thirteen Hawker Sea Fury FB.11 fighters, and No. 816 Squadron, with twelve Firefly FR.4 strike aircraft, re-formed as the first RAN squadrons at *Gannet*/Naval Air Station Eglington in Northern Ireland on 28 August 1948. A recently converted aviator was not considered fully operational until he had undergone twelve months of rigorous work-up in a front-line squadron concentrating on weapons and tactics. This intense training commenced immediately under their RN commanding officers.

Meanwhile there were RAN engine room artificers shivering in inadequately heated barracks at *Condor*/Naval Air Station Arbroath in Scotland as they trained to become aircraft artificers. Scattered around the UK at other air stations were similarly cold drafts of sailors becoming skilled air mechanics, aircraft handlers, safety equipment workers and the multitude of other new trades required. Being the divisional officer for all these personnel involved a tremendous amount of travel for VAT, who would visit all these stations. The ratings under training would remember those visits when he would listen closely to their requests and complaints, writing them in his little black notebook.[5] Among a multitude of minutiae he was instrumental in getting approval for the men to wear "AUSTRALIA" shoulder flashes on their uniforms. In Australia *Albatross*/Naval Air Station Nowra commissioned in August 1948, although its numerous support organisations and facilities would take several years to come fully into being.[6]

Glory, alongside in Portsmouth, was being used as a barracks ship for those standing by as

---

5   As recalled by Naval Airman John "Snodgrass" Buchanan while training at *Gamecock*/Naval Air Station Bramcote in 1948/49.
6   Schools for aircraft engineering, electrical maintenance and radio maintenance needed establishing in addition to schools for aircraft ordnance, photography and meteorology. Pilot and observer training schools were also required plus a school of aircraft handling with a dummy deck for practice using surplus RAAF Spitfires.

Sydney's commissioning crew. This Colossus-class utility or light fleet carrier was a wartime construction designed as a half-way point between fleet carriers and escort carriers. Essentially, she was a scaled down *Illustrious*, whose designed 30 knots required 80,000 shaft horse power. Limiting the Colossus-class to 25 knots enabled the cheaper option of two sets of existing cruiser main machinery totaling 40,000 shaft horse power to be used. With their enclosed moulded bows, clean stern and tall well-placed island the class were as pleasing to a seaman's eye as an ungainly carrier could be.

Some of these unfinished Colossus hulls were completed post-war as the Majestic-class with upgraded catapults, arrester gear, lifts and reinforced flight decks to handle the larger and heavier new aircraft types. HMS *Terrible*, laid down in April 1943, thus commissioned at Devonport as the third HMAS *Sydney* on 16 December 1948. Having commanded the aircraft-less *Ruler* and *Vindex* for six months post-hostilities, Captain "Black Jack" Armstrong DSO had been penciled in for command of this first Australian carrier. Unfortunately, the doctors pronounced him unfit for sea service, so the carrier commissioned under Captain Roy Dowling DSO.[7] Among the numerous official guests were Admiral Sir Louis Hamilton, Rear-Admiral Edmund Anstice and Commander VAT Smith who, with this commissioning, personally saw one of the principal objectives of the naval air plan achieved.

The two squadrons of the 20th CAG embarked on the *Sydney* on 8 February 1949. An intensive work-up period for the ship and CAG soon saw the flight deck crew landing and stowing an aircraft every 30 seconds. On 17 March Acting Lieutenant Daniel "Danny" Buchanan became that rarest of aviators, a reverse ace during a single sortie. In a rough sea with little wind Danny's Firefly bounced over the barrier and crashed into the forward deck park destroying five aircraft.[8]. It was a solace that no-one was injured and all were RN loan aircraft. No. 805 Squadron's Sea Fury pilots, in contrast, won the traditional case of champagne from commander (air) when they achieved an accident-free deck landing work-up.

It had been hoped to get 600 ex-RN ratings to help man the carrier, but an overwhelming response saw 1,100 accepted for RAN service with 700 of them aboard *Sydney* when she sailed for Australia in April 1949.[9] Once again this highlighted how problematic the formation of the RAN FAA would have been if not for the unstinting support, training, men and materiel of the RN FAA. The Australian crew members had acquired 150 new English brides while standing by at the dockyard and those wives travelled separately by liner.

With the CAG embarked there were 56 new aircraft and 1,635 officers and men aboard, including

7   Later Vice-Admiral Sir Roy Dowling KCVO KBE CB DSC (1901-1969), he was in command of the gunnery school at Flinders Naval Depot when the college transferred there. Surviving the sinking of *Naiad* off Crete in 1942 he commanded *Hobart* in the Pacific and was present in Tokyo Bay at the Japanese surrender.

8   Later Lieutenant-Commander (P) Daniel Buchanan (1919-1956), a demobbed Sub-Lieutenant (A) RNVR Avenger pilot who joined the RAN in January 1948. He saw service in Korea aboard the destroyer *Anzac* then commanded No. 816 Squadron and the corvette *Junee*. When Commander (Air) of *Albatross*, his Vampire crashed into the sea on the night of 8 October 1956. His body was never recovered.

9   Of the first 25 aviators when the 20th CAG formed fourteen were RN and eleven RAN.

The HMAS Sydney badge.

The new carrier HMAS Sydney ferrying the 20*th* CAG with all of its aircraft and air stores to Australia in 1949.

the ship's band, who played *Waltzing Matilda* on first entering Australian waters.[10] When the aircraft were disembarked by lighter in Jervis Bay on 25 May 1949, and towed the 33 kilometres to *Albatross,* the Australian FAA truly came into being. As all settled down for refresher flying the newly functioning air station had just increased the local population by ten percent.

While VAT was overseeing the UK side of the FAA's training and formation in 1948 and 1949, the fourth naval member overseeing the new FAA in Australia was Commodore Guy Willoughby. With VAT's considerable RN service, it was not surprising that Willoughby had been Commander (Air) of *Glorious* when he embarked with No. 825 Squadron in 1938.[11] There can be no doubt that VAT's extensive RN contacts, and his standing with them, helped clear many an administrative hurdle over the years to come.

On 25 August 1949 *Sydney* became the new flagship when Rear-Admiral Harold Farncomb, who had commanded *Attacker* in the Mediterranean in 1944, hoisted his flag as Flag Officer

10 On 5 April 1948, 25 Hawker Sea Fury FB.11s and 25 Fairey Firefly AS.5s were ordered for the 20th CAG. Eventually 101 Sea Furies and 108 Fireflies were taken on RAN strength.

11 Later Rear-Admiral (P) Guy Willoughby CB (1902-1997) who qualified with No. 3 Naval Pilot's Course in 1925 and embarked an Osprey on the cruiser *York* in 1934. Chief Staff Officer to Rear-Admiral Eastern Fleet Aircraft Carriers in 1944 aboard *Illustrious* he was Director of the Naval Air Division before Australian loan service.

Commanding Australian Fleet. Ably assisted in his staff work by a newly commissioned Jeffrey Britten, once again serving at Australia House, VAT was informed he would be *Sydney*'s next executive officer. As had happened at Navy Office in Melbourne, he was replaced by two staff officers at Australia House, his duties being divided between an aircrew officer and an air engineer officer. A civilian from the Directorate of Naval Air Stores was also added to deal with the amount of extra work required in that area.

Nanette and VAT embarked on the RMS *Orion* in November to return to Australia, accompanied by a third family member, their son Michael having been born sixteen months before. His recent workload is even more impressive given the added pressure of an infant, although Nanette shouldered most of the burden. Foley regretted VAT's departure and recommended him for accelerated promotion. He reported that he was a skillful and systematic staff officer who carried out his duties with commendable efficiency, zeal and foresight. His strong and pleasant personality was coupled with a ready sense of co-operation. Foley further remarked that he was held in high esteem by the Admiralty and that His Excellency the Australian Ambassador in Paris had been very pleased with Commander Smith's work at the Diplomatic (Red Cross) Conference in Geneva, both endorsements beneficial to one on the fast track to more senior ranks.

HMAS *Sydney* Executive Officer   9 January 1950 - 24 April 1952

> She was an efficient aircraft carrier, and I would say as smart as any of the RN carriers in which I served.
>
> VAT Smith, 1992

It is a truism that the captain commands his ship, but his executive officer housekeeps it. On a major warship the executive officer is referred to as the commander or "XO" and coordinates the carrier's routine through the heads of departments such as Commander (Air) and the Engineer Commander. VAT was responsible to the captain for the discipline, order and organisation of the ship's company, assisted by subordinates such as the First Lieutenant, Master at Arms and divisional officers. As commander he allotted duties and meted out justice while ensuring all were in their correct place at the correct time, and that what was not painted was polished. He housekept on a scale that would daunt most. Typical of VAT's self-effacement was to recall how smart *Sydney* was without any acknowledgement of the dominant role he played in making that so.

For the first three months of 1950, VAT was executive officer to Flag Captain Dowling until Captain Harries took command. The Flag Officer Commanding Australian Fleet (FOCAF) was now Rear-Admiral John Eccles CBE, who had been executive officer of the *Ark Royal* for VAT's first six months aboard her at the start of the war.[12] Having commanded *Indomitable*

12   Later Admiral Sir John Eccles GCB KCVO CBE (1898-1966). A Japanese linguist who commanded *Durban* before *Indomitable,* he finished his service as Commander-in-Chief Home Fleet.

in 1944 and 1945 with the Eastern Fleet and then the BPF, Eccles was no stranger to carrier operations and had been especially chosen to help entrench the new carrier into the Australian fleet. Likewise, VAT had years of experience with the routine of fleet and escort carriers which, supplemented by his certain reading of the 235-page bible *Running a Big Ship on Ten Commandments*, stood him in good stead.[13]

The author, Captain Rory O'Connor, had been commander of *Hood*, a very smart ship indeed, and his first three commandments were central to VAT's naval ethos:

1. The Service – the customs of the service are to be observed at all times.
2. The Ship – the good appearance of the ship is the concern of everyone and all share responsibility for this.
3. The Individual – every man is constantly required to bring credit to the ship by his individual bearing, dress and good conduct, on board and ashore.

VAT by this stage had a considerable reputation, both as an aviator and as a serious-minded officer, who would ensure both a "smart" and an efficient carrier. Dowling certainly found him a very able executive officer although he had worried that VAT might have been handicapped by a lack of experience, having been away from general service for so long. He appreciated his loyalty and keenness combined with intelligence, and as a man whose quiet manner came with a strong character. They did not fully mesh as a command team, however, as Dowling, perhaps preferring a heartier leadership style, found VAT's leadership only average and his personality "not outstanding". Despite this he still recommended VAT for accelerated promotion.

When Captain "Darbo" Harries relieved Dowling in April, his quiet and conservative command style fully complemented that of VAT's. The nickname Darbo referenced a well-known jockey who was "always on your back" and VAT had worked under Harries when he was executive officer of *Shropshire,* perhaps modeling some of his own style in partial emulation. Certainly, VAT considered Harries a first-class captain who was surprisingly shy but who understood people far better than they realised and always had the wellbeing of his ship in mind. Harries also "got the birdies" better than most and proved an excellent carrier captain.

The RAN with a carrier was now clearly a fleet rather than a squadron, a rear-admiral commanding instead of a commodore. With the expansion it was appropriate that the Chief of Naval Staff should be a vice-admiral and in May 1950 Collins was promoted, receiving a telegram from the Governor of Victoria General Sir Dallas Brooks:

Congratulations on a "vice" worth having.

After working up the 20th CAG and port visits to Melbourne, Hobart and around New Zealand, *Sydney* sailed for the UK in mid-1950 to embark Nos. 808 (Sea Fury) and 817 (Firefly) Squadrons of the 21st CAG. Her report of proceedings for June remarked that during the Indian Ocean

---

13   *Running a Big Ship on Ten Commandments*, Captain Rory O'Connor, Gieves Limited, London, 1937.

Newly embarked Fireflies of the 21ˢᵗ CAG on the deck of Sydney in the North Sea in 1950.

passage "it had been possible to organise deck games which were played enthusiastically", enthusiastic enough that VAT's medical file records the 37-year-old commander suffered a broken left rib when struck by a hockey stick on 26 June. The squadrons flew from Cornwall to assemble at *Condor*/Naval Air Station Arbroath on the east coast of Scotland. As No. 808 Squadron embarked on 29 August 1950, including Lieutenant Goldrick of that air-minded 1941 college class, VAT could not have helped reflecting on those desperate days of 1941 in the Mediterranean when No. 808 Squadron and his No. 807 Squadron had battled together.

Following a short work up in the North Sea the ship sailed around Scotland's Cape Wrath to run down the west coast of Britain to Portsmouth. Cape Wrath lived up to its name and they encountered a severe Atlantic gale which buckled some bow plating as the ship's stem pounded directly into the breaking swell. After dockyard assistance in Portsmouth, a course was set via the Suez Canal, to arrive back in home port with 23 Fireflies and 35 Sea Furies in time for Christmas leave.

Meanwhile North Korean forces had invaded across the 38th parallel on 25 June 1950, and plunged south until halted at the Pusan perimeter. The UN break-out and subsequent landing at Inchon in mid-September 1950 had pushed further north, occupied the North Korean capital Pyongyang and reached the Yalu River border with Manchuria in places. Through the winter blizzards two Chinese armies crossed from Manchuria and forced back the UN troops. Prime Minister Menzies' concerns about communist aggression, which had led to the introduction of national service that year, seemed vindicated. The navy was expected to train 1,000 conscripts every twelve months and would do dedicated training cruises for the "nashos".

The Colossus-class *Triumph* flew her first strikes with the 13th CAG on 3 July under the US naval commander in support of Security Council resolutions. Putting paid to the much-publicised alleged statement by the Chief of the Imperial General Staff in 1947 that there would be no war for fifteen years, *Triumph* was relieved by *Theseus* and then *Glory* took her place in turn.[14] The RAN had assigned ships to the British Commonwealth Occupation Forces since 1946, basing them out of *Commonwealth*, the naval base at Kure some 24 kilometres from Hiroshima. Already in the area *Shoalhaven* and *Bataan* deployed to Korean waters on 1 July 1950, the first of nine RAN warships that would see active service.

When the 20th CAG embarked in January 1951 they had been farewelled from *Albatross* by that station's new commander (air), John Stenning, VAT's pilot for their "gallant failure" against *Scharnhorst* in 1940.[15] Once onboard, VAT met all the aircrew over informal drinks at lunch. Many of the pilots and observers were new to him and all were amazed when, later that afternoon, he introduced all 35 to Captain Harries virtually name and rank perfect. VAT had developed an uncanny memory for names, knowing almost everyone in the ship and would always address an officer or sailor correctly by his rank/rate and name. It was a personal leadership touch that could not help but bond CAG and carrier.

Newly joined Midshipman Thomas "Toz" Dadswell (1946 class King's Medallist) learned the practicalities of VAT's approach to leadership and discipline when on boat duty in Jervis Bay. As his workboat, full of sailors who had been drinking ashore, approached the ship they saw the commander at the gangway and their shouted comments echoed clearly across the water. VAT ordered Dadswell to standoff. A period of cold spray and bouncing around soon partially sobered the men and they quietened down. As the subdued sailors boarded VAT indicated the vocal ringleaders who were hurried below for defaulters parade. VAT invited Dadswell to his cabin where he forthrightly pointed out that it was the midshipman's fault those men were now on charge. Dadswell should have recognised the situation and kept well clear and out of earshot of the ship until the men had quieted down.

The junior aircrew would grumble about VAT's cleaning and painting parties constantly keeping the ship "smart". At one point off Korea Sub-Lieutenant (P) Frederick "Fred" Lane recalls almost the entire rear starboard aft roped off.[16] Aircrew who would usually go from the wardroom to the ready room via the starboard gallery deck had to go up port side and traverse the hangar or flight deck or go well forward on Deck Three then climb to the galley deck and walk aft. If this was during morning action stations with the numerous watertight doors and hatches closed with clips dogged-down, it was time consuming and arduous.

When he was governor-general of Australia in 1946 Prince Henry, the younger brother of

---

14   Similar to the Ten-Year Rule adopted by the Committee of Imperial Defence in the 1920s and early 1930s which required the navy to draft its estimates on the assumption that the British Empire would not be engaged in any great war during the next ten years.
15   John Stenning had five years loan service in Australia. After two years as *Albatross's* commander (air) he volunteered to cover the next Korean deployment, becoming *Sydney's* commander (air) in turn from January 1953. Subsequently *Sydney* did not relieve *Ocean* until after the armistice.
16   Later Lieutenant-Commander (P) Frederick Lane (b. 1929), a graduate of No. 1 Naval Air Pilots Course at RAAF Point Cook who later trained as a landing signals officer and qualified flying instructor. He commanded No. 805 (Skyhawk) Squadron in 1969.

King George VI, instituted the Duke of Gloucester's Cup for annual award within the navy. In April 1951 *Sydney* was announced as the unit with the highest level of overall proficiency for 1950 and was presented with the cup. While all departments onboard contributed, the captain and commander could deservedly take extra pride in the achievement. It was the first of a long association VAT and his ships were to have with the Gloucester Cup.

Among the usual deck accidents working-up, Lieutenant (P) Robert "Bob" Smith died when his Firefly, caught in funnel turbulence after a late wave-off, hit the landing beacon beside the funnel and plunged into the sea.[17] Exercising with the New Zealand cruiser *Bellona*, a rocket accidentally fired from a Sea Fury and hit her quarterdeck, demolishing their prized whaler. Supposing themselves favourites to win the scheduled pulling regatta in Hobart, feelings ran high, with an Aussie conspiracy against the Kiwis being seriously mooted. Feelings only assuaged when they were informed that the pilot had been Lieutenant Peter Seed, himself a New Zealander.[18]

There was another fatal accident when the 21st CAG embarked for their carrier qualifications several months later. Lieutenant Robert "Bob" Barnett suffered an asymmetric rocket-assisted take-off launch and crashed just off the ship's bow.[19] An hour's search by ships and aircraft failed to reveal any trace of aircraft or pilot so the flying programme was recommenced. This accident rate was markedly low for the time and was seen as an indication of the depth of experience amongst the aircrew, seventy percent of whom had flown in the last war.

Admiral of the Fleet Lord Fraser, now First Sea Lord, asked Collins if *Sydney* could relieve *Glory* for "two or three months operational flying if the Korean business is still going". The Admiralty had first requested the carrier the previous December, but two destroyers were considered then as sufficient commitment. The prime minister agreed on 11 May and three days later an enlarged *Sydney* CAG of Nos. 805, 808 and 817 Squadrons was designated and an even more intensive pre-deployment work-up commenced. This number of aircraft required operating with a permanent deck park. There were no fatalities in this work-up. Embarking three squadrons meant the ship's living spaces were as crowded as her hangar and flight deck but VAT found all his required housekeeping fell into the necessary routine. To ensure this the executive officer and ship's office staff would work long hours, where VAT found himself assisted yet again by Commissioned Writer Jeffrey Britten, who had joined the carrier in March.

Sydney's air group commander would be Lieutenant-Commander Michael "Mike" Fell DSO DSC, who had managed to shoot down an enemy aircraft while flying the obsolescent Gloster Sea

---

17   Ex-Flight Lieutenant Robert Smith (1924-1951) was a Lancaster captain with No. 460 (RAAF) Squadron and joined the RAN in late 1947. His observer Petty Officer Keith "Bunny" Bunning survived.
18   Later Lieutenant-Commander (P) Peter Seed (1924-1995), an ex sub-lieutenant (A) RNZNVR who was mentioned in despatches for Korea, commanded No. 808 Squadron and was lieutenant-commander (flying) for a year at *Albatross* while VAT was in command.
19   Ex-Flight Sergeant Robert Barnett (1924-1951) flew Kittyhawk fighters in New Guinea with No. 78 Squadron, RAAF, and joined the RAN in early 1949. The use of rocket assisted take-off gear was discontinued.

A Firefly of No. 817 Squadron with Korean "invasion stripes".

Gladiator biplane.[20] When the *Ark* had swapped her No. 800 (Skua) Squadron for *Furious's* No. 807 (Fulmar) Squadron off Gibraltar in April 1941, VAT and Mike had passed each other in the air. That the CAG did particularly well over Korea VAT always felt was a tribute to Fell who made the most of his very experienced aircrew, while taking the most inexperienced as his own wingmen.

Other RN loan officers in *Sydney* were the Commander (Air) Launcelot Kiggell DSC, lieutenant-commanders flying and operations and the flight deck officer.[21] A mere three years from *Sydney's* commissioning, it was inevitable that the majority of the new FAA's senior ranks were still British. Of aircrew commanders ashore and afloat there were seven RN and two RAN, while there were seventeen RN lieutenant-commanders and five RAN.[22] Only No. 805 (Sea Fury) Squadron had an RAN commanding officer, Lieutenant-Commander Walter "Jimmy" Bowles.[23]

Rough seas had caused several mishaps and barrier entries with minor injuries only. One Sea Fury was lost although the pilot, Lieutenant Peter Goldrick, was rescued.[24] When they sailed for Korea on 31 August with *Tobruk*, work-up continued with the aircraft now sporting the "invasion stripes" VAT had first seen in 1944 off Normandy. Apparently, the US air force could mistake a Sea Fury for a Yak-9 in the stress of combat. The first day of September saw the signing of the ANZUS treaty where an attack on either Australia, New Zealand or the US in the Pacific would see them unite against the common danger. With civil unrest in Rabaul,

---

20   Later Vice-Admiral (P) Sir Michael Fell KCB DSO DSC* (1918-1976) who had commanded No. 805 (Martlet/Wildcat) Squadron in the Western Desert, aged 24. Mentioned in despatches flying off *Illustrious* during the Sicily landings, he was awarded an immediate DSO striking *Tirpitz* off *Searcher*. Fell was commander (air) of *Emperor* during the invasion of southern France and was awarded a DSC for operations in the Aegean.

21   Commander (P) Launcelot Kiggell DSC MiD (1916-1980) had joined the RAF in 1935 before transferring to the FAA in 1939. A No. 815 Squadron flare layer/bomber at Taranto, he commanded No. 841 (Albacore) Squadron in 1942. His final appointment before retiring in 1958 was fleet air officer for the Mediterranean Fleet.

22   The only Australian aviators senior to VAT were Captain (O) George Oldham DSC, Captain Superintendent Sydney/Captain of the Dockyard after commanding *Australia*, and Commander (O) Claude Brooks (KM) serving as Chief Staff Officer to the Flag Officer-in-Charge NSW. Neither served on carriers during the war.

23   Later Commander (P) Walter Bowles DSC (1920-1994), a former RNZNVR Wildcat and CAM ship fighter pilot who joined the RAN in 1948. He was lieutenant-commander (flying) in *Vengeance*.

24   Lieutenant (P) Peter Goldrick sheared away his port oleo and slewed violently, missing wires and the barrier on 17 July, toppling over the port side into the swell. Seeing the shadow of the carrier passing overhead he delayed getting out of the cockpit before surfacing on the starboard side of the ship's wake. He entered in his logbook: "Deck Landing Practice. Splash 0:05. Deck Landings – 1".

a show of force was flown over the area in passing. Another Sea Fury ditched with an engine failure on passage to Yokosuka, the pilot achieving a record time for getting into his dinghy and deploying a fishing line, but the enthusiastic rescue destroyer rushed in too close and tipped him out.

By September 1951, the latest UN offensive was essentially static, holding near the 38th parallel and only fighting for local tactical advantages. Armistice negotiations began at Panmunjom on 25 October and General Ridgeway halted offensive ground operations. As the second harsh winter of the conflict froze the ground, there was active defence only along the trenches of the 155-mile front. At sea the navies of nine nations blockaded North Korea, and the carrier aircraft of two of those navies, in conjunction with UN air forces, conducted an interdiction campaign. With *Sydney's* arrival the RAN became the third navy to commit a carrier to the theatre and only the fourth navy to ever send a fixed-wing carrier into combat.[25]

The day before *Sydney* arrived in Kure, Harries wrote that VAT had:

> Performed the onerous and difficult duties of executive officer of an aircraft carrier with complete success. His professional ability and strength of character has been exercised to ensure harmonious co-operation between the Carrier Air Group and the Air Department on the one hand and the rest of the ship on the other. A thoroughly good seaman with high personal, moral and professional standards. In my opinion the service is fortunate in having such an officer available for service in the higher ranks both of naval aviation and of general service.

Harries recognised that VAT needed to round off his experience, recommending that he be given his own command as soon as possible. His leadership was once again marked highly, and immediate promotion was recommended.

When *Sydney* secured to No. 5 berth on 27 September, opposite a *Glory* showing the wear of nine war patrols, *Glory's* marine band played *If I'd known you were coming I'd have baked a cake*. The three-day handover included swapping the Australian Fireflies for *Glory's* cannon armed Mark 5s, also borrowing the USN loaned Sikorsky HO3S-1 rescue helicopter and crew.[26] Nicknamed *The Thing* by *Glory's* fixed-wing fixated 14th CAG, its rescue and plane guard abilities had Harries describing it within days as "invaluable"! *Glory* departed for a much-needed refit in the strategically vital capital-ship dry dock at Garden Island Dockyard and *Sydney* sailed for her first war patrol screened by *Tobruk*.[27] Fell led the first operational sortie on 5 October, one of 47 that day. Soon an average of 54 sorties were being flown in the short winter days.

---

25   After the Royal Navy, Imperial Japanese Navy and the United States Navy. Several other nations such as the Russians and Germans had used seaplane carriers and catapult ships on active service.

26   Produced under license in the UK by Westland as the WS-51 Dragonfly.

27   The Captain Cook Graving Dock for capital ships was first mooted in the crisis year of 1938. The largest civil engineering project in Australia to that date, construction began in July 1940. It was the working shore lights of this project that backlit *Chicago* and *Canberra* during the midget submarine attack of 1942. When it opened in March 1945, the emergency docking of the *kamikaze* damaged *Illustrious* had already occurred three weeks before.

Photographs from the deck of Sydney with New Jersey in the background.

The usual pattern for a two-week war patrol was to sail from Kure or Sasebo, do four days of operations off Korea's west coast from Point Oboe roughly abeam Seoul, then steam south to replenish from the small fleet train for a day, back to Point Oboe for another four days, and then return to Japan. All quickly got used to this patrol pattern and the aircrew welcomed the break during replenishment. Of course, for the majority of the ship's company, and for VAT, that replenishment day of taking on ammunition, bunker fuel, avgas and air stores was anything but a rest day. Neither was it restful for the CAG maintainers as they repaired battle damage and ensured maximum serviceability when the ship returned to Point Oboe. Time in port was equally hectic with the many ongoing duties of a carrier's executive oficer amidst the whirl of ceremonial visits, exchanging calls and social activities.

Much is made of the record number of sorties in a day achieved by various light fleet carriers during the Korean War. Both before and after *Sydney*, in consecutive carriers' deployments, that daily record was competitively sought and surpassed. For three years, from 2 July 1950 when *Triumph* arrived on station, until the armistice of 27 July 1953 while *Ocean* was on war patrol, the record was held and broken seven times.[28]

The most recent record of 84 in a day had been set by *Glory* on her eighth war patrol. What is remarkable about *Sydney* is that she surpassed that record on only the fifth day of her first war patrol, clearly indicating a fully worked-up ship's company and CAG. Competition was not restricted to the Commonwealth carriers, they also competed with the smaller US carriers. Several days before, the *Rendova* had achieved a USN record of 50 sorties, only five above her usual 45, while *Theseus* the previous April had launched with her single catapult faster than *Bataan* had managed with two.

After dawn action stations, with all ship's guns manned, twelve Sea Furies launched from

---

28   Records to September 1951: *Triumph* 19 July 1950 37 sorties; *Theseus* 3 February 1951 66; *Glory* 9 September 1951 84.

0626 in Event "A". Immediately the deck parties prepared the next event aircraft which needed fuelling, arming, ranging and launching before the first strike could land. Two Sea Furies and eight Fireflies launched from 0745 in Event "B", and Event "A" aircraft returned at 0800 for turn-around servicing, fuelling, rearming and ranging. This cycle repeated itself throughout the daylight hours available. Inshore of *Sydney* was the battleship *New Jersey* ("Big Jay"), light cruiser *Belfast* and destroyers. Each event had up to three aircraft allocated to spotting for the awesomely destructive 16-inch guns of the battleship and the 6-inch guns of *Belfast*, while 11 October also recorded the largest sea bombardment of 1951. The commander of the Seventh Fleet, Vice-Admiral Harold Martin, an aviator himself, was aboard *New Jersey* and declared that the spotting was the best they had experienced.[29]

Fireflies attacked troops in and around the township of Tongchon. The fifth event launched eighteen Sea Furies from 1200 and at one point there were 31 aircraft in the air. Goldrick flew three times - as did almost every other pilot - striking Kojo with rockets, spotting for *Belfast* and flying a CAP for a total flight time of five hours. On the eastern slope of a ridge less than two kilometres from a beach 2,000 enemy troops were seen digging in expecting a landing. The final Event "G" launched twelve Sea Furies from 1545 in a strike against those troops. After seven events, the last recovery was at 1649 setting a new record of 89 operational sorties flown. Three aircraft returned with flak damage.

This was as much a ship's record as it was the CAG's. Everyone from parachute riggers to cooks, stokers to sick-berth attendants, needed high spirits and brilliant teamwork to safely achieve such a figure. The flight deck team worked in a continuous watch as also the ordnance teams sweating to bring up and load the tons of bombs and rockets expended. Aircraft maintainers had to additionally work long hours through the nights before and after to maximise aircraft availability. It was not unusual for between 30 and 40 percent of aircraft to return unserviceable because of flak damage or other issues, with all needing to be serviceable again by the next morning.

In terms that VAT's cricketing uncle would have appreciated *Sydney* was signaled by Rear-Admiral Alan Scott-Moncrieff who declared:

Eighty-nine sorties in one day is grand batting by any standard, especially in the opening match.[30]

Collins in Navy Office received a personal message of congratulations from the First Sea Lord for this outstanding performance on *Sydney's* first war patrol. Paraphrasing *Sydney's* motto, the work-up had been thorough and she had proven ready! With this first war patrol, and on this day, the RAN demonstrated the successful establishment of a carrier aviation capability for the nation.

---

29   Over 10/11 October *New Jersey* expended 184 x 16-inch, *Belfast* 529 x 6-inch and the destroyers 284 x 5-inch and 309 x 4.5-inch rounds. *Sydney* expended 88 x 500-pound bombs, 648 x 60-pound rockets and 23,335 x 20 mm cannon rounds.
30   Later Admiral Sir Alan Scott-Moncrieff KCB CBE DSO* (1900-1980) who commanded a sloop and a destroyer in WWII. During the Korean War he was Flag Officer Second-in-Command Far East Station and the in-theatre commander of Commonwealth naval forces.

Typhoon Ruth and its aftermath.

Everyone who served in Korea that October remembered Typhoon *Ruth*, which occurred shortly after that record-breaking day. *Sydney* was in Sasebo refueling and re-arming when the warning was given that there was a typhoon in the offing. As the harbour was crowded, Captain Harries made the decision to put to sea and face the typhoon there since remaining in harbour carried the risk of vessels losing their moorings and damaging other vessels. At 1030 on 14 October the carrier slipped and headed out to sea.

Pitching heavily with torrential rain and the sea churning brown, a maximum roll of 22 degrees was experienced at 1527. That it was not more was because the carrier was hove-to making only two knots to maintain steerage way with Captain Harries keeping the sea very fine on the starboard bow. This allowed the waves to roll down the starboard side and kept damage to a minimum. While nowhere near the 52 degrees VAT had once experienced in an Atlantic gale aboard *Tracker*, maneuvering to avoid submarines, the situation was serious with the 45-foot waves washing over the side a motor dinghy, forklift truck and a Firefly. Stokers were tending the boilers and turbines with a foot of water in the machinery spaces.

There was only room for 24 aircraft to be secured in the hangar, so the remaining thirteen were lashed down aft of the island. The whip of the stern collapsed the under-carriages of some aircraft and as tons of green water regularly swept the length of the flight deck lashings broke and aircraft slid across the deck into the gun sponsons. The aircraft handlers risked their lives on the flight deck and in the hangar to secure aircraft and equipment as lashings eased and then broke with the ship's pitching and rolling. The escorting destroyers, especially the Netherlands *Van Galen*, had an even more unpleasant time in the mountainous seas and a USN troop transport with 500 troops aboard was blown ashore.

VAT had hard-won experience of both man-made and storm-induced damage to ships and aircraft. As *Sydney's* executive officer he headed the damage control organisation and for 36 hours without rest or pause he worked with his seaman and engineering damage control parties to keep the ship and her crew safe. One of the continuing problems was that in these extremely high seas the ship took a lot of water into the intakes of the ventilation system. These intakes, flush with the side of the ship, had within them electric fan motors to circulate air. Taking sea water into the air intakes the motors would short circuit and start an electrical fire. Not every fan could be shut off and all fires needed immediate attention before they became dangerous, especially as fumes from ruptured fuel tanks spread.

VAT (left) in the wardroom hosting a ship's company fancy dress party on Christmas Day, 1951.

On return to Sasebo, one beached ship had clearly dragged her moorings right through *Sydney's* previous anchorage. In southern Japan 572 people had died and 221,118 homes were destroyed. Half of *Sydney's* aircraft needed repairs, two were retrieved from the gun sponsons, seven were written-off and three sent to the maintenance carrier *Unicorn* for major repair. VAT succinctly observed that Typhoon *Ruth* was something extraordinary and *Sydney* had been very lucky.

They spent Christmas 1951 in Kure and Captain Harries continued to report that the health, morale and disposition of the ship's company was most satisfactory. Rear-Admiral Collins made a Christmas broadcast from Melbourne to the RAN ships in Korean waters. For the aviators the occasion was celebrated with the concentrated intensity of young men under wartime stress. Sailing for her sixth war patrol on 27 December one squadron diarist wrote:

> It can be said without exaggeration that more than half the squadron was relieved to be once again at sea and enjoy a little sobriety.

The patrol statistics are a stark indication of *Sydney's* mettle. Of the 38 aircraft embarked, the fourth patrol from 18 to 30 November saw them hit by flak 43 times and five were lost. Over 43 days of flight operations during *Sydney's* seven war patrols the CAG flew 743 Firefly and 1,623 Sea Fury sorties, 90 aircraft were damaged by flak and thirteen lost with nine shot down. Small calibre flak damage was so common, a version of a bicycle puncture repair kit was used to patch the holes. Over half a million 20mm cannon shells and 8,655 rockets were fired with 1,162 bombs delivered. In retrospect, it seems incredible that only three aircrew were killed. The number would have been higher if not for the rescue work of *The Thing*, affectionately referred to as *Uncle Peter* after its registration letters UP-28.

Handover to a refreshed *Glory* came in Hong Kong at the end of January 1952, with Fireflies and stores returned to *Glory* and *Unicorn*. Reluctantly *Uncle Peter* was also returned. There they heard the news that King George VI had died. All official functions were cancelled and sailing was delayed until the Royal Proclamation of the accession of Queen Elizabeth

The new Queen's Korea Medal (left) was awarded for service in Korea between 1 July 1950 and 27 July 1953. The reverse showed Hercules fighting the hydra, a symbolic representation of communism. The United Nations Service Medal (Korea) was awarded to those from twenty member states who served with the United Nations forces in Korea from 27 June 1950 until 27 July 1954.

had been read. When they stopped in Fremantle, a lightning strike by waterfront workers saw Harries have six Sea Furies lashed in a line athwartship forward and six aft, enabling a pinwheel manoeuver so they could depart tug free. When the blasts from the revving aircraft blew coal dust over the lounging strikers there were no apologies.

As *Sydney* arrived in Jervis Bay to disembark her CAG on 3 March 1952, Commander John Stenning led the welcoming fly past of four Sea Furies and four Fireflies. Already ashore at *Albatross* was Peter Goldrick, recovering from being shot in the arm while striking gun positions along the Yesong River on 5 January. Shepherded back to Point Oboe by the rest of his flight he landed safely aboard and was flown back to Australia from Japan.[31]

Glory made conscious efforts to take back her record from *Sydney*. This she achieved in the longer daylight hours of 17 March 1952, flying 106 sorties in ten events. The Fifth Sea Lord signalled:

Congratulations on your fine century.[32]

At 1045 on 6 March contingents from *Sydney*, and the recently returned *Tobruk* and *Murchison*, were formed up for a march through Sydney. The great majority of the Australian public supported their armed forces presence in the continuing Korean conflict. Five days earlier, 3,000 had cheered the launching of the new destroyer *Voyager* at Cockatoo Island Dockyard. Three days before, there had been a rousing send-off for the soldiers of the 1st Battalion Royal Australian Regiment heading to join the 3rd Battalion in Korea. Now crowds, undiminished in their enthusiasm, lined the streets to cheer the marching sailors in their white summer uniforms, as people in the buildings overlooking George Street threw paper and streamers down on the marchers in a "ticker tape shower".

On the saluting dais in front of Sydney Town Hall, flanked by the naval ensign and national

---

31   Later Captain (P) Peter Goldrick (1927-2002), one of the first RAN qualified flight instructors and jet pilots. He commanded Nos. 816 (Gannet) and 725 (Gannet/Dakota) Squadrons, the frigate *Stuart* and shore establishment *Penguin*.
32   *Ocean*, under the hard driving command of Captain (P) Charles "Crash" Evans DSO DSC, who had been *Sussex's* Osprey pilot with the Australian Squadron in 1935, flew 123 sorties on 17 May 1952. *Glory* matched this during her third deployment on 5 April 1953.

The impressive parade of 900 men from Sydney, Tobruk amd Murchison marching through the city of Sydney on 6 March 1952. VAT Smith was leading but is just outside the frame of this photograph.

flag, stood the Governor-General of Australia Sir William McKell GCMG to take the salute. At his special invitation the captains of *Sydney, Tobruk* and *Murchison* were by his side, watching the men of their warships winding past.

Leading those men as parade commander, preceded by the colour party with the ensign of his service, was Commander VAT Smith DSC. He was wearing a black mourning armband for a king whose coronation procession he had watched, and who had personally presented him with that DSC.[33] Proudly marching at the head of 900 men to the acclaim of his fellow Sydneysiders must have been one of VAT's most memorable moments.

Sydney and her CAG were not the first naval aviators to operate under United Nations auspices. That honour was already held by the RAN's original observer, Commander Henry "Chesters" Chesterman OBE.[34] In September 1947, the UN requested military observers to report on the conflict in the Netherlands East Indies and Chesterman was sent as a naval observer on the staff of the Australian Consul General Batavia. With Australian army and RAAF colleagues they commenced their mission several days before the British observers arrived. Australia, and the RAN, thus having the honour of fielding the very first UN peacekeepers.

VAT would ruminate that being a United Nations war it had been an odd sort of war, relatively restricted in geographical area and conducted a long way from Australia's traditional areas of interest. Much later he would look back on those cheering crowds, recognising there could be

---

33   The temporary flagship *Australia* had fired a 56-gun salute on the death of the king and a 21-gun salute for the new queen. In Korea *Bataan* and *Cardigan Bay*'s 56-gun salutes were fired, in a more effective manner, "at the queen's enemies".

34   Commander (O) Henry Chesterman OBE (1901-1985) joined the college in 1915, watched the German Grand Fleet scuttled at Scapa Flow and saw active service in the battleship *Ramillies*. Qualified with the 11th Naval Observer's Course in 1927 he survived two ditchings. Awarded the US Legion of Merit by Admiral Kinkaid for service on his staff in WWII he was Resident Naval Officer Brisbane.

no comparison between the public attitude then to that of many during the Vietnam War. That war was still a decade away for Australian servicemen, who would spend a decade fighting there.

The drama and dash of Korean flight operations, with its close air support for the Commonwealth Division and bold rescues of downed aircrew behind enemy lines, can obscure the mortal grind of aircrew losses in training and as squadrons worked up to their operational tempo. During the six months of *Sydney's* deployment eight Australian FAA aircrew were killed flying in Britain and Australia.

The much-anticipated homecoming after active service was quickly followed by a rush of CAG engagements and weddings, among them Peter Goldrick who had been wearing a scarf knitted for him by Caroline Purcell the freezing winter morning he was shot through his right arm. He had promised to bring it home and he did, promptly marrying her.[35] For Nanette and VAT their son Mark was born nine months later on 6 December 1952.

After his Korean service Darbo Harries was made a Companion of the British Empire, the citation noting:

> … this most efficient carrier created a sortie record and consistently kept up a very high rate of sorties, which could only have been achieved by high efficiency of all hands from hard training under the supervision of Captain Harries.

That his award very much reflected on his commander was recognised by Harries when he wrote about VAT in mid-April:

> Perhaps I may be forgiven for saying that the ship's performance on the Far East Station has proved his outstanding qualities as a naval officer. I could not have wished for better support from my Second-in-Command. He is strongly recommended for immediate promotion to the rank of captain.

Following this handsome tribute from Harries the FOCAF, now Rear-Admiral John Eaton DSO DSC appended:

> Fully concur. I was much impressed by the efficiency of this officer on my visit.[36]

As well as the expected decorations and mention in despatches for the CAG aircrew, including a DSM for *Uncle Peter's* USN pilot for his daring rescue behind enemy lines, were awards to some

In 1992 VAT commented that "The winter weather in Korea was severe although it was not as bad as on the Murmansk run".

---

35   In the vast collection of the Australian War Memorial in Canberra is item REL38595, the navy blue scarf knitted by Caroline which Peter held firmly onto with his left hand when being lifted out of his Sea Fury and rushed below to the sick bay. His bloodstained cloth chit, with a message in Chinese and Korean carried by aircrew in case they were shot down, is item REL32854.
36   Later Vice-Admiral Sir John Eaton KBE CB DSO DSC (1902-1981) who had commanded four destroyers during the war and a cruiser after. Before retiring he was Deputy Supreme Allied Commander Atlantic under the NATO organisation.

of the carrier's complement who made those aircrew achievements possible.[37] From within the air department, operations room and engineers, exceptional service was recognised. *Glory's* commander had received a mention in her deployment and Harries report on VAT makes clear similar was merited. With his self-effacing nature, feeling he was lucky to have already been recognised several times and knowing that only a very small percentage of those deserving could be cited, VAT likely steered consideration towards others he would have felt were more deserving.

Schofields: establishing an air station   25 April 1952 to 17 July 1953

After time as a MONAB supporting the British Pacific Fleet, Schofields had been handed back to the RAAF. In the 1947 naval air plan VAT had designated the base as a maintenance station and training school for air technical ratings. Commodore (O) Arthur Pedder, Fourth Naval Member, evaluated the site in November 1950 and, as it was near the de Havilland works at Bankstown and the industrial areas of Sydney, agreed.[38] On Anzac Day 1952 VAT joined RAAF Base Schofields as commander of the RAN air section. He was leading an advance party tasked to turn the establishment from being an RAAF base into a naval air station.

VAT was essentially a detachment commander since he reported to Captain (O) George Beale DSO OBE at *Albatross,* Schofields briefly becoming *Albatross II.*[39] It was planned that the station would include an aircraft repair yard and be the headquarters of captain (air) Australia. VAT found his initial months at Schofields "interesting" as it was an extraordinary job the like of which he had never previously experienced. As the air force wound down from its establishment of 890 airmen and 120 officers, VAT commenced the naval build up with his initial staff of ten.

This staff included engineering, electrical and supply branch commanders. The supply commander was an RN loan officer but VAT's commander (L) was his 1927 classmate George Knox who had served with him in *Bulldog.* Knox had become an anti-submarine specialist and commanded *Orara* and *Quiberon* during the war. As the post-war navy became increasingly technology focused, Knox transferred to the new electrical (L) branch when it was instituted in 1948. VAT's engineering commander was Stuart St Vincent Welch (1928 class) who had mislaid his cap in 1932, when due to be presented with the King's Medal. Numbering twenty by the summer, it was a happy wardroom under VAT as president of the officer's mess.

Towards the end of the year Captain Beale praised VAT's application and capacity for getting things done. Using his considerable knowledge and ability he applied these attributes to "the numerous problems involved in getting the navy a footing at Schofields and of making it suitable as a naval air station". Never hidebound in his problem solving, one example was

---

37   Chief Aviation Machinist's Mate Arlen Babbitt was also awarded the US Navy Cross, as was his aircrewman Aviation Machinist's Mate Callis Gooding.
38   Later Vice-Admiral Sir Arthur Pedder KBE CB (1904-1995), an observer course mate of George Oldham's in 1930 he had spent considerable time with the Naval Air Division and commanded *Khedive.*
39   Captain George Beale DSO OBE (1905-1974) was seriously injured when a Fairey IIID spun into the sea during his 16th Naval Observer's Course in 1929. Wounded when air staff officer in *Illustrious* he was captured in Crete and became head of the escape organisation in his POW camp. He commanded *Nairana* as a training carrier after VE Day before her transfer to the Netherlands Navy as the *Karel Doorman.*

when VAT adopted the air force practice of a single senior NCO's mess instead of the navy's separate messing for petty officers and chief petty officers. It was possibly the only combined senior sailors mess in any Commonwealth navy at the time.

In December 1952 Captain (O) Dennis Sanderson DSC was appointed Captain (Air) Australia and VAT became his chief staff officer.[40] Sanderson quickly recognised that VAT had exceptional ability, integrity and drive and commented on his tact, manifest in the transition of Schofield's from light blue to navy blue. When *Nirimba*/Naval Air Station Schofields commissioned on 1 April 1953, Sanderson also assumed duties as the station's commanding officer and VAT those of his executive officer. With this commissioning the need to use RN training establishments for junior ratings finally ceased. *Nirimba's* three technical schools of air electrical, air ordnance and air engineering with their highly trained alumni kept the FAA flying ashore and afloat for many years.[41]

Sanderson reported that VAT was extremely competent as his chief staff officer with a facility for quick and clear expression of his logical and reasoned opinions. As the station's executive officer, he was an efficient organiser and administrator, whose leadership and beneficial influence was felt in all the affairs of the station. As with the senior sailors' mess VAT had displayed imagination and foresight in the development of this new air station.

Sydney had been busy while VAT was at Schofields with more than just the normal workups, exercises and port visits. Embarking Nos. 805 and 817 Squadrons she led eleven RAN ships to support the five RN vessels, including the escort carrier *Campania*, in Operation *Hurricane* at the Montebello Islands off Karratha, Western Australia. When a plutonium implosion device in the hull of the frigate *Plym* exploded on 3 October 1952, the UK became the world's third nuclear power. With a commonwealth contingent embarked the carrier was one of nine at the July 1953 Spithead Coronation Fleet Review, where No. 817 Squadron flew in the 36-squadron review fly past by 327 naval aircraft. *Sydney* next took over from *Ocean* for a post-armistice Korean deployment that finished in May 1954.

Not long after commissioning it was considered that the air station at Nowra, in conjunction with private contractors at de Havilland's and elsewhere, could cope with the aircraft repair side, so that function was abolished. When it was later decided there should be only one carrier air group, this left only ground training for *Nirimba*. With these two changes the captain (air) structure also became superfluous. VAT was not there for those changes, having moved on to Navy Office, where he had instituted them under Treasury pressure. He would comment in future years that he was pleased to see how *Nirimba* prospered as the RAN Apprentice School, feeling that the commissioning staff had ensured a good beginning.[42]

---

40   Captain (O) Dennis Sanderson DSC (1911-1979) won his DSC with No. 825 (Swordfish) Squadron over Norway and commanded No. 817 (Albacore) Squadron aboard *Victorious* and, post-war, the sloop *Snipe*.

41   Air ordnance mechanics - armourers - had the simple motto that "Without air ordnance there is no need for a fleet air arm!"

42   With the modernisation of Australian industry in the 1950s *Nirimba* was re-established in 1956 as the RAN Apprentice School using a college style selection board for its twice-yearly intakes. Until 1993 its graduates, including the successful introduction of young female apprentices in the 1980s, kept the RAN efficiently operating at the forefront of naval technology.

CHAPTER 11

CAPTAIN IN COMMAND 1954 – 1962

Navy Office in July 1953 was still at Victoria Barracks, across St Kilda Road from Melbourne's Shrine of Remembrance. It was the seat of the Australian Commonwealth Naval Board under the Minister of State for the Navy, the honourable William McMahon MP.[1] His First Naval Member, Vice-Admiral Sir John Collins KBE CB, was Chief of Naval Staff, Commodore First Class David Harries CBE was Second Naval Member and the Fourth Naval Member, with responsibility for the FAA, was Commodore Edward Price OBE.[2]

VAT Smith as a newly appointed captain, 31 December 1953.

The board had its own secretariat of public servants while the naval staff were divided into divisions, naturally, such as the Plans Division and the Operations Division. Aviation came under the Naval Air Warfare Organisation and Training Division and VAT took up his appointment as the division's director while still a commander in July 1953. He replaced an RN loan officer as Australians started to occupy the more senior ranks of the new FAA ashore and afloat. In the lexicon of naval acronyms VAT was now DAWOT and worked for the fourth naval member.[3] Six months later he shipped the four broad stripes of a captain when promoted on 31 December 1953. Jumping ahead of "Braces" Bracegirdle and seven other executive officer commanders his immediate senior on the captains list, by six months, was Jack Mesley (1924 class) who had been *Canberra*'s navigator at Savo Island.

VAT's small team of four were an impressive group of officers, two of whom had recently served in Korea with him. Lieutenant-Commander (P) Harold Bailey DSC was ex-RAAF and had been awarded his DSC as the outstanding strike pilot of the *Sydney* CAG. Lieutenant-Commander (P) Jeffrey Gledhill DSC, who had struck at *Tirpitz* in 1944, flew Fireflies over Korea with Bailey. Another ex-RAAF officer was Lieutenant-Commander (O) Ronald Thomson who had won a DFC as a navigator with No. 625 (Lancaster) Squadron. The deputy director was a loan officer, Commander (P) Cedric "Chico" Roberts DSO, who had been

---

1   Later Sir William McMahon GCMG CH PC (1908-1988) who had been both Minister for the Navy and Minister for the Air Force since 1951. He was the twentieth Prime Minister of Australia in 1971-1972.
2   Commodore Second Class Edward Price OBE (1902-1983) had graduated from No. 3 Naval Pilot's Course in 1926. He was the fourth Fourth Naval Member to serve after Commodores Edmund Anstice, Guy Willoughby and Arthur Pedder.
3   DAWOT - the Director of Air Warfare Organisation and Training.

decorated for his command of VAT's old No. 825 Squadron in 1952.[4] Roberts' Firefly had been shot down north of the 38th parallel during *Ocean*'s first war patrol, a US Dumbo aircraft rescuing him and his observer from the water. He would not repeat the classic mistake of a second run over a target in *Ocean*'s nine further war patrols.

It was a fortuitously timed appointment for VAT and the new FAA. Having had a prime role in the birth of a local carrier-based force and then contributed to its success on active service off Korea, he was now called on to navigate the emerging budget constraints on the original scope of the 1947 naval air plan. Like most long-term defence projects, lauded by ministers at their birth, the naval air plan had become subject to an annual round of Treasury parsimony and inter-service squabbling over the available budget. The navy, having had the majority of the defence vote from 1947, found the army and air force budgets were in the ascendence post-Korea, but all three services were subject to economies. Two carriers, three air groups and two air stations were proving a reach too far for the available tax funds. The fourth naval member was not able to salvage everything, and what was retained was due in large measure to his DAWOT.

When VAT became DAWOT it was year D+6 (1953/1954) of the original 1947 naval air plan. Two carriers and two CAGs were meant to be operating, while two Firefly strike squadrons should have already been re-equipped with type "Y" and the first Sea Fury fighter squadron should have re-equipped with type "X". These replacements were to be "the best gas-turbine or jet powered" strike and fighter aircraft then coming into RN service.

VAT had played a key role in seeing a second air station for technical training and maintenance commissioned as planned in D+5. However, the second carrier and replacement aircraft were long delayed, and hopes for a third CAG were fading. With his personality and drive at Navy Office he was quickly seen as a most successful director of a staff division, whose energy saw any task done thoroughly. Price appreciated that his experience, coupled with a quick mind and imagination, allowed him to find workable solutions. In the face of budgetary stress, VAT managed to stay cheerful and buoyant despite the hard decisions to abolish the aircraft repair side of *Nirimba* and cancel the plans for a third CAG. In addition, he pondered the viability of operating two carriers within the limitations of increasing recruitment and manpower retention difficulties.

For five years since *Sydney*'s arrival the minds of successive Fourth Naval Members, and their DAWOTs, had been focused on the second carrier, originally due for delivery eighteen months after the first commissioned. The announcement of the five-year plan in June 1947 had been quickly followed by political ill-feeling over the issue of modernisation. The government correctly felt that the requirement for modernisation, with its inevitable extra costs, should have

---

4   Later Rear-Admiral (P) Cedric Roberts CB DSO (1918-2011). He survived the sinking of *Manchester* and French internment in the Sahara after reaching shore. Flew off *Trumpeter* in the Arctic and *Vindex* in the Pacific. Commanded No. 813 (Firebrand) Squadron off *Implacable*. Roberts enjoyed his time in Australia so much that when he retired from the RN he and his family settled on the NSW south coast.

been foreseen, costed and briefed before the Admiralty formally raised the subject in August 1947. In this, Anstice, and indeed VAT, were knowingly or unknowingly remiss, given their specialist knowledge of the increasing weights and launch speeds of new naval aircraft.

After the loss of the light cruiser *Sydney* in November 1941, a shocked public subscribed £427,000 to a replacement fund. This money was able to be legislated towards the new carrier, but money was still tight and Prime Minister Chifley remained suspicious. When Collins became First Naval Member the government decision of 30 March 1948 was that the purchase of two carriers could proceed, but with no modernisation nor extra expenses until completion of the current five-year plan in 1951-52. Fortuitously, the Vickers construction yard would have been unable to complete the Majestic/*Melbourne* hull before this date anyway.

The year 1949 proved difficult for Collins and Willoughby, his Fourth Naval Member, as the Admiralty briefed that a Majestic-class light fleet carrier would likely be unable to operate Hawker Sea Hawk and Supermarine Attacker jets. Nor could it accommodate the larger planned Supermarine Scimitar and de Havilland Sea Vixen. In any event it would require at least three years of extensive modifications. The naval board knew it was cheaper to modernise the carrier while still in the builder's yard rather than during a subsequent refit and accepted the delay. With some economies of truth on what Collins told the government, work on the second carrier belatedly started in 1949.[5]

By 1950 Collins accepted that even a modernised *Melbourne* could not emulate a fleet carrier and operate the latest jets. The Fifth Sea Lord agreed, while holding out hope that the smaller navalised Venom could be a suitable all-weather fighter. With de Havilland Sea Venoms and Fairey Gannet anti-submarine aircraft embarked, *Melbourne* would still have reasonable capability and operational flexibility.

The original air plan had allowed for a wastage rate that would require fifteen fighter and sixteen strike replacement aircraft per annum. Replacing Sea Furies aboard their own Majestic-class *Bonaventure*, the Canadian navy opted for the McDonnell F2H-3 Banshee fighter that had seen extensive service in Korea. The RAN had yet to think about American equipment in acquisition terms and, given the high level of conversion training still undertaken by aircrew in the UK, the decision to acquire British aircraft types was more a *fait accompli* than the result of any detailed staff work by VAT. The transition to two crew Sea Venom jets and three crew turbo-prop Gannets seemed to him in many ways the natural course to follow and, with continued RN support, worked out smoothly.[6]

The prototype BXS-1 steam catapult, to replace hydraulics, was successfully tested on *Perseus* in 1951. While *Sydney*'s BH.3 catapult could accelerate 20,000 pounds to 66 knots and the

---

5   The Secretary to the First Sea Lord minuted on 27 April 1949 that "Admiral Collins … asked that action might not be taken to bring this matter to the notice of either of the Governments".

6   For example, the complicated Double Mamba turbo-prop engines driving the contra-rotating propellors of a Gannet required a dedicated Mamba Handling Course at *Gamecock*/Naval Air Station Bramcote.

maximum weight of a Gannet was 19,600 pounds, this speed at launch was insufficient. Two BS.4 steam catapults, suitably shortened, were ordered from the UK production run at a cost of £400,000. *Melbourne*'s would be fitted while building, with *Sydney*'s fitted during scheduled modernisation in 1955.

A steam catapult, larger and heavier lifts, stronger arrester gear, a strengthened flight deck,

The two-seat de Havilland Sea Venom FAW Mk.53, with "FAW" meaning "Fighter All Weather". The prototype first flew in 1951.

carrier-controlled approach radar, a large operations room and a mirror landing aid were all necessary additions to *Melbourne*.[7] The carrier, reflecting the expected hazards of the Cold War, was also re-designed to have a central citadel that could be sealed in the event of nuclear fallout. Improved air conditioning and a more modern cafeteria and mess deck spaces were also incorporated.

Opinion initially wavered on incorporating the latest innovation, an angled flight deck, which would cost £95,000 and add six months to the already delayed construction schedule. VAT's elegant staff work saw his team quickly prepare a paper delineating the advantages.[8] Doing away with the barrier crashes inevitable with a straight deck carrier and a forward deck park would have prevented seventeen of the 42 accidents experienced in the previous twelve months. At an average cost of

An advertisement for the Fairey Gannet anti-submarine aircraft, which the RN first ordered in 1951.

£10,000 per accident the saving would be £170,000 for a cost of £95,000. There were the added savings of removing three crash barriers and halving the number of arrestor wires from ten to five. It would clearly be improvident not to incorporate the angle deck concept and accept the delay. On seeing the paper, Collins declared of the vital 5½° "this is a must". VAT's division had measurably reduced the potential for injuries and lives lost during flight deck operations.

---

7   The CCA radar enabled a carrier-controlled approach in bad visibility until the pilot could visually acquire the stabilised mirror landing aid which gave the correct final line of approach to the carrier.
8   Instead of landing on the carrier's centreline, aircraft would land at an angle to the centre of the landing area. This permitted the removal of half the arrestor wires and all barriers. If the pilot failed to engage a wire he simply went around, safely angled clear of the aircraft parked forward.

The vital 5½° of Melbourne's angled flight deck and larger lifts are clearly shown in company with Sydney after that carrier's conversion to a troop transport in 1962/1963.

With two CAGs and only one carrier, the vital deck training was severely limited. To remedy this *Vengeance* was loaned to the RAN and had arrived in Australian waters in early 1953. As well as replacement Sea Furies and Fireflies, she carried three Bristol Sycamore Mk.50 helicopters as the RAN started the first rotary-wing training school in Australia. The RN had proved amenable to loaning *Vengeance* free of charge, as it was grateful for *Sydney's* contributions to the Commonwealth carrier forces in Korea. Manpower was a perennial issue in the low unemployment era of the 1950s. Inflation reduced already low pay, and this combined with poor or non-existent service housing and the normal postings disruption to cause a retention and recruitment problem.

With the Korean armistice, the Treasury Department under the Menzies government restricted the navy's budget, so economies were necessary, and the cruisers *Australia* and *Shropshire* disposed of. *Sydney* would not be modernised and the £200,000 steam catapult awaiting her refit was sold on. There would now only be one operational carrier with a single air group. *Vengeance* was returned to the UK in July 1955 and her ship's company became the commissioning crew for *Melbourne.*

For 24 months from July 1953 to June 1955 VAT and his team laboured over these and other issues in close consultation with their fellow manpower and engineering divisions of the naval staff. As VAT handed over his DAWOT duties, dozens of aircrew, responding to his careful planning, were gathering in the UK at *Heron*/Naval Air Station Yeovilton and *Seahawk*/Naval Air Station Culdrose, where they reformed Nos. 808 (Sea Venom), 816 (Gannet) and 817 (Gannet) Squadrons in August 1955.

The latest *Ark Royal*, a 37,000-ton Audacious-class carrier, had commissioned in February 1955 and the 81,000-ton USS *Forrestal* commissioned on 1 October. These were the first two carriers with angled flight decks, steam catapults and mirror landing aids installed on the initial build. When *Melbourne*, laid down in April 1943 and launched as *Majestic* in early 1945, commissioned on 28 October 1955, she was only the third carrier in the world to be fitted with all three innovations during construction, albeit the smallest at 20,000 tons. The three squadrons embarked in February 1956 for the return voyage to Australia and disembarked at Nowra on 7 May 1956.

Appropriately, it was Captain Galfrey Gatacre DSO DSC* who commissioned *Melbourne*.[9] Gatacre, as Deputy Director of Plans, had briefed VAT in 1945 on future aviation and minuted Hamilton that "surely the introduction of a fleet air arm can be confidently expected" whilst nominating VAT to go to London to prepare a draft plan in 1945.

During *Melbourne*'s delivery voyage *Sydney*, having already done one general service training cruise without aircraft, embarked Nos. 805 and 851 Squadrons in March 1956. This final short period of deck landing and handling training for aviators and flight deck party was to supplement *Melbourne*'s crew when she arrived, since no flying was possible on her ferrying delivery voyage. *Sydney* remained in commission as a training ship until May 1958 when she went into special reserve off Bradley's Head, from where she would be resurrected in 1962 as a fast troop transport.

When *Melbourne* joined the fleet her radar-equipped Sea Venom FAW.53 and Gannet AS.1 aircraft gave the navy an all-weather day/night strike capability, unique in the southern hemisphere, on a platform that could move 800 kilometres every 24 hours. As director of the staff aviation division, VAT had ensured the FAA and *Melbourne* would be a significantly more capable presence in southeast Asia and the Pacific, a presence that would continue beyond his own retirement.

Since July 1954 VAT had been one of the honorary *aides-de-camp* to the governor-general, but his services were not called on. Leaving Navy Office, his deserved reputation was that of an extremely competent director of his division. His excellent knowledge of air matters, as the fourth naval member observed, enabled initiative in his planning which had "successfully launched and piloted various schemes with sound judgement". It was recognised that VAT had a good chance of achieving flag rank, so future appointments were mooted that would best widen his experience to fit that rank. Having been intimately involved with aviation for sixteen years, some general service was mandated.

Fox 1: 28 June 1955 - 28 December 1956

Three 2,020-ton Q-class anti-submarine frigates made up the RAN's 1st Frigate Squadron and VAT was appointed as Captain (F) in *Quadrant* on 28 June 1955. As Captain (F), commonly known as Fox 1, not only did he command his own ship, but he also commanded the squadron. VAT was naturally apprehensive, having not served in a destroyer or frigate since being a midshipman in *Bulldog* with the Mediterranean fleet in 1933. He worried how well he could do the job, get along with the ship's company and whether his ship-handling ability

---

9   Later Rear-Admiral Galfrey Gatacre CBE DSO DSC* (1907-1983) who served in the coal-burning light cruiser *Melbourne* with the Mediterranean fleet in 1925. Commanded *Arunta* with the British Commonwealth Occupying Forces and as captain of *Anzac* in 1952-53 his destroyer spent more time in Korean waters than any other Commonwealth ship. After service in 22 RN and RAN ships, he flew his flag in *Melbourne* as FOCAF, Flag Officer Commanding Australian Fleet, in 1959.

would be up to standard. Also, as someone who had seen "Johnnie" Walker in action, his own ability for frigate anti-submarine doctrine and tactics exercised his mind. One bright spot was that he still got flying pay as long as he kept passing his annual aircrew medicals.

Nanette had her own worries. In a reflection of VAT's postings, Michael had been born in London, Mark in Sydney and the youngest, Piers, in Melbourne

VAT as Fox 1 on Quadrant's bridge in 1955.

only months beforehand. While the family had experienced the domestic upheavals of service life, Nanette was once again joining that most hardy fraternity - naval wives with young families whose husbands were at sea. When VAT flew to Singapore to take up his appointment their boys were six, two and five months. However daunting his new posting was for VAT, it would have been equally daunting for Nanette, who relocated to Brierley Street in Cremorne to be closer to the extended Smith family. There she found her

The HMAS Quadrant badge.

mother-in-law Una, and the boy's Uncle Bill with his wife Enid, were all a great help with baby Piers and the older two boys.

Quadrant was then exercising off Singapore with ships and submarines of the RAN, RNZN and RN. Underway replenishment was being provided by Royal Fleet Auxiliary tankers. The Malayan Emergency had been declared in 1948 in response to communist terrorist attacks, and Australian forces were committed in response, including a Lincoln bomber squadron in 1950. A Commonwealth Strategic Reserve was now being formed to deter further communist aggression in South East Asia and assist in operations against the Malayan terrorists. It was at Sembawang, Her Majesty's Naval Base Singapore, that VAT joined *Quadrant* and assumed command. Dowling, the First Naval Member, was in Singapore and officially called on VAT the next day.

While steaming south to Australia on 3 July, a mail-run rendezvous was made with *Vengeance*, passaging to the UK on completion of her loan, where her crew would man the about to commission *Melbourne*. VAT quickly settled into the normal ship's exercise routine in eastern Australian waters. Often working with RAAF maritime aircraft and Sydney based RN submarines, time was full with training classes from the Torpedo and Anti-Submarine (TAS)

VAT transfers by jackstay from Quadrant to Queenborough on 3 March 1956.

The anti-submarine frigate HMAS Queenborough in Sydney Harbour.

school, exercises for the RAN and RAAF students at *Albatross*'s Australian Joint Anti-Submarine School (AJASS) and also that station's observer courses. Alongside at Garden Island for all of August no-one who ever served under VAT would be surprised to hear of the amount of paint expended on masts, mess decks, bathrooms and flats.

As Captain (F) VAT had a Lieutenant (S) as secretary to assist with squadron paperwork and *Quadrant*'s TAS, gunnery, navigator and engineer officers all had additional squadron duties in their respective specialisations. In December FOCAF, Rear-Admiral Henry Burrell CBE, carried out his annual inspection.

The HMAS Queenborough badge. VAT took command of the ship on 10 April 1956.

Quadrant under Captain Thomas Morrison OBE DSC (1925 class) had won the Duke of Gloucester Cup as the most proficient RAN ship in 1954.[10] Morrison had begun his appointment as Fox 1 having previously commanded a destroyer, and with seven more years of bridge watchkeeping experience than his successor. Hence VAT inherited a first-class team and maintained what was already a very smart ship, with *Quadrant* winning the Gloucester Cup again in 1955 under his command.

While the stress of this command was not visible to his superiors and juniors, that it took a toll on VAT is reflected in his medical records as he suffered boils, rashes and painful bouts of

---

10   Later Rear-Admiral Thomas Morrison CB CBE DSC (1911-1983), he had served in *Hobart* for four war years. Awarded the OBE during the evacuation of British Somaliland and the DSC for operations at Lingayen Gulf, he also commanded *Tobruk*, *Melbourne* and *Albatross* and was FOCAF in 1965.

cellulitis. Now 42, his fitness was not helped by the stress, increasing his smoking habit to twenty or more cigarettes a day. February 1956 found VAT commanding *Quadrant, Queenborough, Quickmatch, Arunta, Kaniere* and the submarine *Telemachus* in a weapons training exercise off Townsville, Cairns and Darwin. The ship's doctor recorded that on 21 February his ECG (electrocardiogram) trace was showing an irregular heart rhythm with missing beats.

On 3 March VAT transferred by jackstay to *Queenborough* for several hours, inspecting that ship's company at divisions and walking around her mess decks, flats and spaces. By mid-March *Quadrant* was once again with the strategic reserve in Singapore, participating in Exercise *Monsoon* with other Commonwealth naval and air forces. VAT found the night jackstay transfer of mail and personnel alongside a darkened *Centaur*, the 24,000-ton Far East duty carrier, "interesting". In Darwin on 10 April, with *Quadrant* being due for a long refit on return to Garden Island, VAT moved with his staff to take command of *Queenborough*.

Even normal passage, as now south to Sydney, was not restful for a frigate captain where a daily programme of exercises and general drills occupied most watches. Instructions in the captain's night order book would generally see him woken several times through the middle and morning watches. VAT led his ship's command team in the Joint Unit Course at AJASS and then practiced their lessons at sea off Jervis Bay with aircraft from *Albatross*. This time his jackstay transfer was to inspect *Quickmatch*.

In the early hours of Monday 7 May, the flagship *Sydney*, together with *Queenborough* and *Quickmatch*, were in Jervis Bay when *Melbourne* anchored at 0435, just over nine cables from the old college clock tower. VAT thus had a ringside view as the second Operation *Decanter* began disembarking Sea Venoms and Gannets from the new carrier at 0600.[11] *Melbourne* was a state-of-the-art carrier and VAT could take pride in the role he had played in her acquisition. Departing the bay two days later, VAT formed his squadron into a screen for the carriers in an anti-submarine exercise before the submarine *Thorough* led *Sydney, Melbourne, Queenborough, Quickmatch* and *Arunta* in a ceremonial entry for the welcoming crowds gathered around Sydney Harbour.

During a visit to Brisbane in June VAT made the usual round of official calls to the Chief Justice, Lord Mayor, General Officer Commanding Northern Command and His Excellency the Governor. More memorable and enjoyable would have been when the Resident Naval Officer Queensland called on Fox 1 aboard *Queenborough*: the navy's first observer Commander Henry Chesterman OBE was calling on its eighth. Chesterman had been VAT's senior watchkeeper aboard *Canberra* in 1935 and flying stories of the intervening years no doubt flowed.

FOCAF reported that VAT was carrying out his duties as senior officer of the frigate squadron efficiently, the reputation of that squadron for anti-submarine work was high and that his own

---

11   *Melbourne* had ferried 21 Gannets, 39 Sea Venoms, 2 Bristol Sycamores, 1 Avro 707 Delta Wing aircraft, 1 Gloster Meteor, 8 Double Mamba and single Mamba engines, 9 Ghost engines and a large amount of freight including a 10-metre yacht for the RAN Sailing Association.

ship was efficient and extremely clean. Rear-Admiral Henry Burrell's sole concern was with VAT's poor ship handling, especially when manoeuvring in close waters, and worried that he took unnecessary risks.[12] He acknowledged that it was VAT's first command and advised a closer study of *Remarks on Handling Ships*. Otherwise:

> I have nothing but praise for this conscientious officer who has ideas, who is thoughtful, and who can express himself clearly. Altogether a promising young captain.

Burrell recommended that VAT next commanded a shore establishment and then an operational carrier to fit him for flag rank, noting that the carrier would give him added ship-handling experience.

Queenborough had rescue destroyer duties astern of *Melbourne* for night flying on 5 September and they deployed north later that month, as it had been decided that the Australian carrier would make an annual appearance with the strategic reserve. For Fox 1 there were visits to Thailand, the Philippines, Hong Kong, Japan, Korea and Borneo between exercises. In the major maritime Exercise *Albatross*, *Queenborough* was particularly pleased to have "got" the US submarine *Carp*. When VAT formed a patrol group 30 kilometres on a "convoy's" port bow it was a scenario he was all too familiar with from his war years in the Atlantic and Arctic. Recorded among all the official visits with ambassadors and governors, VAT made sure to include the squadron's rugby match against Kanto University, and the subsequent reception given by the Japanese Rugby Football Association. The squadron lost 14-3.

Australian forces with the Far East Strategic Reserve included tours of duty by battalions of the Royal Australian Regiment as well as RAAF fighter and bomber squadrons. Over the years, seventeen different ships of the RAN, crewed by up to 1,500 men annually, would serve with the strategic reserve.

The Australian Service Medal 1945-1975 is awarded for declared non-warlike operations. If that service was a minimum 30 days with the Far East Strategic Reserve between July 1955 and October 1971 the FESR clasp is worn on the medal ribbon.

The Australian Service Medal 1945-1975.

Christmas Day 1956 found Fox 1 once again alongside in Singapore where the tradition of ship's officers serving the festive dinner to their ship's company was again followed. Handing over command on 28 December, VAT flew home to celebrate the new year with Nanette and the boys.

The Chief of Naval Staff, Vice-Admiral Dowling CBE DSO, wrote a confidential personal letter to VAT on 16 November. Having been informed he was going to Nowra, VAT knew that another sea-going command was

The FESR (Far East Strategic Reserve) clasp worn on the Australian Service Medal ribbon.

---

12   Later Vice-Admiral Sir Henry Burrell KBE CB (1904-1988) of the 1918 class was a navigation specialist who commanded *Norman* during WWII and then *Bataan*, *Australia* and *Vengeance*. As CNS from 1959 he struggled to reverse the decision to disband the Fleet Air Arm.

necessary to be competitive for further promotion. Dowling allayed any concerns stating that "under present plans you can expect further employment at sea". Harries, his captain in *Sydney*, had been FOCAF since June and his opinion of VAT had not lessened. He held that VAT's outstanding qualities were integrity, reliability and moral courage which made him a "thoroughly good man in the true sense of the word".

Also recognising that VAT was not a natural small ship handler in confined waters, Harries wrote that although lack of experience in fleet work had been evident at the start of Exercise *Albatross*, he had rapidly improved. Having had his own first command aged 35, Harries equitably added:

> Taking into consideration this last commission was his first sea-going command at a comparatively advanced age, I was pleased with the result he achieved in his squadron and particularly with their anti-submarine efficiency. I think it distinctly possible he will achieve flag rank.

When *Queenborough* was awarded the Gloucester Cup as the most efficient ship of Australia's 1956 Olympic year, VAT modestly described it as being due to "very good fortune", having found his time as Fox 1 "most interesting".[13]

Albatross: 14 January 1957 - 29 November 1959

VAT's appointment to command the air station at Nowra, and as Resident Naval Officer Jervis Bay, was a very special one to him. Having had much to do with the wartime transfer of the RAAF base to a MONAB for disembarking aircraft of the British Pacific Fleet, he found it very satisfying to return twelve years later as captain of an RAN air station. It was the navy's second largest shore establishment, with a ship's company of around 2,000 and a wardroom of 90 officers, not counting the squadron aircrew. With six squadrons it was also the most operationally active shore establishment.

The HMAS Albatross badge.

Coupled with training disembarked front line squadrons was the ongoing training of the second line squadrons, with some of that training being carried out at the Jervis Bay airstrip. There were also the courses in various schools for observers, aircraft handlers, safety equipment workers and air mechanics. The RAAF/RAN Australian Joint Anti-Submarine School was a lodger unit.

Nanette and the family welcomed their three years of settled existence, with the boys thriving in the rural environment of the Shoalhaven area. The "patch", or married housing area, had improved considerably from the caravan and converted aircraft packing-case days of the early years, but would still have struck modern eyes as unacceptably meagre. The Smiths found the nearby commanding officer's house very homely with lots of character. Nanette, with a young

---

13   Meanwhile *Melbourne* had left the strategic reserve in early November to be alongside in Port Melbourne on 22 November for the opening day of the XVI Olympiad, the first to be held in the southern hemisphere. Hundreds of her officers and ratings were marshals in the various stadia each day.

family, would have particularly welcomed the staff of gardener, cook and steward. Nowra Hill Public School, responding to the fecundity of young naval couples, had been open for over a year so the older boys were within walking distance of school. The family quickly settled into the patch and its circumscribed social life of camaraderie and good friendships.

VAT and his boys in 1957: left to right Mark, Michael and Piers.

Knowing that the morale of his married sailors depended in large part on the welfare of their families, VAT gave developing the patch a high priority. He organised to move surplus huts from the base to provide a larger village store and a community hall. In the days before near universal car ownership this saved many journeys by pram-laden bus the ten kilometres to the town shops. VAT found the tennis club with its free membership was a great success and the "source of some of my happiest memories". He was remembered as "a good player (left-handed too) and he always took his turn at umpiring". VAT, imbued with the importance of sport to naval teamwork from his earliest college days, naturally encouraged all sports at *Albatross*, even donating a VAT Smith Cup in 1959 for an annual fun relay race.

Given VAT's own youthful enthusiasm for the scouting movement, it is not surprising that Michael and Mark joined the 1st Nowra Hill cub pack. Meeting in the new community hall the pack leader was Sub-Lieutenant Sydney Morris.[14] It was an interest that continued as the family relocated, VAT helping with painting the hall or with the annual bottle drive when time allowed. Mark eventually became pack leader of the Red Hill Canberra cub pack. VAT congratulated him, mentioning that he had also reached that "exalted" level.

Safety as well as morale was of concern to VAT. Commander (Air) was Jeff Gledhill, who had worked under VAT's directorship at Navy Office. He had been commanding No. 817 Squadron until the death while flying of his predecessor, Danny Buchanan, only two months before VAT's arrival. In the previous three years there had been eighteen aircrew fatalities, eight of them while flying from the station. VAT knew it was inevitable that in the business of flying training there would be accidents, and unfortunately some of them would be fatal. The *Melbourne* air group was expected to maintain an embarked operational tempo, and the second line squadrons, preparing their junior aircrew for carrier flying, also operated at a high level of skill.

---

14   Later Lieutenant-Commander (Special Duties Executive Branch) Sydney Morris (b. 1926) who joined as an ordinary seaman aged 17 in 1944 and served in *Hobart*. Demobbed in 1946 he rejoined in 1948 becoming a leading seaman patrolman and then a Regulating Petty Officer. He was commissioned as a Special Duties officer in 1958.

As the captain's wife on an operational air station, Nanette had "ancillary duties" on behalf of the FAA families' welfare. Comforting Danny's recently bereaved widow Anne, they became life-long friends. Nanette would, along with one of the station chaplains, take the lead in consoling wives who had just lost their husbands. A more pleasant duty was preparing and delivering layettes for new mothers while hosting seemingly endless morning teas and other social activities.

Flying at *Albatross* had been in the more laid-back style common to the post-Korean years. Lieutenant (P) Thomas "Toz" Dadswell, then with No. 816 Squadron, saw at first-hand VAT's influence.[15] Without doubting the continued sound airmanship of the squadrons, he set out in his quiet way to smarten things up, given added impetus when Sub-Lieutenant (P) Warren Brown (21) and Midshipman (O) Ian Caird (19) were killed in their Firefly on the night of 19 March. VAT had mourned the loss of many aircrew over the years and begrudged every single one. If the squadron programme showed that you had a sortie at 0900, that had been taken as a guide and no-one worried if the aircraft launched at 0905. Commandment number six of O'Connor's *Running a Big Ship on Ten Commandments* was punctual attendance at place of duty - and that duty was to be in the air at 0900. VAT would appear on the flight line with Gledhill at his side, late take-offs were noted on a clipboard, and commander (air) was asked to explain. In the time-honoured manner Gledhill, in turn, would ask the squadron commander who would ask the squadron duty officer who would ask the individual aircrew to explain.

It did not take long before all squadrons carefully conformed to the published programme. VAT would also suddenly appear at aircrew briefings, take a personal interest and sometimes ask probing questions. During night flying he could often be found at the elbow of the air traffic controller in the tower. The old days of "Kick the tires, light the fires and first off is leader" were gone. Everyone could see that the station's aircrew became more professional in their flying.

In VAT's first year in command there were two aircrew fatalities and in 1958 none, although his final year of 1959 was marred by a tragic four. Not just deaths amongst his aircrew, however, concerned VAT. Many of the ship's company would head to Sydney for their weekends, a journey that could take five hours on the unimproved highway of the late 1950s. The death toll from road traffic accidents, at its worst one death a month, VAT found "awful". Thinking flexibly, he changed the station's working routine. Everyone would start half an hour earlier Monday to Thursday, allowing the weekend standdown to start at 1500 on Fridays. This gave those travelling to Sydney more time to make the trip in the safer daylight hours.

VAT had been aware from day one that a general morale problem existed. In his opinion the ship's company lacked cohesion, had no common cause and exhibited inadequate *esprit de corps*. VAT knew that improvement was needed to benefit the entire establishment. His decades of service gave him the innate belief that "smartness" was the solid base to build

---

15   Later Commodore (P) Thomas Dadswell (KM) AM, (b.1932), a midshipman under training in *Sydney* when VAT was executive officer and then flying Fireflies and Gannets in the late 1950s. Flight Deck Officer in *Melbourne* under VAT he next commanded No. 816 Squadron, flew Trackers and Skyhawks, and was captain of *Albatross*.

on. Thinking up the watchwords "Second to None" in 1958 he went about making changes to rectify the problem. In 1959 he added a second catchcry "Still the Best" as rumours of the demise of the FAA eroded morale once again!

Some initiatives came as no surprise to those officers and sailors who had served in *Sydney* when VAT was the executive officer. They knew him as a strict disciplinarian and had "braced for the rod". For the first month or so of 1957 nothing major changed

VAT inspecting the Albatross guard at divisions.

except the civilian gardeners stopped tending the gardens and started painting the road kerbs, of which there were many kilometres, white. After the gardeners had made some progress VAT began to inspect the various car parks on the station. If he found a car with tell-tale white smears on its tyres, he would leave a note instructing the owner to report to the first lieutenant's office at the end of the day. There the man would be given a pot of white paint and directed to an area which had not been painted. Men under punishment were also detailed to carry out this chore. Two things happened very quickly, the station looked smarter with painted kerbs and the ship's company paid closer attention to how they parked their cars.

VAT also ordered that flying would cease at 1200 on Fridays. This allowed aircraft to be serviced for an early start the following Monday morning, and he decreed that all departments and squadrons were to garden from 1300-1450, or work on any other project to make their part of station look smart. This routine was only interrupted once a month when the whole station would parade for divisions. The armourers decided they would build a fishpond between the gunner's store and bomb carrier workshop. VAT watched the progress with interest on his weekly rounds and he suggested they stock it from the pond outside the wardroom. At his next inspection the leading seaman standing rounds pointed out the fish named Victor, Alfred and Trumper to him but Smithy was hiding under a rock.

It soon became clear that those departments/squadrons that made a good improvement to their surrounds received a Bravo Zulu from VAT, the naval code for well done. Heads of department and squadron commanders with a view to good annual reports and future promotion encouraged their subordinates. Rivalry soon developed between sections and the whole appearance of the station changed for the better. With little effort on his part VAT had developed a more robust sense of pride in the station. All could see how smart it looked!

The gardening was accompanied by improvements to the buildings at *Albatross*. Construction projects were funded, more married quarters were built and some of the WWII huts being used as single sailor's accommodation were replaced. A new air traffic control building and battery workshop was approved, and the Beecroft bombing range was developed further.

As a shore establishment *Albatross* came under the command of Rear-Admiral Hastings "Arch" Harrington DSO (1924 class), Flag Officer-in-Charge East Australian Area.[16] After one year at *Albatross*, Harrington reported in January 1958 that VAT was a very determined officer who was keen, thoughtful and ambitious. He could exercise great self-control but there were occasional impulsive acts. Harrington thought it was through hard work and application, rather than mental brilliance, that allowed VAT, who he had known at the college in 1927, to achieve his aims. He could see the pace VAT was setting for himself but felt that mental resilience, and his great physical endurance, would sustain him, which it did for the next two months.

VAT had always tended towards the supererogatory and it was inevitable in his middle years that his work pace, well above the normal that duty required, would have consequences. For two weeks, in March 1958, he suffered three bouts of fever and general malaise while continuing his normal routine, until finally collapsing at 1230 on 13 March. Surgeon Commander Robert "Mumbles" Coplans found plasmodium vivax in VAT's blood and positively diagnosed BT malaria.[17] Taking a medical history he was dismayed to learn of his patient's recurring bouts of fever since West African service in 1941, and that he had never consulted naval surgeons or had a course of suppressive treatment. It was a dereliction that VAT himself would not have accepted in a subordinate. VAT was prescribed a two-week drug course and was back in his office within days.

Monthly divisions were held on a Friday afternoon. Falling in at 1300 VAT would arrive for inspection at 1330, with the inspections being assisted by heads of department since one man inspecting 2,000 is a long and tedious business. Normally the inspection would be completed around 1400 followed by a twenty-minute march past. At 1430 leave would be piped and libertymen would be on their way by 1500.

On one particular Friday VAT arrived at 1330, got out of his car and looked around. Saying something to the executive officer he got back in his car and drove away. The executive officer informed the parade that the captain would be returning to conduct divisions when all of his ship's company was assembled. Some sailors had developed the habit of hiding in their messes and missing divisions. Avoiding being inspected in uniform, they would already be in their civilian clothes poised to proceed ashore the minute leave was piped.

So now the regulating staff visited every mess and instructed the laggards to get into their No. 1 uniforms and join their departments and squadrons on the parade ground. This took time and

---

16   Later Vice-Admiral Sir Wilfred Hastings Harrington KBE CB DSO (1906-1965) who commanded *Yarra* in the Persian Gulf campaign of 1941 and was executive officer of *Australia* at the battle of Savo Island. Commanded *Quiberon*, *Warramunga* and *Sydney*. Appointed CNS in 1962 where VAT served as his Second Naval Member. His son Simon Harrington also achieved flag rank.
17   Later Surgeon Rear-Admiral Robert Coplans CBE (1911-1989), Medical Director of the RAN. He served with the RN in the Battle of the Atlantic, joining the RAN in 1948 to help establish the new FAA's air medicine specialty. He was Senior Medical Officer during *Melbourne's* delivery voyage and then SMO at *Albatross* and head of the School of Aviation Medicine.

divisions did not restart until 1400. When VAT arrived, he inspected the guard and then inspected every single man of the full 2,000 now on parade. Those who had not expected to be there had unpressed or dirty uniforms which were noted, and they were instructed to report to the guard house on completion of divisions. After his inspection all marched past as VAT took the salute, but any squad

Chief of Naval Staff Vice Admiral Sir Roy Dowling KBE CB DSO (KM) addresses divisions at Albatross. Flag Officer-in-Charge East Australian Area Rear-Admiral Wilfred Harrington DSO is second from left and Captain VAT Smith DSC is second from right.

whose marching was not up to standard was sent around to do it again. The parade finished around 1600 with the point well-made and the problem never recurred.

With his memory for names, VAT already knew many of the old *Sydney* CAG's aircrew, from the New Zealander Lieutenant-Commander (P) Peter Seed, commanding No. 808 (Sea Venom) Squadron, to Lieutenant-Commander (P) Peter Goldrick, now senior pilot of No. 816 (Gannet) Squadron. Soon after settling in, he started dropping into crew rooms for morning coffee. His opening remark would be "Any chance of a clean mug of coffee?". One of the dirty cups lying around the room would rapidly be washed and filled. He would stay for ten minutes and during that time learnt the names and backgrounds of those present. Once met VAT would know the man thereafter. Since jet, turboprop and rotary-wing conversions were now done on station, VAT got acquainted with the coming generation of aviators, who quickly made sure a clean mug was always on standby in their crew rooms.

Effective leadership counts on the personal factor, the "name" business having its own section in O'Conor's *Running a Big Ship on Ten Commandments*. VAT's amazing facility, which he worked at, showed his interest in the individual as a separate identity, earning their respect. Flying commercially in a Vickers Viscount with Harries in 1959, VAT amazed the airliner's first officer by turning to Harries and saying "Admiral, you remember young Powell, he was with us in Korea". Powell, the carrier's most junior acting sub-lieutenant, had briefly joined *Sydney*'s No. 805 Squadron in December 1951 for the final two war patrols, and remembered no contact with the ship's executive officer.[18]

Centralised maintenance was wished on the station at this time by Navy Office. VAT had appreciated

18   Later Lieutenant Andrew Powell (b. 1930), a graduate of No. 4 Probationary Naval Aviators Course, hurriedly flown to Japan in December 1951 with Lieutenant Alan Cordell (1942 class) to replace losses in No. 805 Squadron. Transferred from *Sydney* to *Glory*'s No. 804 Squadron in February 1952, as replacements for their aircrew losses, they helped *Glory* take back that daily sortie record. Leaving the RAN in 1955, Powell flew with Trans-Australia Airlines before working in industry.

the knowledge and leadership of his No. 825 Squadron RAF flight sergeant rigger and fitter aboard *Glorious* in 1938, always thereafter feeling strongly the advantage of squadron maintenance personnel looking after their own squadron's aircraft. He called centralised maintenance a "garage" system which lost the personal attachment between the people in the squadron and that squadron's aircraft. It was not popular with the operators or maintainers or VAT.

The White Ensign Club in Nowra had been founded in 1954 as an off-duty recreational centre in the town for sailors. There was a good and energetic board formed of local residents, with VAT, as captain of the air station an ex-officio member. Despite the board's endeavours, the club was not thriving. One reason was that many servicemen like to have a bet or a flutter in a small way on almost anything and the club did not have any poker machines. Many sailors enjoyed playing the pokies, but VAT's predecessor had opposed their installation. Consequently, sailors went around the corner to the Shoalhaven Ex-Servicemen's Club and played the machines there.

Gambling was in contravention of O'Connor's commandment number nine which stated card-playing was allowed at mess tables and on the upper deck but that gambling, any game of chance played for money stakes, was strictly prohibited. VAT was flexible enough to see that what was a sensible rule for shipboard harmony was not applicable to the Nowra township. He allowed poker machines to be installed, the number of sailors using the club increased and the welcome profits enabled some very worthwhile improvements. One example was helping to set up the *Albatross* Sailing Club on the banks of the Shoalhaven River.

In May 1959, VAT's father George died in Sydney's North Shore Hospital after cardiac surgery. One benefit of being at Nowra for the preceding few years had been the still regular visits to Chatswood for the boys to see their grandparents. As the state's best known "fat stock" auctioneer of sheep, and despite the funeral being held on a Homebush sale day, the attendance of his colleagues at St Paul's Church of England was high. There, George was remembered "as straight as a dart" who "didn't waste a second or a word", qualities which he had passed on to his son.

The New South Wales government at this time had dismissed the Shoalhaven Shire Council and installed an administrator. This decision was unpopular with many people of the shire, and VAT found that where the shire president would have normally officiated, he, as captain of *Albatross*, rather than the administrator, would be invited. One advantage of this unusual situation was that station and shire became closer than had previously been the case, as an increasing number of ex-FAA families settled in the area when their naval engagements expired. That VAT was successful in the role was demonstrated when he and Nanette were given a civic reception on their departure in November 1959.

While VAT was at *Albatross*, the naval college returned from Flinders back to Jervis Bay. He had been appalled by the way the original college buildings had been allowed to run down and gladly accommodated Captain William "Bill" Dovers (1932 class) at *Albatross* as he planned the transfer.[19] It was a happy day for VAT personally when the college returned to Jervis Bay with the 1958 class.

In November 1959 Darbo Harries was Flag Officer-in-Charge East Australian Area and saw that VAT, as when his executive officer in *Sydney*, made it his constant business to ensure that those entrusted to his command carried out their duties in accordance with his own exacting standards. He wrote that VAT's performance in the difficult task of commanding *Albatross* was of a high standard and "he enjoys the respect of all". The "difficult" was most likely in reference to managing morale with troubling talk of "paying off" the FAA, leaving the RAAF as the only flying service.[20] After his annual inspection Harries called the station "a shining example of the service at its best". VAT had indeed made *Albatross* "Second to None!"

With over five years as a captain, VAT, of middling seniority among the 37 captains on the list, was now to be formally assessed for flag rank. Harries strongly recommended his promotion after another sea-going command. Before that promised command, however, VAT was once again off to London. Departing *Albatross* he was presented with a coffee table handsomely inlaid with silhouettes of squadron aircraft.[21] He was towed ashore in a Land Rover by the station's officers and a formation flypast overhead marked the end of a memorable tenure.

Imperial Defence College London 1960

All five of the Smith family travelled on the Shaw Savill liner *Dominion Monarch* to the UK, where VAT was enrolled in the 1960 course for senior officers at the Imperial Defence College on Belgrave Square. Mark had his seventh birthday onboard and all boys remembered the fancy dress parties, deck games and the crossing the line ceremony. During rough weather VAT's sea-legs ensured he never missed a meal in the suddenly emptied dining room.

Imperial Defence College students were from all three armed services as well as the senior public service, and from a range of nations including not

"Don't worry dear — by the time we get there it'll be second to none !"

Albatross's cartoonist obviously expected VAT to sort out the Dominion Monarch's slovenly crew.

---

19   Later Rear-Admiral William Dovers CBE DSC (1918-2007), he served in the destroyer *Nestor* in the Mediterranean in 1941. He was commissioning First Lieutenant of *Quickmatch* before commanding *Swan* with the British Pacific Fleet. Inaugural commander of the Royal Malaysian Navy in 1960 he became FOCAF in 1971.

20   In the station's November 1959 monthly magazine *Slipstream*, which VAT had instituted in 1957, their reporter "interviewed" a Gannet which had ended up in the grass alongside runway 08. "I'd just landed smoothly as usual, in spite of my driver and was trundling gently along the runway, a little worried about all this talk of paying off, when I happened to catch the eye of those two RAAF Neptunes. They were positively smirking at me. I just did my block and headed straight for 'em!"

21   Now in the office of the Commander Fleet Air Arm at *Albatross*.

just the dominions, but Nigeria and the United States. There were five other Australians on the course, two each from army and air force and a senior public servant from the Department of Foreign Affairs. All were selected as having potential for the highest commands.

The quality of the directing staff and lecturers was superb, and VAT appreciated having time to read in the first-class library. He particularly relished the five-week course tour in August/September. Divided into groups to visit either Europe, North America, Africa or the Far East VAT counted himself fortunate to be included in the North American party. Touring establishments not normally open to foreigners, he attended lectures at the Pentagon, State Department, Strategic Air Command headquarters and the North American Air Defence Command under Cheyenne Mountain in Colorado. It was a good grounding for the senior roles he would play in Australia's looming commitment to the war in South Vietnam as a US ally.

The course was a rare opportunity for VAT who, under wartime pressure, had missed the usual single-service staff course. As a joint services course, he fortunately had considerable tri-service experience. It gave him the opportunity to form collegial relationships with a wide variety of officers who were being prepared, as he was, for the highest ranks in their respective services. It was also a much-needed year's respite from the pressures of command to recharge physically and mentally.

In addition to the lectures there were social activities with a movie each Wednesday evening to which wives and friends were invited. Occasional cocktail parties would often have a celebrity guest and in summer there was the mandatory outing to Royal Ascot. It was also an opportunity for Nanette to spend valuable time with her mother, and for the boys to connect with their English grandmother, who accompanied them on their family holiday to Penzance in Cornwall.

When he successfully completed the course at the end of 1960, the post-nominals *i.d.c.* were entered after VAT's name in the seniority list. On return to Australia the house in Cremorne was re-occupied, the boys being schooled at Mosman Prep and Shore, Sydney Church of England Grammar. VAT was happily heading back to sea again, this time in command of both a carrier and a flagship. But first he briefed the naval staff in Canberra on information he had acquired during the Imperial Defence College visit to the USA and Canada.

Carrier Command: 8 January 1961 – 16 June 1962

In many ways VAT's long FAA career had been in preparation for his command of *Melbourne*. Having served in five different carriers since 1932, the size of his new command was in no way daunting and he surprised Harrington, now commanding the fleet, with the confidence and skill with which he handled the big ship. Entering Fremantle, only six weeks after taking command, the sole berth available gave clearance of only 24 metres ahead and astern. VAT calmly stopped abreast the berth and used six Sea Venoms to propel him sideways to secure at No. 8 North Wharf on 18 February 1961.

The notoriously irascible rear-admiral soon realised that his flag captain's observer background made conducting flying operations second nature and would entrust occasional tactical command of sizeable groups of ships to VAT, where he met "all the requirements of this enlarged command with no difficulty". As *Melbourne* began a refit period nine months into VAT's carrier command, Harrington already considered him "almost certain to achieve Flag Rank". The consensus of many was that: "Captain Smith, and only one or two others, operated *Melbourne* as an aircraft carrier".

The HMAS Melbourne badge.

They had been a busy nine months, beginning with work-up for ship and squadrons in January. The first aircraft landed-on in the forenoon of 16 January so the flight deck team could practice handling and spotting the different types. Only nine days later 800 landings had already been made. On 31 January the *Melbourne* Air Group comprised of ten Sea Venoms of No. 805 Squadron, ten Gannets of No. 816 Squadron and an SAR (Bristol Sycamore) helicopter flight embarked. VAT, who had seen the original No. 816 embark on *Ark Royal* in July 1941 and then again on *Tracker* in August 1943, now watched the squadron embark on his own carrier.

The initial deployment was to the Indian Ocean for the annual Commonwealth joint exercise. Ships and aircraft from Australia, Britain, Ceylon, India, New Zealand and Pakistan participated in Exercise *Jet 1961* south of the Nicobar Islands. With the Indian navy acquiring the carrier *Vikrant* they showed particular interest in *Melbourne*'s performance.[22] VAT noted that *Hermes*, with her larger Sea Vixen and Scimitar jets operating with a Gannet AEW.3 airborne early warning radar aircraft, had the edge, although she did suffer the loss of one Gannet and pilot. When his own Gannets, flying surface search, discovered a "raider" at 1400 the well-worked up *Melbourne* was able to launch a six-aircraft Sea Venom strike at 1410. On 3 March, *Melbourne* had the experience of being involved in surface, anti-submarine and air attacks within the span of a single hour.

The next day her underpowered Bristol Sycamore XD654, flown by Lieutenant (P) John Da Costa,

The Melbourne Air Group of Gannets and Sea Venoms in Jervis Bay.

22   The Majestic-class INS *Vikrant* (ex-*Hercules* launched in 1945) commissioned in March 1961 with Hawker Sea Hawk fighters and French Bréguet Alizé anti-submarine turboprop aircraft. Decommissioned in 1997, she had been operating BAE Sea Harriers since 1983 having had a 9.75° ski-jump ramp fitted.

ditched while attempting to hover alongside *Hermes* off the Cocos Islands in tropical heat with insufficient wind.[23] All passengers and crew were rescued by a boat from *Hermes*.[24] Although other aircraft would be slightly damaged in accidents, this was to be the only loss during VAT's command. Considering that there had been four Sea Venoms and two Gannets badly damaged and written-off aboard the ship in 1960, VAT's devotion to ensuring adequate training was clearly paying dividends.

A Sycamore helicopter launching from Melbourne. One was lost when it ditched in the Indian Ocean on 4 March 1961.

Before an eight-day self-maintenance period in Singapore's naval dockyard, the ship visited Bombay, and was in Karachi to dress-ship for Pakistan Day. *Melbourne* and her group of *Vendetta*, *Voyager* and *Queenborough* then joined the USN in the Philippines for the SEATO amphibious Exercise *Pony Express* off Borneo. VAT made time for a jackstay transfer of teams from the Australian ships to compete in an athletics competition on his flight deck, which the carrier won. Nostalgia probably occurred again when No. 825 Squadron, helicopter equipped since losing their Gannets the previous year, cross-decked four piston-engined Whirlwinds from *Victorious*. The command team had time to assess their anti-submarine capabilities and were not impressed.

VAT put to sea from Hong Kong to ride out Typhoon *Alice*, the eye of which passed directly over the harbour, and then returned to Australia via Papua New Guinea and Townsville in June. When the air group disembarked to *Albatross* on 13 June, the two front-line squadrons had flown 1,350 sorties and made 1,700 deck landings, the highest figures since the ship had commissioned and with a pleasingly low accident rate. The Minister for Navy the Honourable John Gorton joined the flagship for the ceremonial fleet entry into Sydney Harbour two days later.[25]

Re-embarking his air group in July, VAT again demonstrated his confidence in, and complete mastery of, his carrier command. Bad weather was causing the scheduled working-up of the squadrons to become well adrift. With an easterly swell in the Tasman Sea and a south-

---

23   Later Commodore (P) John Da Costa (b1934) who flew Fireflies, Sea Furies and Sea Venoms before commanding No. 805 (Skyhawk) squadron in 1968, and the shore establishments *Kuttabul* and *Penguin*.
24   Of the thirteen RAN Bristol Sycamores nine were lost in the nine years between 1953 and 1962.
25   Later Prime Minister Sir John Gorton GCMG AC CH (1911-2002) from 1968-1971. Served as Minister for the Navy for five years from 1958-1963. His craggy features were due to extensive facial injuries when his RAF fighter crashed off Singapore in January 1942.

A pair of Gannets show off their folding wings, with a Sea Venom positioned behind.

westerly wind, VAT decided to gain the lee of the wind by conducting day and night flying operations inside Jervis Bay. He stationed *Vampire* in the northeast corner of the bay ready to get underway as rescue destroyer if required, and manoeuvred in these confined waters for launches and recovery. Settling briefly each time on a south-westerly flying course before having to go-around again, VAT found the cycle "interesting". No doubt the watching cadets at the college found it thrilling.

A very successful admiral's inspection was held in Queensland's Hervey Bay that August before participating in Exercise *Tuckerbox*. This anti-submarine exercise in the Coral Sea saw No. 816 Squadron Gannets get two positive and three probable kills against the three "attacking" submarines. On a visit to New Zealand after the exercise a fleet reception in Wellington celebrated the RAN's 50th birthday with a cake cutting and a Beat the Retreat ceremony aboard the flagship. The golden jubilee cake was cut by Lady Phyllis Collins, our midshipman balloon pilot of 1917 having retired as Vice-Admiral Sir John Collins in 1955 and been appointed Australia's High Commissioner to New Zealand the following year.[26]

VAT's scar turning white continued to be a bellwether sign to his juniors that they should make themselves scarce. Lieutenant Fred Lane, a Flight Deck Officer in this deployment, remembers that the executive officer planned a wardroom party on the quarterdeck while in Auckland. VAT ordered the party to take place in the wardroom and to keep the quarterdeck, a sacrosanct area on any major warship, clear while he attended an evening engagement ashore. On return the quarterdeck was crowded with a local band and loudly partying officers and their guests. Some reports told of a Maori princess lifting the executive officer off his feet as VAT quietly made his way to his cabin. There he sent his sentry to invite that officer,

---

26   Collins had been disappointed to lose VAT shortly after he took command of *Shropshire*. While commanding Task Force 74 he had been severely wounded in the attack that killed *Australia*'s Captain Emile Dechaineux DSC and Harrie Gerrett.

who had commanded *Quickmatch* under VAT when he was Fox 1, to drop by. The officer returned visibly shaken to quietly report the short conversation's parting words "Commander Scrivenor, you may forget this. I never will".[27]

Lane's replacement as FDO was Lieutenant Toz Dadswell, who recalled that VAT normally commanded with a quiet voice but could hand out a blast at ten paces or one hundred metres when necessary:

> The other thing I remember about VAT blasts - and I copped a few as the FDO on *Melbourne* - was that he would give you a real tongue-lashing and five minutes later be talking to you in normal mode. He would not stew like some senior officers. He had pointed out in clear concise language your error and that was the end of the matter unless you were stupid enough to repeat it.

In under eight months *Melbourne* and her air group had exceeded any previous twelve-month records. VAT was riding high, and his fall was a prosaic but painful one. Sailing from Wellington to Melbourne, the carrier experienced strong southerly winds and rough seas on 9 September. Going down the ladder from the bridge to the wireless office VAT slipped and fell,

Launching Gannets from Melbourne while conducting an underway transfer. The line of men trailing past the island are on the jackstay line between Melbourne and the Daring-class destroyer to starboard.

27   Later Captain Robert Scrivenor (1922-1974).). Joined the naval college in 1936 and served mainly in destroyers in WWII. After *Melbourne* he was commander at *Cerberus*. Promoted to captain less than two years later, so VAT must have been scrupulously fair in his confidential personal reports. Scrivenor became Fox 1 himself in *Parramatta*, commanded *Penguin* and was Military Adviser in Bangkok 1967-1969.

fracturing his sixth rib. He obviously did not let it hinder him overmuch, Harrington noting only two weeks later that VAT's physical resilience was remarkable.

With the future of the FAA under serious threat, the recently instituted "Shop Window" day was more important than ever. Embarking numerous dignitaries on 20 September, *Melbourne* and her group of *Vampire*, *Anzac*, *Parramatta* and *Yarra* demonstrated everything from jackstay transfers and anti-submarine mortar firings to Sea Venom rocket strikes. It was an impressive display. The following day VAT took to sea again with 1,000 family aboard for "Family Day" to demonstrate in small measure what their husbands and fathers did in the long months away from home port. When they returned to Garden Island Dockyard, the refit period lasted until early January 1962.

Of course, Harrington, as fleet commander flying his flag in *Melbourne*, was also receiving the benefit of VAT's considerable administrative skills as chief staff officer to the admiral's nine staff. Harrington professed himself well content with his energy and organising ability, particularly commenting on his attention to staff work connected with training. Ensuring good training for the next naval generation had been a feature of VAT's time as a senior officer since *Nirimba*. In summary Harrington wrote that VAT's:

> … knowledge and judgment are excellent, he is most reliable, determined and, I believe, courageous.

The first half of 1962 reflected the previous year with work-up of the ship and air group before deploying north. Looking at two days will suffice to show some of what was involved. On 15 January *Melbourne* exercised tows forward and aft with *Anzac*, exercised replenishment at sea with jackstay transfers and refuelling both abeam and astern, followed by night refuelling. There was anti-aircraft tracking for the guns, officer of the watch ship-handling and manoeuvres followed by simulated steering-gear breakdowns while conducting engine room trials. The next day aircraft flying out from *Albatross* made 260 landings between 0830 and 1715 before the ship anchored in Jervis Bay. *Melbourne* burned one ton of fuel for every two miles steamed and her daily running costs, with 1,300 plus people onboard, dictated maximum value was wrung from every watch at sea.

Before deploying north, they visited Hobart for the regatta, and in the traditional pulling competition *Melbourne* came second to *Anzac*. The captain of the visiting destroyer USS *Vance* made his official call, where he would have been most surprised to learn that VAT had known the destroyer's namesake, the USN liaison officer killed in *Canberra* at the Battle of Savo Island.

After visiting Adelaide, Fremantle and Singapore a short maintenance period was required in Hong Kong with Sea Venoms disembarked for continuation flying at RAF Base Kai Tak. This was repeated in April to the US Naval Air Station at Cubi Point in the Philippines prior to the SEATO Exercise *Sea Devil*. Ships had gathered from Australia, New Zealand, Pakistan, Thailand, the

United Kingdom and the United States under the command of the new FOCAF, Rear-Admiral Alan McNicoll CBE GM (1922 class).[28] On completion of the exercise, for the first time five carriers were berthed in Subic Bay: *Ark Royal, Hancock, Princeton, Valley Forge* and *Melbourne*.

They made memorable visits to four ports in Japan, where VAT had the testing time of remaining fully alert throughout the entire night as *Melbourne* transited the Shimonoseki Strait and the Inland Sea of Japan, with its large number of unlit fishing vessels. Return to Australia was via Guam and Papua New Guinea, where VAT suffered a relapse of malaria on 13 June. *Melbourne* anchored off Townsville three days later, and divisions were paraded on the flight deck where VAT read the appointment of Captain Richard Peek OBE DSC (1928 class) to the ship's company and relinquished his command.[29] Peek, fresh from recommissioning *Sydney*, kept up the high standard and *Melbourne* was awarded the Duke of Gloucester Cup for 1962.[30]

Whatever heights VAT was still to achieve, his carrier command was possibly the true pinnacle of his naval career.

VAT was always "a good oar". Here he is stroke, as Rear-Admiral Harrington's ship's captains row him ashore from Melbourne having hauled down his flag as FOCAF.

28   Later Vice-Admiral Sir Alan McNicoll KBE CB GM (1908-1987), a torpedo specialist awarded the George Medal for defusing unexploded torpedoes in a captured Italian submarine. Also a D-Day planner, he commanded from 1949 the 1st Frigate Squadron and then the 10th Destroyer Squadron. On retirement he became Australia's first ambassador to Turkey and translated *The Odes of Horace*.
29   Later Vice-Admiral Sir Richard Peek KBE CB DSC (1914-2010). A gunnery specialist Peek had been wounded in the same attack on *Australia* that killed Harrie Gerrett in 1944. He was Fox 1 in *Shoalhaven* before commanding *Bataan* and then *Tobruk* off Korea.
30   *Sydney* was recommissioned by Peek on 7 March 1962, but remained in refit, not becoming fully operational as a fast troop transport until July 1963.

CHAPTER 12

ADMIRAL 1962 – 1975

WITH ONLY TWO BREAKS, as Fox 1 in 1955-1956 and then his Imperial Defence College course of 1960, VAT had worked tirelessly for Australian naval aviation since writing the draft plan in 1945. Appointed as the Second Naval Member of the Australian Naval Board of Administration and Chief of Personnel on 6 July 1962, that direct connection now ended. Replacing Rear-Admiral Galfrey Gatacre, VAT was promoted to Acting Rear-Admiral, a rank made substantive six months later.

When the naval air plan was approved in 1947, there were 448 men required in the first year. Over three weeks 4,200 applications were received, 756 for commissioned pilots, 1,470 for rating pilots and the rest for skilled air artificers, air mechanics and naval airmen. By the time VAT was serving in *Sydney* as executive officer the new air branch numbered over 3,000. The allure of naval aviation was strong, politically as well as publicly, but budget and manpower issues caused difficulties in the 1950s and early 1960s.

Prime Minister Robert Menzies, in office from 1949 to 1966, saw communism as the major foreign threat. The ANZUS treaty between Australia, New Zealand and the United States had underpinned the country's security since 1951, while the broader based Southeast Asia Treaty Organisation of 1954 was intended specifically to counter communist expansion.[1] The navy was tasked accordingly, reflected in VAT's postings as commander and captain. From active service in *Sydney* off Korea, to the deployments of his frigate squadron with the strategic reserve, followed by command of *Melbourne* in SEATO multinational exercises, all had been in response to the perceived threat.

VAT's shore postings highlighted the vagaries of being subject to an annual round of Treasury constraints. Reducing the scope of the original naval air plan in the post-Korean economies had seen the role of *Nirimba* circumscribed. Demanding staff work as DAWOT in Navy Office had been needed to achieve at least one modern carrier and a capable air group from 1955 onwards. Towards the end of his time commanding *Albatross* VAT struggled against the morale problems inherent in the threatened demise of the twelve-year old FAA, in addition to the well-established issues of inadequate pay, housing and poor manpower retention rates. With *Melbourne* and her aircraft projected to be obsolete by 1963, the Chief of Naval Staff Vice-Admiral Sir Roy Dowling, and his successor Vice-Admiral Sir Henry Burrell, were struggling as their aging ships, 21 in 1960, required over 60 percent of the available budget on maintenance alone.

---

1   SEATO signatories were Australia, Britain, France, New Zealand, Pakistan, the Philippines, Thailand and the USA, with the organisation's headquarters in Bangkok.

The Chiefs of Staff Committee in July 1959 declared a replacement carrier could not be funded within the £190m defence budget, and the Treasury made only £42.1m available against navy estimates of £47.3m for 1959-60. Lieutenant Athol Townley RANVR, who had depth charged a midget submarine from his requisitioned motor yacht *Steady Hand* during the Battle of Sydney Harbour, was now the Honourable Athol Townley, Minister of Defence. Despite this naval background he was a drinking partner of the Chief of Air Staff, Air Marshal Sir Frederick Scherger, and allowed himself to be swayed by unthinking air force parochialism. In November the demise of the FAA was publicly announced. The Navy Minister, Senator the Honourable John Gorton, recalled of Scherger "he had this bloody thing about getting rid of the Fleet Air Arm".[2]

Gorton and Burrell commenced a rear-guard campaign to reverse the decision. Noting that cabinet supported naval aviation in principle but lacked the funds, they determined there were enough spares to keep flying until 1963. Scherger continued his harassment, even attempting to veto staffed naval projects on technical grounds, which Burrell, rightly, saw as impertinent interference in his own service. Burrell, not comfortable navigating the politics and bureaucracy of government, was also struggling with the increasing technology and costs associated with the 20-year strategic vision for the RAN he had initiated, a vision that included the Fleet Air Arm.

June 1960 was momentous for the FAA. Previous naval ministers, although being the naval board's nominated president, had not regularly attended meetings. Gorton, however, would chair and his five years in the portfolio gave him a solid grasp of his department in all its complexity. Also, one assumes VAT did not miss the opportunity to brief him soundly on naval aviation during the minister's 1959 visit to *Albatross*. At the board meeting of 3 June 1960 Burrell said *Melbourne*, costing £3m per year, should be placed in reserve in 1963. Gorton, strongly disagreeing with his uniformed naval board members, refused to countenance the proposal. It had been a serendipitous day for the future FAA when the corvette *Ballarat* rescued a badly injured Flight Lieutenant Gorton from his life raft in February 1942.

Burrell, well aware that fleet defence would be inadequate without a fixed-wing FAA, was fortunate to have Captain Gledhill as DAWOT from July 1961. Gledhill had studied hard during his six months at the RN Staff College Greenwich. On return in July 1961, he mustered all his new-found administrative skills, adding them to those he had learned under VAT, and fought tenaciously against RAAF connivance in the moves to scrap the navy's fixed-wing squadrons. He would remember that "It took three years, working day and night to turn this around." While some decried the subsequent concentration on anti-submarine warfare for *Melbourne* and her CAG, it did keep Sea Venoms flying over the fleet for as long as possible. It also ensured that a carrier capability, which would otherwise have disappeared, was positioned

---

2   Later Air Chief Marshal Sir Frederick Scherger KBE CB DSO AFC. As chairman of the Chiefs of Staff Committee from 1961-1966 he strongly advocated commitment of forces to Vietnam. In retirement Scherger admitted to feeling a little ashamed that his extreme parochialism had been at the RAN's expense.

for full resurgence when naval commitments and budgets increased. By happenstance this occurred as new aircraft types suitable for a light carrier became available.

In 1961, as Navy Office completed its move to Canberra's Russell Offices, the navy ordered 27 Westland Wessex 31A ASW helicopters. Manned by four crew with a dunking sonar and torpedoes, their Napier gazelle turbine gave a speed of 108 knots and a range of over 400 kilometres. Essentially a Sikorsky S-58 built under licence they, and the two guided missile destroyers ordered from the US, presaged the move to future acquisitions of ships and aircraft from that country. When Burrell returned from leave, he found that Gorton had added the cost of re-commissioning *Sydney* to the estimates. When he remonstrated that it was not affordable, Gorton said he would find the money, and he did! VAT would later be referred to as "the Father of the Fleet Air Arm", but Gorton was its undoubted "Fairy Godmother".

Regional commitments aside, Australia had actively supported UN security measures six times between 1947 and 1962. There was a general recognition that while an Australian presence might not be necessary for strategic reasons, it was both a middle power responsibility and in our diplomatic interests. There was also a view that actively supporting UN forces helped keep conflict far from our shores.

The new nation of Malaysia was established in 1963, prompting Indonesia to pursue a policy of *Konfrontasi* until 1966. This confrontation required substantial RAN involvement, particularly off Borneo, and by late 1964 Menzies, informing Parliament there had been a deterioration in Australia's strategic situation, announced increases in defence spending and manpower. Growing instability in the region grew the defence budget 31% between 1959-60 and 1964-65. As the situation in South Vietnam deteriorated, military advisers were deployed from mid-1962, RAAF Caribou aircraft were sent, and national service was re-instituted in 1964. *Sydney* carried the First Battalion Royal Australian Regiment to South Vietnam in May 1965, the first of 25 voyages she would make to that troubled country.

Naval Board 6 July 1962 - 29 January 1966

Senator John Gorton, Minister of State for the Navy, as chairman of the naval board, reported direct to cabinet. The First Naval Member was Vice-Admiral "Arch" Harrington CB CBE DSO, who was responsible to Gorton for the navy's administration, and also Chief of Naval Staff. As CNS he dealt with issues of policy, strategy and operations through his Deputy Chief of Naval Staff, and the various divisions such as Plans, Air Warfare and Organisation or Intelligence. As Second Naval Member VAT was responsible for all matters of personnel including manning of ships and establishments. The Third Naval Member, Rear-Admiral Kenneth Urquhart CBE, was the senior engineer responsible for ship construction, maintenance and repairs while the fourth, Rear-Admiral Patrick Perry CBE, administered supply and works. The previous direct FAA responsibilities of the Fourth Naval Member had now been divided between all the board members.

An admiral's secretary plays a large role in ensuring his admiral's success and, consequently, is usually a personal choice by the flag officer. As VAT took over the role of Second Naval Member from Rear-Admiral "Gat" Gatacre he had no hesitation in retaining Gatacre's secretary, Commander Jeffrey Britten. Having worked with Britten in various appointments since 1942, including active service off Korea, it proved a harmonious and successful pairing. VAT would write of his secretary's commonsense, tact and reliability which proved of great assistance in their heavy workload.

By this time Britten was a family friend as well as a valued subordinate, the Smith family often staying at Jeff and Jean's holiday house on the coast at Garden Bay. Together the rear-admiral and commander even constructed a shelter for the Smith boys' sailing boat in the rear garden at 15 Fishburn Street in Canberra's Red Hill, with all sailing taking place on Lake George before Lake Burley Griffin was filled in late 1964.

All the board member's wives had an ancillary role to play, given the regular attendance at formal functions and the entertaining inherent as the spouse of an admiral with its assumed social position. It was one Nanette filled with grace. When she hosted in their own home the boys, with teenager's hunger, would compete for the leftover food. VAT, throughout his office years, was efficient enough to keep reasonable hours, rarely arriving home after 1800 unless there were diplomatic or service functions to attend.

The Navy Office relied heavily for efficient administration on dedicated and long-serving civilians, from the board's secretary to the directors of victualling, naval stores and accounts whose continuity in these administration posts released uniformed officers for service at sea. The permanent secretaries of any service department are of strategic influence, occupying as they do the position for lengthy terms in contrast to the several years of their uniformed colleagues. Thomas Hawkins CBE, the naval secretary, VAT found of particular assistance to him in his early days on the board.[3] With Hawkins experience of many aspects of naval, defence and government administration he proved a valuable mentor to the new rear-admiral.

A relaxed VAT holidaying with his family at Garden Bay.

Recovered from another relapse of malaria, VAT

---

3   Thomas Hawkins CBE BA LLB (1898-1976) started his public service as a staff clerk at navy office in 1915, only two years after the formation of the Australian fleet. He served seventeen ministers for the navy and fourteen chiefs of naval staff. As secretary from 1950, Hawkins strenuously protected his service's interests against the claims of other government departments.

joined the board in mid-1962 when the survival of naval fixed-wing flying was still being fought by Gledhill as tenaciously as he had struck at the battleship *Tirpitz* in 1944. As the first Wessex commenced delivery that November, policy reversal was imminent. While VAT would continue at every opportunity as a board member to put his imprimatur on FAA issues, they were only some among a multitude of issues, involving every branch, that he was deeply involved with. Such issues included manning for the new submarine service whose first keels were laid down in UK yards in 1964 and 1965. While he would not have been able to resist keeping a fatherly eye on aviation matters, no other branch ever claimed partiality or lack of attention to its own needs. As he oversaw the increase in naval numbers VAT also instituted the first exchanges with USN officers. Dadswell, now working in a staff directorate under VAT, found the USN was also amenable to *ab initio* training of naval aviators when the RAAF were unable to fully accommodate RAN needs.

In April 1963, eight years after commissioning, *Melbourne* recorded her 20,000[th] deck landing and, rather than paying off, continued in service for another nineteen years. Sam Landau, who had been working in the Department of Defence and was consequently familiar with many of its practices and procedures, became secretary of the naval board when Hawkins retired in 1963.[4] VAT found him an equally helpful colleague remarking "a more loyal friend the RAN never had". Gorton was replaced by the Honourable Frederick "Fred" Chaney AFC, also ex-RAAF, who likewise took a great interest in the service.[5] Chaney told VAT that when he was awarded the navy portfolio the prime minister said to him "never think that you can run your department from the end of the telephone", and he apparently never forgot that advice.

On 8 June 1963, VAT's 36 years of long and distinguished service to the RAN were recognised when he was made a Commander of the Military Division of the Order of the British Empire.

During night operations off Jervis Bay in February 1964, Lieutenant-Commander Toz Dadswell, commanding No. 816 Squadron, had his Gannet in a descending turn above *Melbourne*'s port quarter when a huge ball of flame lit the area - it was the boiler room of the destroyer *Voyager* exploding. While acting as plane guard, on the manoeuvring carrier's port bow, *Voyager* had cut across *Melbourne*'s bow and 82 people lost their lives when she was cut in two and sank.

VAT regretted that the navy did not have the same legislation as the air force which would have enabled a board of inquiry led by a federal judge, rendering the subsequent royal commissions with their latitude for press speculation and sensationalism unnecessary. While the fault was clearly with the destroyer, as the navy's premier "carrier captain" he had learnt that when the wind was light and variable, and the carrier searching for the best flying course, best practice

---

4   Later Sam Landau CBE (1915-1983), part of the war cabinet's secretariat as personal assistant to the Department of Defence's permanent head in WWII and helped establish SEATO in 1954. The naval board members valued his loyalty and professionalism. When the navy department was abolished in 1973 he was, in the face of some uniformed criticism, appointed to Washington as a civilian head of the defence staff.

5   Later Sir Frederick Chaney KBE AFC, Administrator of the Northern Territory in the early 1970s and a strong advocate for aboriginal land rights.

was to station the plane guard astern, completely out of the carrier's way. Once the flying course was found the destroyer could then take up her plane guard station.

In January 1965 VAT changed from second naval member to fourth, from personnel to supply. Harrington reported how very impressed he was with VAT's ability to get new ideas underway and to follow them through, commenting that:

> His determination and patience, not always attributes found in association with one another are remarkable. He may well show himself to be one of our best flag officers.

The sole caution was:

> He should not be allowed to work himself into a state where his health could suffer, thereby affecting his productivity.

Why VAT, lacking the normal paymaster or supply branch background, was made Chief of Supply quickly became clear. He initiated a restructuring of the three civilian supply directorates, namely naval and air stores, victualling and armament supply. With his concept endorsed by the departmental secretary and approved by the minister he moved rapidly ahead to change the status quo. The idea was that the three directorates, instead of being almost entirely independent and separately compartmented, should cooperate to a greater extent and all three be placed under a Director General of Supply. The new organisation was brought into being and had successful results over the years. The Director of Works was also responsible to the fourth naval member and VAT found it absorbing to have a hand in planning facilities that would serve the navy for many years into the future.

A Grumman Tracker aircraft had first landed on *Melbourne* in 1958. A larger variant was cross decked in July 1964 off Subic Bay with Dadswell as co-pilot to the USN aircraft commander. This Grumman S-2E Tracker was a proven anti-submarine aircraft with reliable Wright Cyclone radial engines and an endurance of nine hours. In May 1965, while VAT was chief of supply, a Douglas A-4 Skyhawk fighter/bomber cross decked from the 40,000-ton *Bennington* to *Melbourne* in the South China Sea. Inevitably while onboard, it was "zapped" with a red kangaroo painted on its fuselage. A mix of already delivered Wessex helicopters with Tracker and Skyhawk aircraft was clearly a combination that would keep a modernised *Melbourne* multi-role capable. In October 1965 the board announced the purchase of eight Skyhawk A-4Es and two TA-4Es.

Flag Officer Commanding Australian Fleet
30 January 1966 - January 1967

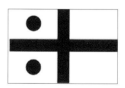

On 22 December 1965, the naval board, with the approval of the governor-general, appointed VAT to be the next FOCAF. With the document proclaiming the appointment was another authorising him to convene courts martial for the trial of any person borne on the books of any of HMA ships.

VAT's rear-admiral's flag which he hoisted as FOCAF.

Few naval officers are ever privileged to hoist their rear-admiral's flag at sea, as VAT did at 0800 on Monday 31 January 1966, from his flagship *Melbourne* at No. 2 buoy in Sydney Harbour. The ship then dressed overall to mark the Australia Day holiday. It presaged a year which was one of the most interesting and enjoyable of VAT's life. January had also seen the ship's catapult conduct 71 deadhead trial launches to confirm its viability for the announced replacement aircraft. As the ship worked-up under Flag Captain David Wells (1933 class) with Wessex, Gannet and Sea Venoms in February, VAT invited Landau to spend several days as his guest. Onboard they would have made sure to dine with his flagship's new supply officer, Commander Jeffrey Britten. Sometimes, with pressing work back at his Fleet Headquarters in Sydney, VAT would transfer there by helicopter while keeping his flag in *Melbourne*.

During the work-up one Gannet, which had ended its landing run hanging overboard from the No. 6 wire, could not be recovered and was ditched overboard. In March 1966 a RAN task group exercised off the east Australian coast with the USS *Hornet* and her ASW Group One. To VAT it seemed an embarrassment of riches to have a 37,000-ton Essex-class carrier in an anti-submarine warfare group but it reflected the pervasive threat from "hostile" submarines perceived at the time by Western nations - a threat which had fortuitously kept *Melbourne* in commission. After VAT and his command team attended a fleet tactical period in the shore-based trainer at *Watson* on Sydney's south head, his flagship led *Yarra*, *Stuart* and *Supply* out of Sydney Harbour on 24 March. A course was set north via Rabaul and Manus for an "up top" Far East SEATO deployment.

Arriving in Singapore, *Ark Royal* was wearing the flag of Rear-Admiral Charles Mills.[6] With the same seniority, as both rear-admiral and captain, the question of which ship would salute which was adjudicated in Australia's favour, since VAT had got his commander's brass hat first. VAT had private discussions about the future of the RN FAA and made suggestions to help secure its future. While VAT and his English counterpart had unshaken faith in the importance of naval aviation, the success of carriers in the 1982 Falklands War saw their retention in the RN and that service fared better than the RAN in the final decades of the century.

Melbourne's habitability, especially for machinery space watch keepers, was marginal in tropical waters. Four hours on watch in 54°C caused ten cases of heat exhaustion in one week after leaving Singapore. In the Sulu Sea on 28 April, a landing Sea Venom engaged the number two arrestor wire which broke during the pull-out. As the slowed aircraft toppled off the flight deck Lieutenant (P) John Da Costa successfully ejected but Lieutenant (O) Edward "Ted" Kennell (29) was lost.[7]

With the announcement that Australian military forces in South Vietnam would be increased to 4,500, the 5th and 6th battalions of the Royal Australian Regiment were deployed under

6   Later Vice-Admiral Sir Charles Mills KCB CBE DSC (1914-2006), a D-Day planner like VAT, he commanded the destroyer *Concord* off Korea and helped plan the Suez invasion of 1956. In retirement he became Lieutenant-Governor of Guernsey.
7   John Da Costa had survived the ditching of his Sycamore helicopter during VAT's command of *Melbourne* in 1961.

Operation *Hardihood*. On 30 April *Melbourne*, *Yarra* and *Vampire* assumed defence stations, rendezvous being made that afternoon with *Sydney* and *Supply*. Escorting *Sydney* with her embarked troops and equipment to Ganh Rai Bay off Vung Tau, the flagship remained in defence watches with two Wessex at Condition One alert for launching with depth charges. Gannets carried out dawn and dusk surface searches and a Sea Venom flew the midday search. Three weeks later the first national serviceman, Private Errol Noack (21), was killed while on patrol. In the first week of June the flagship, with *Yarra* and *Vendetta*, again escorted *Sydney* with embarked troops to Vung Tau and the 1st Australian Task Force secured their new base at Nui Dat, 30 kilometres north-east in Phuoc Tuy province.

While VAT's group were in Hong Kong the arrival of *Gull* and *Curlew* made six RAN ships in the harbour. He began a round of admiral's sea inspections beginning with *Vampire* on 17 May, and inspecting *Melbourne* herself in June. Typhoon *Irma* slowed passage in the South China Sea to the annual SEATO exercise off the Philippines with assembled RN and USN carrier groups. Each respective admiral was made Officer-in-Tactical Command for a period and VAT found the comparison as each admiral carried out their duties "interesting".

Onboard *Melbourne* VAT had a small staff separate from the ship's officers. It was not a complete staff by any means as he had left many at his Fleet Headquarters on Garden Island, but it worked in practice. VAT's experience and firm belief was that a fleet benefited from having an admiral afloat as much as possible. Return to Australia was via Penang and Fremantle with VAT hosting the minister for the navy for some of the passage. The remainder of the year was the usual busy round of exercises off Australia and port visits.

VAT welcomed the newest units to his fleet, *Perth* in February and *Hobart* in August. A teenage Mark Smith was very impressed with the soda fountain of the American built destroyers whose single dispenser would produce lemonade or cola at the touch of a button. After almost four years of settled life in Canberra, with VAT's appointment as FOCAF, Nanette moved the family to the navy owned *Chatsworth* in Potts Point, less than five minutes' walk from his headquarters. For the boys this had the advantage of being able to see from the windows the flagship entering and leaving harbour. They had transferred from Canberra Grammar to Shore, the older two staying on as boarders for several years to prevent extra disruption to their education when VAT moved back to Canberra after finishing as fleet commander.

VAT hosted the Japanese Maritime Self Defence Force Training Squadron and never forgot the sight of the Chilean Sail Training Ship *Esmeralda* moving up Sydney Harbour with all sails set and yards manned. They visited New Zealand and then a large Australian Maritime Exercise was held in October with sixteen RN, three USN, one RNZN and eight RAN ships in the Coral Sea and Jomard Passage area. VAT did not ruminate on the desperate days of May 1942 when six allied ships braced to battle the 29 Japanese warships of the Port Moresby invasion force reported heading south to the passage, but did comment on the comparative ease with which units of these different navies worked together, a unity only achieved with practice.

In January 1967 VAT hauled down his flag and handed command of the fleet to Rear-Admiral Richard Peek OBE DSC, just as he had handed over his command of *Melbourne* to Peek in 1962, and joined Navy Office on promotion to flag rank.

A medal was established in 1993 to recognise those who had supported Australian operations in Vietnam for relatively short periods of time. For his service in *Melbourne* as FOCAF escorting *Sydney* to Vung Tau twice in 1966 VAT was awarded the Vietnam Logistics and Support medal.

The Vietnam Logistics and Support medal.

The campaign honour "Malaysia 1965-1966" was retrospectively added to *Melbourne*'s honour board, and those of Nos. 816 and 817 Squadrons, for their operational support of the Federated States of Malaysia during the confrontation, which ended when a peace agreement with Indonesian was ratified in August 1966.[8]

Deputy Chief of Naval Staff   20 January 1967 - 2 April 1968

As DCNS VAT ran the office for his chief, Vice-Admiral Sir Alan McNicholl. He was McNicholl's gatekeeper through whom all divisions - plans, operations and equipment - reported, as did naval intelligence and the policy divisions for tactics, weapons, aviation and submarines. Even the naval weather service and scientific services came under VAT's administrative control. All these disparate elements needed to be efficiently coordinated through him as the main conduit supplying the naval board with information. He was also then equally responsible for instigating the board's consequent decisions. In all this he particularly valued the wisdom, common sense and humour of the Honourable Charles "Bert" Kelly which were displayed when he was minister for the navy.[9]

The appointment proved to be an incredibly busy fourteen months as the build up to the war gathered pace and the FAA prospered. In February a clearance diving team flew to South Vietnam to begin their dangerous work in those murky waters, while in March *Hobart* deployed to join the US Seventh Fleet, where she operated on the gunline as far north as the Red River delta near Hanoi. Over the next five years, as the board rotated destroyers every six months, 102,546 rounds were fired by those ships. *Sydney* and her escorts continued a regular logistic shuttle of troops and equipment. *Oxley*, the first boat of the new Australian submarine service arrived in Sydney that August and the submarine base *Platypus* was commissioned in Sydney's Neutral Bay.

In October a RAN Helicopter Flight deployed to Vietnam for a twelve-month tour under Lieutenant-Commander Neil Ralph.[10] *Melbourne* arrived in San Diego at the end of the month and embarked fourteen S-2E Trackers, ten A4-G and TA-4G Skyhawks, two weapon system trainers and 800 tons of stores. In this they were assisted by Dadswell who had travelled from

---

8   British Commonwealth forces had peaked with 17,000 in Borneo and 10,000 in Malaysia and Singapore.
9   Later Charles Kelly CMG (1912-1997) a farmer and passionate supporter of free trade policies.
10   Later Rear-Admiral Neil Ralph AO DSC, who joined as a naval airman in 1952, becoming an observer in Firefly and Sea Venom aircraft. In 1958 he qualified as a pilot in Sea Venoms then flew Sycamore and Wessex helicopters. He also commanded Nos. 725 and 723 Squadrons, *Torrens* and *Albatross* before retiring as DCNS.

Washington to be the RAN's liaison officer. On return to Garden Island Dockyard the carrier entered an extended refit in preparation for operating the new fixed-wing aircraft, and Lieutenant-Commander Da Costa commissioned No. 805 (Skyhawk) Squadron at *Albatross* on 10 January 1968, returning a strike capability to the FAA.

The newly delivered A-4 Skyhawks returned a significant strike capability to the FAA, with No. 805 Squadron reforming in January 1968.

An expanding navy upgrading its ships, weapons and systems while contributing units to active operations in Southeast Asia made for tremendous work pressure and VAT's doctor recorded him experiencing ventricular ectopic heart beats. One of the continuing discussion items was the possible replacement of *Melbourne*, the matter dragging on for years since there were no cut-and-dried solutions. Almost from its inception, the FAA had had some problem or crisis to overcome, with VAT consoling himself with the thought that the fact they were overcome had added to the FAA's quality and strength.

For his achievements in these senior appointments VAT was made a Companion of the Military Division of the most Honourable Order of the Bath in 1968. The citation referred to his exceptionally strong sense of duty and leadership, determination, integrity and reliability. His final confidential report from McNicoll simply stated that, as he had been appointed the next CNS, "comment would be superfluous". Selecting the professional head of the navy is a cabinet and ministerial choice as well as a service one and VAT, although lacking the political connections enjoyed by McNicoll, had had no contenders to the appointment.

First Naval Member and Chief of Naval Staff
3 April 1968 - 23 November 1970

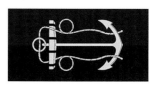

Promoted to vice-admiral on becoming the professional head of the RAN, VAT knew he had been fortunate to have had experience as both second and fourth naval members, and doubly fortunate having been DCNS for the previous fourteen months. This meant

The flag of the Naval Board from 1920-1976 and now used by the Chief of Navy.

that immediately on becoming CNS he was fully informed on the most current matters. Given the heavy commitments to operations in Vietnam, and the ongoing modernisation of the navy's ships and weapons this proved a boon.[11]

In a tradition originating with the First Sea Lord in 1914, VAT, as Chief of Navy, would now use green ink in his formal correspondence. The signal, written in green, that VAT had transmitted to all ships and establishments on assuming command reflected in sentiment those he had first heard as a young teenager from governor-generals addressing graduating classes at Jervis Bay. He

---

11   Even the Fleet Band completed a short tour in Vietnam entertaining the troops. In addition there were navy medical teams, staff officers and some aircrew bolstering numbers in the RAAF's No. 9 Squadron.

stated his profound belief that:

> … it is upon the RAN that the wealth, safety and strength of Australia so greatly depends.

He also saw his role as ensuring that the navy met the commitments the government placed on it.

With their shared histories it was inevitable that VAT chose as his secretary the newly promoted Captain Jeffrey Britten. By this

The Naval Board makes a 1969 call on Governor-General Baron Casey. From left: RADM Hugh Stevenson, VADM VAT Smith, Baron Casey, RADM Richard Peek, Samuel Landau, RADM Bryan Castles and RADM William Graham.

time VAT's regard ensured his support for the award of an OBE in the 1968 Queen's Birthday Honours List for Britten's long service to the RAN. When VAT and Nanette were subsequently invited by the Indian Government for a two-week visit, they were accompanied by Britten, as staff officer, for an itinerary that ranged the breadth of the sub-continent from Kashmir to Cochin. Among the military installations visited time was made for the couple to visit the Taj Mahal.

When the naval board made official calls on state or vice-regal occasions, they would wear No. 1 Full Dress. This was a gold-braided ceremonial frock coat with epaulettes, gold laced trousers with full dress sword belt plus medals, decorations and orders. Looking quaintly Victorian on such occasions, between them these six men represented 214 years of dutiful service to Australia with knowledge hard gained in peace and war.

The Third Naval Member and Chief of Technical Services, Rear-Admiral Bryan Castles, is a good example of how many people VAT "knew'" and had influenced, by this his fifth decade of service.[12] Castles was an RANVR lieutenant aboard *Shropshire* in 1943 when he first met a naval college educated officer who assumed no superior "airs" towards the young volunteer electrical engineer. Castles was struck by VAT's "search for knowledge", his willingness to listen and learn from others, and his:

> … dedication to his fellow officers and men and to the RAN … the like of which I never experienced again.

They served together again off Korea where Castles saw VAT at his best with the ability:

> … to bring *Sydney* to its peak of efficiency and at the same time create a very happy ship's company.

He now witnessed VAT operating at the highest level.

---

12   Rear-Admiral Bryan Castles CBE (1915-2006), after discharge from the RANVR he served with the RN before returning to the RAN and commanding the Electrical School at Flinders post Korea. Later he was Fleet Electrical Officer.

Australians and New Zealanders deployed to South Vietnam peaked in 1968 at over 8,000 from all three services. The Tet Offensive of that year morphed from a tactical defeat for Hanoi to a strategic victory as confidence and public support in Australia and the US for the war rapidly waned, eventually coalescing into active opposition. Uncertainty also affected the government as Prime Minister Gorton, while continuing to support the war, refused to increase Australia's commitment.

As soon as he was settled in office, VAT visited the fleet in Sydney at the end of April, making sure to walk around the refitting *Melbourne* and six other vessels from a patrol boat to the submarine *Oxley*. *Otway*, the second submarine, had just commissioned, to be followed by *Ovens* and *Onslow* in 1969. Mid-1968 found the minister for defence requiring a reorganisation of defence joint planning by creating a tri-service planning staff. No stranger to organisational change, VAT was never hidebound, always willing to be convinced of a new policy's benefits and never automatically inimical for the sake of tradition.

A revised group pay structure, giving commonality across the services, was introduced, where pay would be differentiated according to trade and skill. Although no-one had their pay reduced it still proved divisive, as there were clear winners. This discontent could not be addressed by the board as quickly as VAT would have liked, with the navy being no longer able to act unilaterally in the matter.

VAT and his second naval member, Peek, both wished for conditions of service to reflect the changing ethos in Australian society and the improved economy. Peek himself had had the searing experience, while on an unaccompanied posting to the UK in 1946, of being denied permission to return to Australia and his newborn son when his wife died in childbirth. It solidified a life-long concern for the welfare of his subordinates. When a defence committee in January 1970 confirmed the remit to keep service pay and allowances comparable to civilian rates, Peek and VAT continued to press for pay improvements.

While Peek considered that everything had been downhill since his final sea command and had a contempt for "the duplicity of politicians", VAT had been more exposed to staff work, was more comfortable with the bureaucracy, and lacked Peek's cynicism. Wherever possible more humane policies were adopted, such as the option to discharge two months after joining, which was good for the individual and meant the navy did not waste costly training resources on a dissatisfied rating.

Hobart, operating in company at night north of the DMZ in June 1968, was hit by missiles fired by a US air force F-4 Phantom, killing two and wounding seven. It was exactly the sort of incident that VAT's duties ashore at Normandy in 1944 had strived to prevent. The USN inquiry quickly assigned a *mea culpa* to the air force and recommended improved identification and communication procedures. The navy board was satisfied with this process and accepted the findings.

In January 1969 as the UK reduced its Far East presence, Australia announced it would retain bases in Malaysia and Singapore. A continued RAN and RNZN presence in South East Asia was considered necessary and Gledhill, returned to his country of birth as Australia's defence representative, assisted with Anzac policy. VAT believed continental defence also required an Indian Ocean presence and encouraged the development of naval facilities in Western Australia, eventually sending the first trial deployment there in 1970. A parliamentary committee concluded a replacement carrier was desirable if it could be afforded and VAT assigned Captain Geoff Woolrych (1944 class) to head the project team.[13]

By February 1969, defects were delaying *Melbourne* becoming fully operational after her extended refit. VAT visited the carrier, personally inspected the problems, and promptly detailed his third naval member with his engineering specialists to put things right. Given this level of board attention there was rapid improvement, with 1,000 fixed-wing deck landings being completed by the new Skyhawks and Trackers during their work-up.

Sailing for SEATO exercises in the Far East on 5 May *Melbourne*, under the command of Captain John Stevenson (1935 class), had embarked her new CAG of Nos. 805 (Skyhawk), 816 (Tracker) and 817 (Wessex) Squadrons.[14] Also onboard was the secretary of defence with VAT, to watch flying evolutions before disembarking the next day. *Melbourne*'s motto was "Vires Acquirit Eundo" ("She Gathers Strength As She Goes") which was particularly apropos with the expanded capabilities the new-look CAG gave her. Able to operate as an anti-submarine warfare carrier, or as a maritime strike carrier, *Melbourne* could also conduct offensive operations against ground forces and installations. Once again VAT had had a major role in ensuring a capable FAA component that could be deployed in the country's interests.

The most serious matter which arose during VAT's stewardship of the navy was the collision between *Melbourne* and the US destroyer *Frank E Evans* on 3 June 1969. In a telephone call with Admiral Tom Moorer, USN Chief of Naval Operations, VAT agreed to an initial joint USN/RAN board of inquiry. Perhaps expecting the same probity shown in the *Hobart* inquiry the previous year, where the USN quickly assigned blame to the US air force, VAT was unprepared for the disreputable actions of a US rear-admiral focused on reducing his own service's culpability.

VAT never doubted the ability and contribution made by the RAN members of the board but found several points in the report unsatisfactory. Being an ad-hoc international board, it could not be recalled by the Australian naval board. Strongly feeling that Captain Stevenson was fully entitled to have every opportunity to have his case absolutely and clearly understood, VAT, cognisant that a court could condone as well as condemn, instructed that a court martial

---

13   Later Rear-Admiral Geoffrey Wololrych AO (1930-2006) who boldly married when a sub-lieutenant and then saw active service in Korea aboard *Anzac*. Commanded *Derwent* and *Vampire* before becoming FOCAF in 1983, where he dealt with a fleet newly bereft of a carrier.

14   Captain John Stevenson (1921-2019) had survived the sinking of *Nestor* in June 1942 and served under VAT in *Shropshire* and *Sydney*. He had been Naval Equerry to Prince Philip during the Olympic Visit of 1956 and commanded *Barcoo*, *Anzac* and *Vendetta*.

be convened. This was done and Stevenson, as expected, was honourably acquitted. Where VAT severely erred was in not immediately supporting an innocent Stevenson by returning him to his command or, if that was politically fraught, ensuring an appointment that would have demonstrated his, and the naval board's, unequivocal support.

In October 39,000 people attended the air show at Nowra marking the FAA's 21st birthday. The visiting First Sea Lord, Admiral Sir Michael Le Fanu GCB DSC, presented a silver salver from the service that had done so much to establish naval aviation in Australia.[15] Leading the official guests was a proud VAT Smith, who had flown in from Canberra with other members of the board.

With thoughts never far from his men on active service VAT's 1969 Christmas message reflected that at a proverbial time of peace and goodwill, there would be little peace for those RAN units serving in Vietnam. The navy was expanding to meet its tasks, with inevitable problems and difficulties, but he was firmly convinced any shortcomings would be corrected if all played their proper part. Finishing his term as CNS a year later he handed over 53 ships in service, the largest RAN fleet since 1945. His years on the Naval Board since 1962 had helped ensure a balanced fleet whose versatility, flexibility and capacity for rapid deployment could respond to a wide range of situations.

In September 1968, VAT made the first of his visits to RAN units in and off Vietnam, including the helicopter flight at Camp Blackhorse, 28 kilometres north of Nui Dat, where he flew in a Bell Iroquois and a Cobra gunship.[16] The following year he visited them at Camp Bear Cat southeast of Bien Hoa in Dong Nai Province. Some then, and later, thought that recognition for this unit was insufficient. Around 208 members of the FAA, including those with the RAAF's No. 9 Squadron, served between 1967 and 1971. Not every courageous act could be rewarded, nevertheless VAT ensured that twenty percent of the flight's personnel were recognised with honours and awards, well in excess of the mandated two percent granted front-line squadrons he served with during WWII. As someone who had seen five of his own flight killed or mortally wounded within a tragic two minutes at the Battle of Savo Island, VAT would have been thankful there were only five deaths in the Helicopter Flight Vietnam's four deployments and four years of operations.[17]

Unit citations for gallantry were not then in the Australian honours system, and the wearing of the numerous American and Vietnamese awards bravely earned, such as Air Medals and Crosses of Gallantry, was not countenanced by the prevailing imperial system. While several RAN destroyers were awarded US Meritorious Unit Commendations, as was Clearance

---

15   Inscribed on the salver was "Presented by the Fleet Air Arm, Royal Navy, to the Fleet Air Arm, Royal Australian Navy, on the occasion of its 21st anniversary, 12 October 1969".

16   Some junior aircrew claimed VAT was in country to get a medal, not understanding that 30 days of official visits or one day posted on the strength of a formed unit were required to qualify. In any event, such an unseemly motive would have been inconceivable to VAT, who did not qualify for, and never wore, the Vietnam Medal.

17   Lieutenant-Commander Patrick Vickers MiD (31) 22 February 1968; Lieutenant Anthony Casadio (22) and Petty Officer O'Brian Phillips (32) 21 August 1968; Acting Sub-Lieutenant Antony Huelin (25) 3 January 1969; Leading Aircrewman Noel Shipp (24) 31 May 1969.

Diving Team Three and No. 817 Squadron, no similar citation was granted the 135th Assault Helicopter Company, HFV's parent unit.[18] VAT had been particularly impressed with the work of the HFV whose performance was second to none, and he "felt proud to belong to the same service". In 2018 the governor-general retrospectively approved an Australian Unit Citation for Gallantry to the RAN HFV.

In the Queen's Birthday Honours list of June 1969 VAT was awarded a knighthood in the Order of the British Empire. When Collins received his knighthood, he had commented that:

> One's wife takes no share in service promotions or decorations, and it gave me deep satisfaction that this knighthood honour would also reflect on her.

VAT receives his knighthood.

VAT perhaps had similar feelings, but when Nanette found herself addressed as Lady Smith in the local supermarket, she immediately demanded her interlocutor neighbour "tone it down". Nanette's home counties British accent continued to sound "posh" to Australian ears, her nephews thinking she spoke like the queen, and she could be reserved on occasion. One of VAT's aides was struggling to make conversation on a long official flight. When she went to use the aircraft's bathroom he exclaimed "Ah, the Relief of Ladysmith, I believe". Conversation was not resumed on her return.

A new five-year programme was announced in March 1970 by the Minister for Defence, the Honourable Malcolm Fraser. The board had achieved, among other items, an additional ten Skyhawks, more helicopters and several HS748 aircraft to replace ageing Dakotas. Two more submarines were ordered, but the challenge of manning even six boats meant VAT did not take up the option for any more. The money saved went to other more pressing operational needs including design studies for the next generation of destroyers.

In all this VAT had the unstinting support and departmental administrative expertise of Captain Jeffrey Britten. Writing in his now accustomed green ink VAT observed that his secretary had loyalty, a wide-knowledge of naval matters and could work quickly and thought clearly. Almost in projection of his own personal reports VAT found in Britten an alert officer who worked hard, was always ready to offer sound advice, had applied common-sense and

---

18   No. 817 Squadron was awarded a Meritorious Unit Commendation for rescue operations on the night of 3 June 1969, following the collision between *Melbourne* and *Frank E Evans*.

ADMIRAL VAT SMITH

imagination to their myriad problems and was completely trustworthy. VAT and Britten had formed a commendable partnership that had lasted through various appointments since that critical year of 1942.

VAT had clearly established a good relationship with Fraser, being chosen by him to become the next Chairman, Chiefs of Staff Committee. Since the prime minister was now John Gorton, who first knew VAT from his days as minister for the navy, the choice was quickly confirmed in cabinet.

Chairman, Chiefs of Staff Committee
23 November 1970 - 22 November 1975

The Australian joint service flag used until 1984.

Until 1958, when the respective navy, army and air force chiefs of staff gathered, the most senior at the time chaired their meetings. Following a review greater centralisation was recommended, and Chairmanship of the Chiefs of Staff Committee was established as a formal appointment. The incumbent, reporting directly to the minister of defence, became the government's principal military adviser. Scherger, the third chairman, was promoted air chief marshal towards the end of his term, thereby strengthening his already assertive role by outranking the three service chiefs. Holding four-star rank (admiral, general or air chief marshal), the chairman was the most senior officer of the Australian armed forces.

On 23 November 1970, Sir Victor Smith became Chairman, Chiefs of Staff Committee and was promoted to admiral, the first graduate of the Royal Australian Naval College to achieve that rank.[19] After 43 years' service his direct connection with the navy ceased. VAT was not legally in command, but was senior adviser to the services, overseeing their present and future. Five years later, in large measure due to the organisational changes he managed, the first Chief of Defence Force Staff was appointed ten weeks after his retirement. Now simply titled Chief of Defence Force the new incumbent did have command authority over the Australian defence forces, likewise the CNS exercised direct command of the RAN as the naval board was abolished.

One of VAT's staff officers described him as:

> … a man of rare distinction and ability, modest and under-spoken, yet with a commanding presence and manner, a warm personality and a keen sense of humour.[20]

While many with a modest nature find the surroundings of higher service difficult, this was never apparent in VAT's demeanour although, when CNS, he had been known to slip away from social occasions after the initial round of formalities with instructions to his staff

---

19   While a few RN officers who had served with the RAN achieved admiral's rank, there had only been one RAN four-star prior to VAT. Admiral Sir George Hyde KCB (1877-1937), the first naval member since 1931, was promoted in 1936, dying a year later while still serving.
20   Later General Peter Gration AC OBE (b1932), who commanded the 1st Australian Civil Affairs Unit in South Vietnam and was the Chief of Defence Force 1987-1993.

captain to "carry on". A good listener, able to quietly probe for the information he needed, VAT's solid, reliable persona was appreciated by all, politician or public servant, serviceman or civilian.

Just as VAT had not favoured the FAA over other branches of the navy when on the naval board, so now the navy was never favoured over the other two services. Perhaps it was this lack of hoped-for partisanship that led to some adverse comments. His brief service with *Assault*, reinforced by experiences ashore at the Normandy bridgehead and then dealings with the RAAF on behalf of the British Pacific Fleet and at Schofields, had left VAT uncommonly tri-service in experience and outlook among

VAT signing the guest book at Merdeka Palace in 1972 when calling on Indonesia's President Suharto.

his naval contemporaries. His five years as chairman were turbulent, with an increasingly unpopular war and a new Labor government initiating fundamental changes to defence organisation and strategy. Always a problem solver, VAT's motto was "Convince Me", where nothing would be rejected simply because it was a change to how things had been done.

There were many naval college families, son following father, and Mark Smith joined the 1971 class at Jervis Bay, one of 73 cadet midshipmen in that year's expanded entry. Almost half withdrew before graduation, in Mark's case after two years at the University of New South Wales as the college experimented with arts degrees, in addition to the usual science and engineering courses. VAT's response was typically analytical, initiating an informal discussion with three other admirals, not to change Mark's mind, but trying to understand the reasons for the disproportionate rate of resignations. With never an admonishing word and the full support of his father, Mark continued tertiary studies in the UK and pursued a career in journalism.

Michael, the oldest, had loathed being a boarder at Shore and did his final years of secondary education at Canberra Grammar. Briefly considering farming he instead went to the University of Sydney and on graduation joined the public service for a career in the Department of Foreign Affairs. Piers attended selection interviews for RANC but did not continue his application, attending the Canberra College of Advanced Education after which the financial sector beckoned.

VAT travelled to London with the defence minister in March 1971 for SEATO and other Five Powers defence conferences. The work proceeded without excitement; all nations concerned still appreciative of both organisations' value. When VAT found himself welcomed by Prince

Philip to dinner at Windsor Castle for the second time in two weeks, he felt comfortable enough to joke that perhaps the prince should send him a mess bill. Anzac Day occurred during the conference and VAT helped represent Australia at the impressive ceremonies held in Westminster Abbey and at the Cenotaph.

For some years VAT had watched his mother Una decline into dementia. Moved to a nursing home overlooking Chatswood Park it was distressing to see the woman who had been a staunch support for Nanette during his absences at sea become so diminished, to the point where she no longer recognised him. Una Smith died in September 1971.

A SEATO military advisers conference was held in Bangkok in September 1971, where the lessening importance of the organisation was becoming apparent. In response military representatives from the United States, Australia and New Zealand attended a conference in March 1972 in Hawaii. This was hosted by the United States Commander in Chief Pacific, Admiral John McCain Jr, whose son Lieutenant-Commander John McCain III was still a prisoner of war in North Vietnam, his Skyhawk having been shot down four years before. With only the three nations represented, the exchanges were frank and saw information being shared which would not have occurred with a larger quorum. In June VAT hosted a SEATO Military Advisers meeting in Canberra which addressed the political changes caused by President Nixon's visit to Beijing and the renewed North Vietnamese offensive.

VAT was a guest of the Japanese Self Defence Force later in 1972, where he addressed their National Staff College. He found it an enlightening visit with some of his hosts clearly of the view that their defence policies were inclined to be too restrictive. Certainly, the questions he invited revealed a sound knowledge of Pacific strategy. On the way back to Australia he visited Indonesia where he was granted an unusually long talk with the president, General Suharto. He also renewed his acquaintance with the defence minister General Maraden Panggabean and throughout felt not the slightest antagonism towards Australia from a nation that had been eyed with caution for many years.

All through these years the Vietnam War had been continuing. VAT's views had been changing and he now thought the Australian contribution should be wound down. A five-day visit to Vietnam in March 1971 with Fraser specifically focused on force reduction, including the return of No. 2 (Canberra) Squadron, tanks, engineers and support troops. The final RAN HFV returned in June and the last RAN destroyer left the gun line in

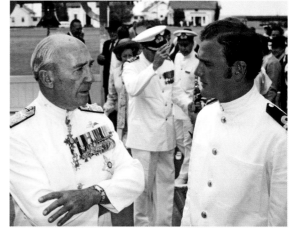

VAT at the 1972 RANC graduation parade at Jervis Bay, chatting to Acting Sub-Lieutenant James "Jim" Stapleton.

October.[21] VAT felt confirmed in the drawdown policy when the senior US commander in South Vietnam had, very diplomatically, told VAT he was having to fight the war with one hand tied behind his back.

In 1972 the armed services were at a post-WWII peak when elections were held in December, with victory going to the Labor party after 23 years in opposition.[22] The Honourable Lance Barnard became minister for defence as well as minister for the navy, army and air force.[23] VAT observed that Barnard took the greatest interest in his portfolio and worked very hard at it. Naturally the new minister saw that his party had been given a clear mandate for their policies and set about them. In this his powerful Secretary of Defence, Sir Arthur Tange, was a willing instigator.[24]

After a short period, the ministerial directive for examination of the Defence organisation, which resulted in the Tange Report, was issued. Initiating its recommendations, as five ministries - the three armed services plus defence and supply - were merged, saw considerable opposition with some uncomfortable at increased civilian oversight. VAT held it was his clear duty to facilitate the wishes of the new government and, in any event, recognised that reorganisation was required, viewing the report as a worthwhile first step. Any contemporary or subsequent view of a weak chairman being overridden by Tange presupposes that the changes did not have VAT's approval, when in fact much bore his endorsement.

This equitable approach resulted in VAT's appointment as chairman being extended to five years, with the government wanting his continued steady and undemonstrative hand at the helm of the institutional changes. VAT was one of the few not intimidated by Tange, who was his own age and a keen rugby fan. Tange in return valued his "unprejudiced judgement and unwillingness to be swayed by special pleading from any quarter", stating that their association, suit and uniform in mutual support, had been unique in his career.

The former prime minister the Honourable Gough Whitlam AC, whose term of office overlapped VATs, recalled that:

> Sir Victor had the administrative responsibility for the armed forces of Australia and
> Papua New Guinea throughout three years of exceptional changes - amalgamation of
> departments, attractive conditions of an all-volunteer Defence Force, development of
> a uniform code of discipline and review of defence treaties with our neighbours and
> arrangements for shared bases in Australia. These changes would not have been possible

---

21 No. 723 Squadron, even though a second-line unit, was awarded the battle honour "Vietnam 1967-71".
22 The size of the three services had grown 69% from 48,000 to 81,000 while the RAN, 11,100 strong in 1962, had grown 55% to 17,200.
23 Later The Honourable Lance Barnard AO (1919-1997) who had fought at the Battle of El Alamein and suffered a permanent hearing impairment from his war service. He and his wife adopted two Vietnamese orphan girls in 1971. After leaving politics he was ambassador to Sweden.
24 Later Sir Arthur Tange AC CBE (1914-2001) was for 30 years one of the most influential public servants in Australian government. Secretary in the Department of External Affairs and then High Commissioner to India he served as Secretary for the Department of Defence from 1970-1979.

if there had not been complete confidence and trust between the Prime Minister and the defence ministers on one hand and the Chairman of the Chiefs of Staff Committee on the other hand.

Sir Victor enjoyed the respect and affection of the Chiefs of Staff, the heads of departments, the representatives of other countries and ministers on both sides of politics. He was a great leader of the defence force and a great servant of the Australian people.[25]

In March of his retirement year, 1975, the first Sea King Mk.50A ASW helicopter was delivered, and the 16th VAT Smith relay race was run at *Albatross*, each of those sixteen years having seen VAT working in the highest levels of the service. It had taken a toll on his health, especially the physical and psychological stress of his years as CNS, which had caused a resurgence of the rashes and other symptoms he had suffered when Fox 1. As was common given the sun exposure unavoidable for an executive officer, there had also been regular excisions of skin cancer, the first in March 1962 when he attended the Hong Kong Military Hospital while *Melbourne* was in port.

VAT had been a supporter of more Australian symbols of nationalism in the navy's insignia, badges and ensigns. At the naval board meeting of 21 January 1966, as well as moving forward with ordering Grumman Trackers and the construction of twenty patrol boats, it was decided to adopt a distinctive Australian white ensign with a blue federation star instead of continuing to sail under the RN ensign with its St George's cross. Although a Knight of the British Empire, he proudly attended the first meeting of the Council of the Order of Australia in May 1975, replacing an imperial honours system with a national one. He was even prouder when, in the first list of awards, he was named a Companion in the Military Division for eminent service as Chairman, Chiefs of Staff Committee, which took order of precedence ahead of his British knighthood.

In language not dissimilar to the 1926 letter informing George Smith that his son had been selected for appointment to the Royal Australian Naval College, VAT received a letter on 30 October from the naval board which:

> ... hereby posts you for discharge to shore on retirement to date 24th November 1975 and directs you to report to your duty.

This was duty to his country and service that VAT had reported to for half a century,

VAT rang the current CNS's secretary, Captain Ian Crawford (1949 class), to enquire what musical salute would be played at the parade to mark his retirement.[26] Told that the designated tune was *Rule Britannia* VAT said he did not think that was appropriate for an Australian admiral. When Crawford repeated that it was the musical salute laid down, VAT quietly

---

25   Letter dated 21 December 1998.
26   Later Rear-Admiral Ian Crawford AO, who served in *Ceylon* off Korea when a midshipman then specialised as a supply officer. He was briefly secretary to VAT when FOCAF.

explained that he didn't care if the band played *Pop Goes the Weasel*, but if they played *Rule Britannia* he would walk off the parade.

On 23 November 1975, at a ceremony in front of the Department of Defence offices in Canberra, VAT retired from the Royal Australian Navy. The 100-man guard of honour was drawn from all three services and in attendance were his army successor and the three service chiefs, as well as the Secretary of Defence Sir Arthur Tange. The new Minister of Defence, the Honourable James Killen, in farewell appreciation commented that VAT's career had been one of true service to the nation, carried out with impartiality and in the highest traditions of his service. As VAT departed the musical salute being played was *Advance Australia Fair*.

The Governor-General of Australia Sir John Kerr held a retirement dinner at Yarralumla in VAT's honour. On the left is Lady Anne Kerr and on the right is Lady Nanette Smith.

Melbourne with Wessex, Sea King, Tracker and Skyhawk aircraft embarked continued in service for seven years after VAT retired.

CHAPTER 13

RETIREMENT

V AT ESCHEWED ANY OFFERS to sit on defence industry boards as he and Nanette settled into a quiet retirement in their unpretentious Canberra home, where they continued to attend services at St John's Anglican Church. Having officially opened the Naval Aviation Museum at Albatross in 1974 VAT continued to advocate for the museum over the years, seeing it as a memorial to those naval aviators who had lost their lives flying. VAT took a quiet pride when referred to as the "Father of the Fleet Air Arm", becoming patron of the ACT branch of the Fleet Air Arm Association. For his encouragement through the early years of the Australian Naval Institute, he was made an honorary life member, and also became patron of the ACT Divisions of the Navy League and reserve cadets.

During the Silver Jubilee royal tour to Australia in 1977 Her Majesty Queen Elizabeth held an investiture at the governor-general's residence in Canberra. As sovereign head of the Order of Australia she invested VAT, wearing formal civilian clothes, with the insignia of a Companion of that Order.

VAT's lifelong interest in rugby continued, and he became patron of the ACT Rugby League Association. Playing tennis into his 70s, he was also patron of the ACT Tennis Association

VAT being invested in the Order of Australia by Queen Elizabeth II in 1977.

VAT proudly wearing the insignia of a Companion of the Order of Australia.

and the RAN Sailing Association. Never aloof, where once he would introduce himself to his neighbours as "My name's Smith, I'm in the navy" it was now "I used to be in the navy". In later years, attending a naval air show he was a personable elderly gentleman who would chat happily to people without ever drawing their attention to his own role in the display they were seeing.

VAT was often called on to officiate at naval events. When the memorial to *Canberra* was unveiled on the shore of Lake Burley Griffin in August 1981 VAT made the commemorative address. He also spoke at the installation of the *Melbourne* stained glass window in Garden Island Dockyard's chapel. At the RAN's 75th Anniversary in 1986 he opened the Naval Historical Society of Australia's museum. He had supported the historical society through its early struggles when he was CNS and remained a loyal member in retirement.

Philanthropy also occupied the elderly couple. For eighteen years Lady Smith was on the committee for Marymead, a home for needy children founded by Catholic nuns, but non-denominational. She served as president for three years. VAT, still upset at his infant nephews' abandonment by their father when his sister died from complications of childbirth, became president of the ACT division of Birthright. This Australia-wide organisation assisted single parents with dependent children and at one point 7,000 children in the ACT were being supported.

Wary of being "an old seadog growling" VAT refrained from public comment on current affairs or defence policy matters, although this did not prevent him quizzing a still serving Commodore Dadswell on the latest FAA concerns. Having ensured future CNS's would have full command autonomy after the Navy Office was amalgamated within the Department of Defence, he was disturbed to hear in later years that the chief of navy's authority was being eroded, but made comment only in general cautionary terms.

He continued to weigh his words and was sparing of those criticising the navy. However, when the Hawke Labor government decided in 1983 to not replace *Melbourne* and to disband the fixed-wing squadrons, he joined three other retired chiefs of navy in opposing the policy. When *Melbourne* was towed to China for scrap the Peoples Liberation Army Navy studied her for years as they initiated their own carrier program. In Australia it was almost 30 years before another RAN "flat-top", the 27,500-ton *Canberra*, commissioned in 2014 under the white ensign.

On their 50th wedding anniversary, as they had in 1944, the celebratory cake was cut by Nanette and VAT both holding his naval sword as their family looked on. Once while in hospital, unable to follow *Harman*'s rugby league navy team from the sidelines as usual, the entire team visited his bedside unshowered having just won their grand final.

Anzac Day 1998 saw VAT admitted to hospital for a routine procedure to remove skin cancers on his legs. Unfortunately, he suffered a serious arterial aneurism during the operation and declined in hospital for the next three months, visited daily by Nanette, until his death on 10 July 1998, aged 85.

Admiral Sir Victor Smith AC KBE CB DSC MiD RAN (Rtd) was accorded a funeral with full naval honours on 16 July. Hundreds of defence personnel lined the funeral procession route as 140 sailors pulled the gun carriage on which the casket, draped with the white naval ensign and with a wreath of white roses from Lady Smith, was carried as the RAN band played and aircraft from *Albatross* flew overhead in formation. Among the retired admirals as pall bearers was Dr Cameron "Cam" Webber who had been a staunch support through VAT's final three months in hospital. In the ANZAC Memorial Chapel of St Paul, with his cap, sword and medals displayed, Commodore Toz Dadswell AM (Rtd) read the eulogy and VAT's grandson Nicholas read the poem *High Flight*, which had been found among VAT's papers. The Naval Psalm was led by the National Chaplain of the Fleet Air Arm Association, Monsignor Frank Lyons and the 450 mourners sang the Naval Hymn and repeated the Naval Prayer, whose words VAT had spoken almost weekly since the age of thirteen.

With a watching destroyer anchored just off the naval college, VAT's ashes were scattered by the family in Jervis Bay from a Torpedo Recovery Vessel.[1]

The portrait below of VAT as Chairman, Chiefs of Staff Committee, overlooked the Smith family dining room in Canberra for many years. Nanette, entertaining naval officers to dinner one night, opined that she did not particularly like it as she had never seen him looking that stern. In unison, and to a man, the guests replied "Oh, we have!"

This portrait now hangs in the wardroom at *Albatross*, Naval Air Station Nowra, unremarked by the young naval aviators. Should they aspire to a consequential life of leadership with integrity and professional excellence, then Victor Alfred Trumper Smith's inspiring example would be a worthy guide as they continue to make the Australian Fleet Air Arm "Second to None".

The portrait of VAT as Chairman, Chiefs of Staff Committee, which now hangs in the wardroom of HMAS Albatross.

1   The ashes of both Lady Nanette Smith (1923-2017) and Michael Smith (1948-2007) were scattered at the same location in Jervis Bay.

APPENDIX A – VAT SMITH'S MEDALS

Insignia of a Knight and a Commander of the British Empire.

Row 1:
Companion of the Order of Australia; Knight of The British Empire; Companion of the Bath; Distinguished Service Cross

Row 2:
1939-1945 Star; Atlantic Star - France and Germany Clasp; Africa Star; Pacific Star

Row 3:
Defence Medal; War Medal 1939-1945 - Oak Leaf Mentioned in Despatches; Australian Service Medal 1939-1945; Australian Active Service Medal 1945-1975 with clasps Korea and Vietnam

Insignia of a Companion of the Bath.

Row 4:
Korea Medal; United Nations Service Medal for Korea; Vietnam Logistics and Support Medal; Australian Service Medal 1945-1975 with clasps Japan and FESR

Row 5:
Defence Force Service medal - six clasps/two Federation Stars; National Medal; Australian Defence Medal; Republic of Korea War Service Medal

ADDITIONAL:

 Arctic Star

 South Korean Presidential Unit Citation

Neck badge of a Companion of the Order of Australia.

ACKNOWLEDGEMENTS

A consequential figure such as VAT Smith has long deserved a biography. However, it needed the encouragement and assistance of my naval college classmates turned outstanding naval historians, Vice Admiral Peter Jones AO DSC (Rtd), Dr David Stevens AM and the late Rear Admiral James Goldrick AO CSC, to complete the project. Building on the works of Peter Jones, Desmond Woods OAM and Tom Lewis OAM, VAT's surviving sons Mark and Piers Smith, helped immeasurably.

Collections curator Ailsa Chittick gave ready assistance in primary research at the Fleet Air Arm Museum managed by my old Wessex squadron mate Commander Stuart "Stu" Harwood (Rtd). Captain Laurie Watson (Rtd) (1961 class), doing outstanding work with the Naval College Historic Collection, was unfailingly helpful as was Marcus Peake of the Fleet Air Arm Association of Australia and Bob Guest of the Naval Historical Society. Rob Garratt, Naval History Section Sea Power Centre - Australia under Captain Alastair Cooper (ADFA 1988), readily opened their archives. Lieutenant Commander Mike Galvin (Rtd) (1974 class) and Edmund Goldrick assisted using their respective college rugby and research expertise. Captain Andrew Whittaker (Rtd) went above and beyond in his efforts on my behalf.

The quest for historical accuracy by the excellent aviation artists Drew Harrison and Juanita Franzi was praiseworthy and their artwork, coupled with the diagrams by Katrina Knapp of Studio-Nine, have greatly enhanced this story. Peter Ingram of Avonmore Books is doing much to further the published aviation history of the RAN, his early commitment to this project and his considerable editorial expertise have been invaluable.

I served under Commodore Thomas "Toz" Dadswell AM KM (Rtd) (1946 class) who commanded the Naval Air Station in the early 1980s when naval aviation was yet again facing an uncertain future. A staunch advocate for the memory of the man he served under during five different appointments, his recollections proved deeply valuable to this story of the father of Australia's Fleet Air Arm.

Jeffrey "Jeff" Britten   *Thomas "Toz" Dadswell*   *John Collins*   *Gorton and VAT*

SOURCES

Archives

National Archives of Australia
A3978 Officers (RAN) personal Record
Commonwealth Naval Board Minutes
Navy Lists RN and RAN 1927–1975
RAF Combat Reports Air-50/313/14
RAAF Unit History Sheets, No. 9 Squadron Mar 41 – Feb 44, NAA A9186/23/1339945
Reports of Proceedings, HMA Ships and Establishments, AWM 78
The National Archives, Kew.
US Naval History and Heritage Command

Online

history.navy.mil
kbbismarck.com "With Gallantry and Determination" by Mark E Horan.
naval-history.net
royalnavy.mod.uk
royalnavyresearcharchive.org.uk
armouredcarriers.com
images.navy.gov.au

Published

Admiral Sir Victor Smith, Tom Lewis, Journal of the Australian Naval Institute, Issue 124.
A Few Memories of Sir Victor Smith, ANI Press, Canberra 1992
A Very Rude Awakening, P Grose, Allen & Unwin, 2007
Ark Royal, K. Poolman, London, 1956
As Luck Would Have It, Sir John Collins, Angus and Robertson, 1965
Australia's Argonauts, Peter Jones, Barrallier Books, 2016
Battleships of the Scharnhorst Class, Koop & Schmolke, Seaforth, 2014
Bring Back My Stringbag, Lord Kilbracken, London, 1996
By Skill & Valor, James Atkinson, Spink and Son, 1986
Churchill's Arctic Convoys, W Smith, London, 2022
Collins of the Sydney, A Macdougal, Clarion, 2018
Convoy, P Kemp, London, 1993
Escort Carrier, J Moore, London, 1944
Flagship, Mike Carlton, Penguin, 2016
Fleet Air Arm 1920-1939, Ray Sturtivant, Air-Britain, 1998
Flying Navy - New Zealanders Who Flew in the FAA, D Allison, Auckland, 2009
For Those In Peril, V Cassells, Sydney, 1995
From Sea to Sky 1910-1945, Sir Arthur Longmore, London, 1946
Hitler's U-Boat War The Hunters 1939-1942, C Blair, Random House, 1996
Hitler's U-Boat War The Hunted 1942-1945, C Blair, Random House, 1998
History of the Royal Australian Naval College, F B Eldridge, Georgian House, 1949
HMAS Canberra Casualty of Circumstance, K Spurling, Sydney, 2022

HMAS Canberra, A Payne, NHSA Sydney, 1991
In All Respects Ready, David Stevens, Oxford UP, 2014
Mermaids Do Exist, Vice-Admiral Sir Henry Burrell, Macmillan, 1986
Naval Historical Society of Australia March 79 Sep 98 Aug 21 Lecture 1970
Observers and Navigators, C G Jefford, London, 2014
Operation Neptune, B Schofield, London, 1974
Pacific Profiles - IJN Floatplanes in the South Pacific, J Claringbould, Avonmore Books, 2022
Royal Australian Navy 1942-1945, G Gill, Canberra, 1968
Royal Navy Aces of World War 2, A Thomas, Osprey, 2007
Royal Navy Torpedo-Bombers VS Axis Warships, M Willis, Osprey, 2022
Schlacht-schiff Scharnhorst, Heinrich Bredemeier, Munchen, 1962
Seagulls, Cruisers and Catapults, Ray Jones, Pelorus Press Hobart, 1989
Sea Power Centre Australia *Semaphore* publications
Sir Victor Alfred Trumper Smith, Desmond Woods, Australian Dictionary of Biography, 2013
Solomons Air War Vol 1 August-September 1942, Claringbould & Ingman, Avonmore Books, 2023
Some Recollections of a RAN Midshipman 1927-1933, Naval Historical Society, 1970
Squadrons of the Fleet Air Arm, Ray Sturtivant, 1984
The Arctic Convoys, B Schofield, London, 1977
The Battleship Scharnhorst, S Dramiński, London, 2020
The Bridge, Peter Lalor, Allen & Unwin, 2006
The Fighting Captain, A Burn, London, 1993
The Flight of the Pelican - a History of Nirimba, Ron Robb, Sydney, 1993
The Third Brother - The RAAF 1921-1939, C Coulthard-Clark, Melbourne, 1991
The Royal Australian Naval College Magazine No.16 Dec 1928/No17 Dec 1929/No.18 Dec 1930
The Shame of Savo, B Loxton and C Coulthard-Clark, Sydney, 1994
The Supermarine Walrus, G Nicholl, London, 1966.
The Swordfish Story, Ray Sturtivant, London, 2000.
U-Boats Destroyed, P Kemp, London, 1997
Walker RN, T Robertson, London, 1958
War to War Australia's Navy 1919-1939, Bob Nicholls, AMHP, 2012
Wings and the Navy 1947-1953, C Jones, Sydney, 1997
With The Carriers in Korea, John Lansdown, London, 1997

Unpublished

Smith Family papers
Chesterman Family Papers
Munro Kerr Family Papers
Hall Thompson Family Papers
Early Scouting in New South Wales, JX Coutts, manuscript

INDEX OF NAMES